TE… DC… GS

A London child's view of World War Two.

For Jacqueline Hollings and her younger sister and brother growing up in Colindale, a part of Hendon, the war brought changes and hardships they could never have imagined. Having lived a carefree pre-war existence, eight-year-old Jacqueline and her family soon faced nightly bombing raids, disruption to school life, food rationing and freezing winters, yet despite the hardships there was a spirit of camaraderie. Seventy years on Jacqueline returns to her childhood through her vivid memories, painting a picture of a little girl with a gift for music growing up against the bewildering backdrop of wartime Britain.

TEDDY BEARS & DOODLEBUGS

Teddy Bears & Doodlebugs

by

Jacqueline Hollings

Dales Large Print Books
Long Preston, North Yorkshire,
BD23 4ND, England.

British Library Cataloguing in Publication Data.

Hollings, Jacqueline
Teddy bears & doodlebugs.

A catalogue record of this book is available from the British Library

ISBN 978-1-84262-847-8 pbk

First published in Great Britain in 2010 by The Book Guild Ltd.

Cover illustration by arrangement with The Book Guild Publishing

Published in Large Print 2011 by arrangement with Book Guild Publishing

Dales Large Print is an imprint of Library Magna Books Ltd.

Printed and bound in Great Britain by T.J. (International) Ltd., Cornwall, PL28 8RW

Dedicated to the memory of
ROSE, STANLEY and DOROTHY

Contents

Preface

We were watching television when my youngest son suddenly asked me what it was like in the war. I was initially stumped for an answer; it seemed so long ago. Those anxious times had long disappeared into the deepest recesses of my mind. Matters of career, marriage and family have occupied me since, almost eradicating all thought of those dark, fearful days of my childhood.

His question had been prompted by media coverage at the end of the 1980s, which marked the 50th anniversary of the outbreak of war in 1939. As we watched the story unfold on the screen, my memory gradually awakened and a kaleidoscopic jumble of incidents, images, sounds and emotions from the past began to sharpen into focus with increasing clarity. All sorts of details surfaced of life under conditions of war. But before I could provide an answer that would satisfy, a little research was necessary to make sense of all these snippets of imagery, to slot them properly into the context of the war's progress and to portray successfully an accurate picture of life for one typical family trying to deal with the routine of each day under such traumatic conditions.

From films, television documentaries, film archives, war diaries and autobiographies, we all know of the war's major events – Dunkirk, Pearl Harbor, the Blitz, the Battle of Britain, the Holocaust and the Normandy landings, and of its great leaders and heroes. But what of the civilians at home? How did they all cope? How did it affect the children?

Although less dramatic, the account that follows is another facet of that same epic. It is one that could also perhaps take its place among the records of such a momentous period in our history. Not the great battles, dramas, heroics, victories and defeats being played out abroad, but how those events influenced and touched the life of an ordinary little girl growing up amid the upheaval of those times.

So, for my son who raised the question that started my mind coursing back to reflect and ponder on a bewildering and stressful episode in my youth, for others who may also be curious (and with the possibility of my grandchildren one day making a similar enquiry), here is the story of our family's involvement in the drama of those six epoch-making years, written and recorded as one grandma remembers, seventy years on, before the details are forgotten and lost forever.

1

Getting Ready

As I was only eight years old when war began I had very little notion of what it was about. I had no understanding of the significance of the extraordinary events happening in the world, and no conception of the explosion of social values about to take place. I had no idea why we were fighting another war so soon after the previous one. Whenever the subject was raised adults spoke in hushed tones and refrained from discussing the darker issues when children were within ear-shot. So we remained ignorant for some time of the implications and political issues involved.

Explanations for the mysterious goings-on in the streets and parks, the diggings, the accumulation of sandbags, and sticky stuff covering windows were at first brief and vague: 'In case war comes'. Detailed explanations came later. I had no idea who Hitler was or why he was so evil. A child accepts and lives each day as it comes, trusting the adults around him, giving little thought to the future. But I could sense that everyone was fearful, so I was affected by the atmosphere of gloom surrounding us all.

We lived on a newish housing estate in north-west London within a few stones' throw of Hendon Aerodrome. Dad worked for the *Daily Mail* in Blackfriars, central London, but at home he was gardener, musician, carpenter, photographer and breeder of budgerigars. Mum had been a ballet dancer but her three youngsters now kept her busily occupied, her dancing but a fast-fading memory. My sister Bronia aged seven and my brother Michael aged four completed the family.

Our lives pre-war were carefree. I've vague memories of day trips to Margate, holidays at

Eastbourne and a holiday camp on Hayling Island. Children enjoyed much more freedom than they do now. Bronia, Michael and I spent a lot of time wandering about and playing with friends in our neighbourhood, exploring woodland and fields nearby, and picking wild blackberries. The Silk Stream, a meandering brook, was heaven. We loved to jump across it via slippery stepping-stones, and search for dabs with our fishing nets. We took them home in jars of water but I cannot recall their eventual fate. We were often stung by nettles but learned to soothe the stings with dock leaves. During our blissful days in the sunshine we were slow to notice the developing political storm or the clouds of doom which were gradually descending upon the adults around us.

Even before war began people must have been fairly sure it was coming for there was evidence all around us of preparation and protection. The huge piles of sandbags propped against public buildings were to protect them from bomb blast. Strips of sticky tape were stuck in patterns on windows to prevent splinters of glass causing injury after an explosion. Tube trains and buses had their windows almost covered by closely woven net, leaving only a small diamond-shaped space in the middle for passengers to peer out. Every station had its identifying name signs blacked out so that enemy spies could not find out where they were. For the same reason all signposts were removed from street corners.

It was thought necessary to have a complete blackout of London and elsewhere after the war started. All lights were to be turned out so German aircraft crews would be unable to target our cities accurately. Practice blackouts were held beforehand. My mother bought some strong black material recommended for the purpose and hung some at each window of the house. No crack of light was to be seen from outside. If there was the smallest chink of light showing we soon had a knock and shout from a passing policeman or Air Raid Warden.

Kerbs were painted white at intervals, and white dotted lines appeared along the centres of roads to help both pedestrians and drivers. It was very dark and eerie after nightfall and everyone had to carry a torch, but we were discouraged from venturing forth at night.

Newspapers and radio broadcasts were peppered with the puzzling word 'war' but nobody explained to me what it meant. It was obvious that everyone was dreading it so, when Dad told us on Sunday morning 3rd September 1939 that there was to be an important announcement on the radio at 11.15 a.m., I felt a sense of foreboding without understanding the reason why.

We gathered around the wireless, as we then called it, to listen. The official declaration of war against Germany that morning was immediately followed by a spine-chilling wailing siren, which added to my fear. We had a neighbour with us at the time whose immediate reaction was to run home as fast as he could, which was quite comical. As always in times of crisis, Mum's reaction was to make a cup of tea. I followed her into the kitchen to toss a hundred questions at her. What *is* a war? What is going to happen? What was that wail? What does it all mean? I was told years later that my little face was as white as chalk and my whole body visibly shaking.

Dad spent the rest of the day continuing to dig a huge hole at the end of our small garden. He explained that an Anderson shelter was to be erected in the hole so that we could sleep in it and be safe from any bombs that Hitler's planes may drop. 'Who is Hitler?' I asked. 'He is a nasty, evil man in Germany who plans to conquer the whole world, so we have to stop him. He pretends to be friendly but events have shown he cannot be trusted. We think that he is preparing to invade our country, but we cannot allow him to do so. If he succeeds we shall all lose our freedom.'

The garden was Dad's pride and joy. Along the back fence was an aviary he had designed and built himself, containing about thirty budgerigars. Its design, and the way it was incorporated into the garden's layout of rockeries, circular flowerbeds, a fish pond and lawns, had won third prize in a competition organised by the Cage Birds Annual. This was no small achievement considering the tiny size of the garden. As he dug, his heart must have been heavy, not only because of the war, but because he was having to dismantle the rockery and fish pond and replace them with a shelter made of ugly corrugated metal. But, typical of his ingenuity and imagination, he managed to organise things so that the rockery could be rebuilt to continue up and over the shelter. When all was finished we could not see it from the house. The entrance was cleverly concealed, positioned at right angles to the back fence. The following spring the shelter was hidden under a mass of mauve and yellow flowers.

Inside it, he built a pair of bunk beds along one side for my sister and me, a small bed along the opposite side for my brother, and into the remaining space he somehow managed to squeeze a bed just large enough for Mum and himself. A curtain, made from an old thinning blanket, was used to draw across the beds for privacy. There was also a shelf where matches, candles and a torch were kept. The door had a little square peep-hole which could be opened by sliding its cover sideways.

Beyond the back fence was a large, rough unused field backed by houses on three sides. Dad had earlier cut a gate into the fence to form a back entrance enabling us to take a short cut through the field to the buses and the Underground tube station. When we first began to use the shelter in the days before Hitler started bombing us, we children would lie on our bunks listening for Dad to return from work. As soon as we heard the fence gate creak we all shouted 'Goodnight!' and he would slide open the peep-hole in the door to reply. Sometimes he came into the shelter to tuck us up and have a little chat before joining Mum in the house.

There was yet more digging to be done. Posters everywhere instructed us to 'Dig for Victory'. The field behind us was carved up into strips of allotments and used by the residents whose gardens backed onto it. Our allotment was alongside the back fence, bordered by a path which led from the gate. Dad spent much of the autumn of 1939 digging, planting and sowing his patch with assorted seeds and vegetables in neat rows. We were lucky to have use of the field and so not have to spoil more of our garden.

All metal objects that could be spared were called in for scrap to help build aeroplanes, guns and ammunition. I recall a horse-drawn cart wending its way around our little cul-de-sac, the collector calling out for any spare metal. Mum gave him some items, as did some of our neighbours.

The metal railings that had surrounded the bed of laurel bushes in the centre of the road were dismantled. That was good news for the children. Henceforth we could dive into and through the bushes to reach our friends and homes on the other side – much more fun than walking around! We played games, built camps, hatched plots and made plans among those bushes. They became a main centre of play during our childhood.

A large brick shelter was built at the entrance to our road. Perhaps it was reinforced in some way but at the time I could not see the point of it, wondering how it could be any more safe than the houses nearby. Our family never used it, but while it was being erected local children played Houses, Battles and Camps inside it in the evenings after the builders had left and at weekends. We re-arranged all the loose bricks to make walls and sorted ourselves into friends and foes, English and German or cowboys and indians, 'firing' at each other from opposite ends and taking refuge behind our own walls.

I soon found that its outside walls were marvellous for playing ball games. After school I played hours of 'Dropsy' and

'Double Dropsy' with a ball against the wall. When my two friends and I had perfected our skills we progressed to throwing two balls at the same time. I never reached the dizzy heights of juggling with three balls as my friend did, but I watched her do so with a mixture of awe, envy and admiration.

Skipping, hoop-rolling, hopscotch and top-spinning were other favourite pastimes. I was once able to keep my little wooden top spinning all the way to school with the help of a stick and string – but only once. It was fun to find who could keep the top spinning for the longest time.

Every man, woman and child in the country was issued with a gas mask. There was a real fear that Hitler would be nasty enough to use gas as a weapon. Gas masks were unpleasant to wear, smelled strongly of rubber, fitted tightly around our faces and were claustrophobic. We never noticed that Mum, who suffered from asthma, managed to avoid putting hers on but she insisted that we became used to wearing ours. She regularly held a gas-mask drill. As soon as we heard her ringing the little bell, we had to stop whatever we were doing to see how quickly we could get the masks on and properly fixed. We never enjoyed this, but complied reluctantly.

Wooden poles supporting flat, square pieces of wood began to appear at roadsides. It was explained that if the surface turned green it would indicate that poison gas was in the air and we were immediately to put on our gas masks.

Tiny babies had special masks into which they could be inserted and zipped. Infants under two years old had masks that covered their heads and chests. These were decorated with pictures of Mickey Mouse but that did not prevent many children from kicking and screaming against being placed into them.

Nobody was allowed out without carrying a gas mask. Each was kept in a square cardboard box and hung over the shoulder by a long strap. They were often subject to misuse and careless treatment so had to be regularly tested. When we had visitors, or when we were visiting relatives and friends, we had to check that everyone had his mask before leaving. It became common to chant a silly rhyme at the door when saying goodbye.

'Got yer gas mask?
Got yer torchlight?
All right?
Goodnight!'

Invariably followed by laughter.

Hitler never used gas against us during the war – but we weren't to know that at the time and had to be prepared.

The Government asked all able-bodied women to become ambulance drivers, join the Women's Voluntary Service (WVS), work in factories, help farmers by joining the Land Army, train as auxiliary nurses, Red Cross workers etc., or enlist in the Armed Forces.

Those with young children were exempt from other work but Mum wanted to Do

Something, so she appealed to the headmaster of the local infant school to include Michael among the new intake, although he would not be five until early November. At first he said 'No, rules are rules', but he later wrote to Mum saying he could not forget the forlorn look on her face, so he was prepared to make an exception in Michael's case. She was delighted as it meant she was now free to do her bit for the war effort.

At first she tried part-time work in a factory, but that did not last long (perhaps because of her asthma). Later, she joined the Hendon Food Office helping with the issue of ration books to everyone in the Borough of Hendon. She enjoyed this, made new friends, and found there were perks such as having access to everyone's records and discovering the ages of all our neighbours! She never let on, of course, but it amused her to be in possession of their secrets. Somehow she always managed to be home before we returned from school and during school holidays.

After the initial fright and panic caused by the siren that followed Neville Chamberlain's broadcast on 3rd September (the siren had been a false alarm) all became strangely quiet at the lack of news concerning the war's progress. Life continued much as normal, with everyone going about their usual routine tasks, attending school, going to work and, in my case, daily piano practice. The war seemed unreal and far away, although I noticed trenches being dug in local parks and open spaces, mounds of earth left between, and poles and stakes pierced into the ground (to prevent landing of enemy planes so I was told).

Cinemas and theatres had closed but gradually opened again. There were announcements about petrol rationing, what to do if an air-raid Alert sounded, how to obtain one's ration book, and where young men were to report for enlisting into the Army, Navy or Air Force.

The sky became filled with hundreds of

floating silver barrage balloons (to stop the enemy flying too low) and the dark blacked-out evenings ensured that most of us stayed indoors after then.

The country settled down into a sort of restive calm, going about its daily business wondering, watching and waiting…

2

What Now?

The atmosphere of quiet unease at home continued into the autumn, through winter and into spring. News began to filter through of German U-boats prowling the Atlantic and successfully attacking our shipping. Hitler's armies continued to overrun Europe, and Poland surrendered. In April, the Germans invaded Norway.

All fit men under the age of twenty-three

were called up into the Armed Forces and reported for their medicals. Food gradually became more scarce and ration books were issued to everybody to ensure fair distribution of food. Each page of the book was given a label such as meat, cheese, bacon, sugar or butter, etc. and was divided into coupons, which shopkeepers either crossed or cut out whenever a purchase was made.

Anyone could be stopped at any time to have his identity checked, so it was essential for us all to carry an identity card and number. During the first few months of the war while all was still quiet on the home front – a period known as the 'Phoney War' – visits between family and friends continued much as before, but visitors always took food with them for their hosts, i.e. butter, sugar or tea, as rationing severely restricted the amount available.

Although we lived in north London, most of our relatives lived south of the Thames in Thornton Heath, Norwood, New Malden and Thames Ditton. We continued to make journeys across London to see them, espeially my maternal grandmother, known to us as Nanna. She and Grandpa lived in Thornton Heath and our trips across the City by tube train and bus remained without incident for some months, but once the Blitz brought the war to our very doorstep all non-essential journeys were stopped. Posters went up everywhere asking 'Is Your Journey Really Necessary?', making us feel a trifle guilty when travelling about.

Christmas always arrived for us the moment Nanna entered the house. She and Grandpa arrived two days before Christmas Day carrying suitcases, and bags bulging with mysterious parcels. Nanna took a childlike delight in the festivities, never losing a child's wonder, awe and happiness of the occasion. She was not the sort to allow the inconvenience and austerity of war to spoil the family fun and fully entered into the spirit of things as ever.

I cannot recall a Christmas without a tree

but where my parents obtained one during wartime I have no idea. There it was, resplendent with lights and tinsel as usual in the corner of the lounge when we came down to breakfast on Christmas morning. We never saw a hint of decorations until that moment, so Christmas Day held a special magic for us. Mum and Dad must have worked like demons the previous evening to make sure all was ready by morning. Presents surrounded the tree, but we were not to open any until after dinner was over and the kitchen tidy.

On Christmas morning I caught Nanna bending secretively over the parcels enjoying a sneaky read of the labels. At my shout of 'Nanna!' she guiltily jumped aside, laughed, and said she was just checking to see if they were all there!

At Christmas the small kitchen was out of bounds to everyone except the two cooks. However, curious at hearing strange noises coming from within, I opened the door to find both Mum and Nanna doubled up with hilarity and hunched over a messy splosh of food splattered about the floor with the half-roasted chicken. They were both rocking with helpless uncontrolled laughter as they scooped up the greasy mess, rescuing as much as they could and replacing it in the roasting tin. One of them had taken the tin out of the oven to baste the chicken and vegetables, then dropped the lot. As she spooned it back Nanna spluttered through her chuckles, 'What the eye don't see, the heart won't grieve over', and Mum added to me, 'Don't you dare tell the others'.

Our family enjoyed their Christmas dinner as much as ever that year, the cooks still quietly giggling. Nanna's looks and behaviour belied her age by about twenty years. She and Mum were great pals and we all loved her dearly.

The winter of 1939–40 was exceedingly cold and bleak, with deep snow lying on the ground for weeks. Supplies of coal nearly ran out resulting in sudden and frequent power cuts. A supply of candles had to be kept at the ready, and our little Valor stove was often in use as an alternative method of cooking and heating. Outside the ironmonger's were queues of people clutching cans whenever it was rumoured that a fresh supply of paraffin was in stock, and I was often sent out to buy some.

We were all asked to conserve energy, turning out lights that were not in use, using only six inches of water in our baths and lighting only one fire in the house. In those pre-central-heating days the family sat huddled around the living-room fire or paraffin stove. Mum did as much cooking as possible on the open fire and we often sat in front of it toasting bread at the end of long-handled toasting forks. Dripping on toast was a supper favourite.

Neighbours helped each other in many ways. They shared each others' ovens, each one taking her turn at cooking friends' dinners.

There was ice and frost on the windows at night; downstairs and up, inside and out.

Bedrooms were always freezing and we wore our dressing-gowns in bed. Mum rolled us in flannelette sheets before tucking us under blankets and eiderdowns. It took at least half an hour before we were warm enough to sleep.

Each day began with Mum on her knees raking out the cold ashes from the fire of the previous day, her hands blue with cold. After the hearth was cleaned she placed scrunched-up balls of newspaper under fresh pieces of coal or wood before applying a lighted match. A large sheet of newspaper was held against the surround to act as bellows to draw up the flames. With the fire burning brightly and the chill off the living room we were called down to breakfast, usually a saucepan of porridge simmering on the stove in the middle of the room. Before we braved the snow in the twenty-minute walk to school, Mum warmed our socks, scarves, mittens and pixie-hoods on the stove so that we would have a warm start.

But before long the tops of my Wellington

boots were chafing around my legs causing sore red rings, and my hands were stiff and frozen. I suffered badly from chilblains so my toes were itchy and painful all day at school, and walking became difficult. One time they were so bad I stayed home for two days. On the second day I opened the door to the school's attendance officer who demanded to know why I was not at school. When I explained about the chilblains he said if I could walk to the door I could walk to school, and to see that I did so next day. Nanna made me a pair of leather spats with fur-fabric trim to wear over my shoes to keep my feet warm. They weren't very popular with me because other children did not wear anything like it and I hated to be different. When I was finally persuaded to wear them they proved fairly effective, but it was many years before the chilblain problem was solved.

Piano practice was a problem during winter because the lounge was always so cold. If there was insufficient fuel to allow the luxury of a second fire I wrapped a blanket around my thighs and legs, wore several thick old woollies, rested my feet on a rubber hot water bottle, had another on my lap, and gradually increased the blood-flow through my fingers by playing scales up and down the length of the keyboard. It took ages before I stopped shivering but eventually I was glowing with warmth, and my fingers were relaxed and supple enough to tackle the music.

One day, Dad arrived home early to find me cluttered up inside blankets and woollies at the piano. I was fearful of his reaction because he believed in Being Tough and not letting minor inconveniences such as freezing cold get in the way of One's Duty. To my surprise he was really pleased. 'That's what I like to see – using your initiative to counter difficulties, and not using the cold as an excuse for not practising.'

After rising one bitter February morning we discovered that all the budgerigars in the aviary had frozen to death. I had never known my parents so upset. One bird had been brought into the house when very young and lived in a cage in the living room. We called him Boysie and he developed a lovable, cheeky personality, was a friendly little character and a constant chatterbox. He taught himself to imitate the sounds around him.

Visitors were startled to hear him call out clearly and quickly in his shrill, repetitive, staccato tones, 'You naughty children – hello Boysie – hello – stop it – stop it at once – Jacqueline, Bronia, Michael – hello – do you hear me?' – on and on and on. He paced up and down in his cage by the door when he wanted to be let out (we called it The Lambeth Walk) and every day we allowed him out for a while to fly around, eat with us off the table and perch on our heads. Boysie was one of the family, giving us hours of pleasure at a down time in our lives.

Burst pipes and flooding became a common occurrence during that hard winter, adding to the many difficulties and general misery. Colds were frequent and severe.

Mum's favourite remedy was to lie us on the floor in a row in front of the fire and rub some Vick into our chests.

Another change in our garden came the day Dad decided to adapt the aviary into a chicken coop, to supplement both meat and egg rations for the family. Inside the enclosure at one end he built a box in which he laid some straw, leaving a small entrance in one side for the chickens to come and go. At the top of the box he carefully positioned a notice, painting on it in black letters, 'Please Lay Eggs Here' with an arrow pointing to the entrance beneath. Michael amused us by reminding Dad that chickens cannot read! Nevertheless the hens obeyed the notice and kept us supplied in eggs, laid in the right place, for most of the war.

Owning chickens brought its problems, not least of which were rats. My parents acquired an airgun but were not skilled enough to shoot many, and the menace remained.

Every now and then, especially at Christmas, a chicken was killed for eating. Neither Mum nor Dad wanted to carry out the execution so a neighbour's help was sought. We looked the other way as the hen's neck was wrung. Sometimes a hen stubbornly clung to life, so the job had to be finished with a hatchet. I shall never forget the moment one hen ran around the garden headless. We were told it had something to do with its nerves suffering shock reaction. I have never eaten chicken since without recalling that incident and feeling guilty because I did not become a vegetarian on the spot.

There was often a smell of boiling vegetation, peelings and food refuse emanating from the kitchen. It was an awful stench, which I can still recall. Some of it was for feeding the chicken but most became pigswill and was tipped into a bin, collected and passed on to farmers for their pigs. Pig farming was part of the Government's campaign for Britain to feed its own citizens as far as possible, imports by sea having been interrupted by the German navy. Hitler was claiming that his ships were successfully strangling Britain into submission, but this was a lie put out by his propaganda minister, 'Doctor' Goebbels.

My reports from school were usually good, so when one of them included the comment, 'does not concentrate in History', it caused enough concern for Dad to take me aside for a serious chat. I sat on his lap, swinging my legs against the sideboard while we studied together all the teacher's remarks.

I asked him what 'concentrate' means. He said it was what I was *not* doing at that moment. I was too busy swinging my legs and trying to tuck my toes under the sideboard's protruding drawer handles to pay much attention to what he was saying.

So what is history? This was our next topic. 'It is the story of lives long ago, of each person's contribution to man's progress and development, the growth of nations, scientific knowledge, laws, inventions. The reasons behind why we do this and that, what and how we think, the way we behave,' explained my father.

Like all children I found it almost impossible to comprehend the fact of anything existing before I was born. History lessons at school were boring stories of unreal people who had no relevance to, or influence upon, our own lives. But Dad pointed out that history never stops, it is a continuous story. It is *now.*

'We should learn how things were long ago so we can understand life today and work towards a better future. We are fighting a war because of past mistakes. We must learn from those mistakes and never repeat them.' He added that my grandchildren and great-grandchildren would one day read about Hitler, Churchill and the war in their history books.

Here was a new concept for me. History is *now?* From then on I perceived history in new light. After music, history became my favourite subject and I had no further trouble.

Rationing for a few items of food began in January 1940. We were allowed 4 oz ham, 4 oz bacon, 4 oz butter and 8 oz sugar each week. Meat was becoming scarce and was rationed later, the limit being approximately 1lb per week. There were no bananas, few oranges and not many sweets. I am convinced that Michael owes his exceptionally strong healthy teeth to the absence of sweets during his early childhood. Our diet consisted basically of the aptly named and dreaded tripe, which I loathed: rabbit, sausages and Spam. In her cooking, Mum used reconstituted eggs, which were in the form of a dark yellow powder. It was useful but not very popular. Occasionally we had whale meat; the taste of which was not unlike rabbit.

Mum was often short of money. When she couldn't afford to feed us she sent us to the British Restaurant in the High Street, where we were given a basic meal for six-pence each. Outside the restaurant was a huge circular water tank. It provided water for fighting fires caused by incendiary bombs. As it wasn't needed for some time, the surface became covered in green slime and exuded an unpleasant smell.

At the beginning of the war all able-bodied young men, other than those in vital services, e.g. food distribution, farming and the manufacture of weapons, were enlisted into the Armed Services. This was achieved according to age groups, the youngest going first. By the end of 1939 all the 18–21 year olds who had passed their medicals, had joined the Army, Navy or Air Force. During the first months of 1940 the 21–28 year-old age groups were called up in stages.

As Dad was thirty-one when war began he had a few months to go before his call-up papers were due. While waiting, he decided to join the Local Defence Volunteers, later known as the Home Guard. An appeal had gone out for men between the ages of 18–65, not in the Forces for various reasons, to provide an army at home for those who wished to help defend their country if invaded. These men were often teased for being amateurs. It was forgotten that the majority of the older men were veterans of the Great War twenty years earlier and the Boer War at the turn of the century. We became used to Dad in khaki uniform, and his rifle standing sentinel in the hall with the strictest of instructions never, *never* to touch or go anywhere near it.

The dreaded day arrived when Dad's enlisting papers came and he had to report for a medical. Over dinner soon afterwards he suddenly asked, 'How would you like to see me in Navy uniform?' Having introduced us to the news of his impending departure, he enlightened us further. It was actually, he said, a branch of the Navy known as The Royal Marines, and explained that a Marine was a combination of soldier and sailor with something of the skills and training of both. He thus gave us the impression that a Royal Marine was someone extra special. In our ignorance of war, as is the way with children, we felt pride and excitement – sentiments not shared by Mum and Dad who must have had totally different concerns and feelings as they finished their meal in a quiet and subdued mood.

Dad had given me my first piano lesson when I was four, and had coached me daily very successfully until about Grade 5 standard. But now that his call-up was imminent he had to make other arrangements for my musical training. He took me to the Guildhall School of Music and Drama in Blackfriars, central London, for an audition, and applied to Hendon Education Authority for a grant to cover the fees. We were all relieved and pleased when I passed the former and was allowed the latter, and my many years happy association with 'the Guildhall' began.

I travelled regularly on the Northern Line of the Underground into central London for a piano lesson every Saturday morning. By this time all station names were obliterated and train windows were covered with sticky mesh to minimize the effect of bomb blast. Not being able to see out easily to find where I was, I soon learned to recognise every nuance of sound along the line, memorising overground tunnel and bridge positions, the distances between each stop, and which side of the train the platform was situated at each station. I knew, for example, that when my ears popped I was under Hampstead Heath, between Golders Green and Hampstead stations.

Leaving the two younger children with a friend, Mum took me for the first three Saturdays, making sure I learned the way and how to change at Charing Cross for the Metropolitan Line. After that I was on my own – every Saturday morning during term time right through the war and afterwards until I was sixteen, when a change of teacher meant a switch to Thursday afternoons. At eighteen I became a full-time music student. Mum must have been quite frightened for me and very relieved each time I returned safely, especially as these journeys coincided with the start of air-raids and bombs, and I was still only nine.

Throughout the spring and summer of 1940 there was a lot of digging at the far end of the school field. I watched the men at work from the classroom window wondering what they were building. First they dug a row of long deep trenches, which were laid with concrete to make solid floors. Corrugated metal sheets were erected at the sides and over the top to form a round roof over each. They looked like rows of giant tunnels. Earth was thrown over the roofs so that, when finished, all I could see were rows of long mounds covered by freshly growing grass with a door at the end of each. We discovered all too soon what they were for as the new autumn term got under way.

News of the war was very discouraging that spring and summer. Hitler's troops had overrun Denmark, Norway, Belgium, Luxembourg and Holland. In June they had reached Paris and nobody seemed able to stop the Nazi menace. The British Army was trapped in France at Dunkirk, and was rescued from the beaches by a flotilla of small boats from England, but a lot of men were lost. The British also had to be evacuated from Norway.

There was a very real fear of invasion, for German troops were now only just across the Channel and must surely be poised for attack. The feelings of doom and dread were strong because we were now fighting Hitler on our own.

Our Government seemed ineffectual so there was a huge sense of relief when Neville Chamberlain resigned and Winston Churchill became Prime Minister of a National Coalition Government. Immediately there was a change of mood in the country. Churchill's gift of oratory was such that his speeches were very inspirational, and we listened to him on the radio as he stirred us all to greater effort, increasing the people's courage, fortitude and their determination not to give in. We were all to stand up and fight for freedom against tyranny. He promised us blood, toil, tears and sweat before we achieved victory. He introduced the 'V for Victory' sign with the first two fingers of his right hand, using it as a salute wherever he went. Everyone adored him.

The Red Cross first aid, ambulance and rescue services, Civil Defence and WVS were gradually getting organised so that they would all be ready to spring into action with an immediate response in the event of an air raid with its inevitable casualties. They needed to rehearse their planned procedures to ensure maximum efficiency. One of their practices was held locally with the co-operation of our school, and they asked for as many children as possible to pretend to be refugees, wounded, homeless or lost – and wait for 'rescue'.

Thinking this would be a fun and welcome diversion from normal routine Bronia,

Michael and I joined in. For a while we patiently endured having labels pinned to our chests with our names, addresses and details of pretend injuries, constantly being bandaged and re-bandaged, carried on stretchers here and there, herded into vans (which proved too much for Bronia. She thought she was being kidnapped and ran home screaming); and generally being shunted about aimlessly.

I never knew if the exercise was considered a success, but to me it all seemed a shambles. Michael and I eventually found our way home bewildered, thirsty, hungry and exhausted, not quite fully understanding what it was all about.

The plans to evacuate children from London and other big cities into the country and places of safety at the outbreak of war did not affect our family but, unknown to us, Mum and Dad had been quietly making alternative arrangements. These were so momentous that they kept their plans secret until almost the last moment, breaking it to us as gently and gradually as they could.

The first clues that something was afoot came when we were taken to the local welfare clinic for inoculations and vaccinations. There were many children lined up waiting their turn and we became increasingly apprehensive as the queue of children in front of us got smaller and some of them screamed in pain at the sight of the needle. We decided to be brave and Michael and I braced ourselves successfully for the prick, but Bronia faltered and shed a few tears.

The clinic was in the old part of Hendon. Dad had often taken me there on various errands and I knew it well. I recall many disabled men sitting on the pavements, often with no legs, sometimes blind or badly scarred from burns or old wounds. Crutches were lying at their sides. They were begging for money or morsels of food – sad reminders of the Great War which had ended only two decades earlier and which was still strongly embedded in adult memory.

Another street memory from those days was the organ grinder who produced mechanical music by turning a large handle at the side of the organ. A battered old cloth cap lay nearby, slowly filling with coppers thrown in by passers-by who had been lured by a tiny monkey wearing a bright red fez on his head and sitting atop the organ. Prompted by my father I asked the monkey's name. 'Jacky' was the reply. Ever since then I have nurtured an abhorrence of being called Jacky as I always think of it as a monkey's name!

On the way home from the clinic Mum explained that we had been injected with a substance to keep us fit and well during our journey.

'What journey?'

'The long journey on a big boat.'

'When?'

'Quite soon.'

'Why?'

'You are going to stay with Uncle Maurice while the war lasts. You are very lucky – you will be happy and safe with him.'

'Where does he live?'

'New Zealand.'

I was perplexed. I had never heard of Uncle Maurice, nor of a place called New Zealand.

'Where is New Zealand?'

'It is a long way away, across the water.'

Perhaps it was her use of the word 'water' rather than 'sea' which threw me, but I spent quite a while after that puzzling over which lake or river Mum was referring to.

My little brother soon worked out it was the Thames. After we had crossed the river at the top of a double-decker bus, he asked in his high loud voice, 'Are we in New Zealand now?' I wondered why everyone in the bus smiled.

Soon afterwards Nanna, who kept us supplied in woollen garments throughout our childhood, knitted little jumper suits in mottled grey and brown for Bronia and me. As we tried them on it was explained that they were for the sea journey.

But suddenly all talk of the trip ceased. Days before we were due to sail, a ship carrying evacuees was torpedoed by German U-boats, despite having a huge red cross painted on its side to identify it as a civilian vessel, rather than a warship. S.S. *Benares* sailed from Liverpool for Canada on 13th September 1940 with more than one hundred child evacuees aboard. It sank on 17th September. Of the people on board 256 drowned, including about eighty children, while thirty-one children survived, having been tossed into lifeboats, and returned home feted as heroes. The overseas evacuation scheme was immediately stopped. I nursed vague feelings of being let down and of missing out on an exciting adventure.

It was only after having children of my own that I realised the enormity of the sacrifice my parents had been prepared to make. Sending one's children abroad must have been a dreadfully agonising decision. They could not have known when, if ever, they were likely to see us again, but apparently they had thoughts about joining us in New Zealand after the war. Most children who were evacuated abroad had no conception of the reality of the situation and were totally unaware that a possible six years of separation from loved ones lay ahead.

Over forty years later I asked her how she would have coped with her emotions and the trauma of seeing her young family sail away. She looked at me in silence for a few moments, unable to speak. Instead, her eyes moistened and a solitary tear trickled slowly down her cheek. Realising I had stirred deep painful feelings long repressed, I changed the subject. I never referred to it again.

We were to learn more about Uncle Maurice and his family in the years to come. He was not actually a uncle, but Dad's first cousin whose family had emigrated to New Zealand in 1913 when he was but a lad of six. In 1940 he had a small daughter who used to watch the passenger liners sailing into Wellington Harbour, wondering which one we were on. After his initial letter to my parents offering to have us for the duration of the war, he and his wife regularly sent us food parcels and little gifts, especially at Christmas.

My interest in this far-flung branch of the family having been awakened, I began writing to them regularly, vowing that one day I would make that journey to New Zealand. It was not until 1975 that I was able to do so for the first time, and to meet the family which so very nearly became my own.

Radio began to do a magnificent job in helping to raise our spirits. Programmes like *Music While You Work* were broadcast to keep up morale in factories. *Workers' Playtime* was composed of groups of entertainers who toured factories and workshops, broadcasting from the canteens. There were excellent comedy shows to get the nation laughing. I was nine by now, reading newspapers and listening to the radio like everyone else, becoming more aware of what was going on.

We were all preparing and bracing ourselves for the expected invasion, wondering when it would start. But we felt all was ready – we had dear old Winnie at the helm now, more than a match for that little twerp across the sea. What a blessing we did not realise just how *unready* we in fact were. The general mood would have been very different had we known the truth.

3

This Is It

Without warning, war arrived on the Home Front in the late summer of 1940. The exact date eludes me but we happened to be visiting Grandpa Hollings in New Malden at the time. Grandpa had driven our family from there to Teddington for the afternoon to enjoy a lazy boat trip on the Thames in warm sunshine. This peaceful idyll was unexpectedly shattered by the blood-curdling sound of a wailing siren which we knew was the air-raid Alert. We had to find cover immediately but were caught in the middle of the river. Frantic rowing got us quickly to the bank where we joined other groups of people in a boathouse, the only shelter we could find. Worry and concern were expressed on their pale faces; frightened children were clinging to parents. No one knew what best to do or what to expect. Parents' instincts were to get children home as soon as possible, but common sense dictated that we stay put until we heard the All Clear siren.

The thuds, bumps and bangs of an air-raid could be heard in the distance; sounds that would become all too familiar in the weeks to come. We felt curiously safe clustered together inside the boathouse but everyone was thoughtful and quiet.

Eventually, after two or so long hours, the All Clear sounded and we made our way back to the car with relief but totally unprepared for the sights that met us as we drove slowly along New Malden High Street. Many shops had been flattened, and there were scenes of chaos amid dust and piles of rubble.

Grandpa's house around the corner was intact, but we were all still in a state of shock as we returned home later to Colindale by bus and tube, reflecting what might have been had we stayed in New Malden instead of deciding to spend the afternoon in a boat.

That was our last journey to South London for a very long time.

Our Anderson shelter in the garden now proved its worth as we began to sleep in it regularly. It had been made as cosy as possible by Dad, with Mum adding her own homely little touches. The air-raids were increasing in number and often disturbed our sleep. A wailing siren warned us of German planes approaching over Kent, and was soon followed by a cacophony of various noises, low drones of plane engines, boomphs, bangs, bumps and thuds of bombs near and far, windows rattling from a blast, shaking walls, quivering earth tremors, whines of descending bombs, and the constant crack-crack of the anti-aircraft guns (which we found strangely comforting). All this was accompanied by flashes in the sky, and the beams of searchlights scanning across it looking for planes. A tremendous feeling of relief always followed the All Clear, a one-note siren, but often that was short-lived when another raid came soon after.

Gradually people learned to cope and became more prepared for the nightly interruptions. The surface brick shelter at the entrance to our cul-de-sac was now in full use night after night. Two women fought over what they considered to be the safest bed in a corner, each competing with the other to grab it first. In the end they fell out completely, not speaking to each other for years. This was the exception for most people were very friendly, helping each other as troubles, worries and difficulties arose.

There was a wonderful spirit of camaraderie. People saw the funny side of things, remaining surprisingly happy and resilient despite the most harrowing situations, hardships and suffering. No one ever doubted that we would finally win the war, even during the darkest days.

We all worked together to achieve that end, even children. Michael joined Bronia and me in learning to knit. We bought lots of khaki coloured wool to knit scarves for soldiers, navy wool for sailors, and sometimes knitted various coloured squares which were sewn together for blankets.

By now, Dad was a Royal Marine stationed at Dover, and undertook spells of duty manning the anti-aircraft guns on top of the cliffs. He was to shoot down as many enemy aircraft as possible as they flew over the coast, before they could drop their bombs on London. We lay awake in the shelter, wakened by the sirens and other raid-related noises, listening intently and fearfully to the various tones of plane engines. We became skilled in detecting the difference between Theirs and Ours. When one of Theirs droned overhead we shouted, 'You missed *that* one Daddy!'

We were rarely aware of Mum sleeping in the shelter, because of the curtain perhaps, or because we were asleep by the time she joined us. But looking back I do wonder whether she really did sleep there very often. Her asthma made her hate small enclosed spaces so perhaps she avoided the shelter whenever possible.

One incident stands out. We were all asleep in the shelter about 2 a.m. when I was awakened by Mum groping around for the torch, slowly creaking open the door and crawling into the garden. Some while later, still awake and mystified, I felt something run through my hair and over my pillow. A mouse! So that was it.

I admired Mum's self-control in remaining so quiet for she detested the creatures. Although I did not share her fear of mice, I had no desire to share my bed with one, so I also decided to leave the shelter and creep out. I had hardly settled into bed in the house when Bronia followed. Michael, I learned years later, was very indignant at finding himself alone when he awoke in the morning!

It was not until breakfast next morning that Mum realised we had followed her into the house. We had a good laugh about it although she never admitted to any knowledge of the little visitor.

It was years before we finally allowed her to forget the night she was far more scared of a little mouse than of Hitler's bombs!

Newspapers began to tell of fierce air battles over Kent. They weren't referring to it yet as the Battle of Britain, but we sensed its importance as we read of pilots' heroism, trying to force back the enemy and protect London and the nation from the Luftwaffe. Daily bulletins included lists of casualties and losses but there always seemed to be more losses on their side than ours. We suspected this was mere propaganda, but the reports were in fact accurate.

Often the dreaded sirens came during daytime, prompting a mad dash into the surface shelters. If we heard a falling bomb we fell flat on our faces to protect ourselves from the explosion, bracing ourselves for the boomph and shudder of its landing. One little boy continued to throw himself down at any sudden noise for some months after the war had ended; a habitual and entrenched reflex action which his mother found difficult to cure.

The raids steadily became more frequent, regularly occurring night after night. The sirens announcing that enemy planes had been spotted approaching the south coast woke us up at any time, but mostly between 9 p.m. and 2 a.m., often later. This meant a very sleepy and bleary-eyed populace having to make a supreme effort to get up next morning. It became the rule that if a raid continued after 3 a.m., school would start at 10 a.m. next day.

Each morning children found the streets littered with pieces of shrapnel (bomb splinters), which they collected. The largest, most spectacularly jagged bits were proudly displayed on the mantelpiece as ornaments. Boys especially would compete with each other for the best pieces, but this was discouraged because sometimes small unexploded shells or bombs were left lying around proving very tempting for children. For example, we were warned via school talks and posters not to touch the small oblong objects called Butterfly Bombs, as they could explode when handled or kicked – and often did.

Our school routine was disrupted by daytime raids. As soon as the Alert sounded, each class was led into the shelters at the far end of the field (for that is what the trench-mounds were which I had watched being built from my classroom). Each class had its own shelter. Along the side were uncomfortably hard wooden benches on which we had to sit and wait for the All Clear. After a few of these interruptions, letters were sent to parents suggesting that each child take a flat cushion to school, with a tuck box of basic rations, possibly a card game and also a long pencil rubber. The latter was to insert between the teeth of the child should he suffer from fear or hysteria.

For each of us Mum made a cushion folded from a square piece of old blanket, using one of the folds to form a pocket to hold the rubber, a game of Snap, an apple and a biscuit. She added a handle to make carrying easier. Her design was unique and served its purpose well.

We were not far into the autumn term before the school suddenly closed due to the discovery of an unexploded shell embedded into the corner of a classroom. It was closed for eight weeks. During that time small classes were held in some of the children's homes, parents having volunteered use of their living rooms for a week at a time on a rota basis. I remember reciting the eight times table, being one of a class of twelve children sitting around my own living room.

Every parent who had participated in this emergency arrangement received a potted plant from the teacher as a thank you. Each house was used twice. A little boy at number six had pulled all the large red berries off his mother's pot-plant after his class's first week at his house. When the second week came round, little did his teacher realise that all the berries were fixed onto the plant with sewing pins!

The nation took its new King and Queen to their hearts after they toured bomb damage in the East End of London, and talked at length to the people. King George VI and Queen Elizabeth were much admired for not leaving London during the Blitz, despite Buckingham Palace being bombed and badly damaged.

Throughout the Blitz I continued the Saturday morning journeys by tube train to the Guildhall School of Music in Blackfriars for piano lessons. I became very used to the journey which was surprisingly rarely interrupted by an air-raid, thank goodness, but I could see the aftermath of the previous week's nightly destruction as I emerged into the street from the Underground. After the lesson I sometimes wandered the streets near St Paul's Cathedral and found gaps where buildings had stood, craters, dust, rubble, smoke and piles of debris.

In those days there were no automatic doors on the Metropolitan Line trains. Being so small I found it very difficult to find the strength to pull down the big heavy handles that opened the doors, and found myself having to go on to the next station a few times. I then walked back to Blackfriars along Queen Victoria Street, seeing yet more devastation.

My most vivid memories of the Saturday trips remain those of the central London tube stations being utilised as shelters. The platforms were covered with sleeping men, women, and children cuddling their teddies, some on crude bunk beds, and of family groups eating sandwiches, brewing tea and heating soup on camp stoves. I had to pick my way through them and over their belongings to reach the exit. The impression was of a huge jumble of humanity covering each platform.

During one awfully tragic night, many people were killed while making their way down into Bethnal Green Underground tube station for shelter. One person slipped at the top of the stairs causing a domino reaction, which crushed everyone below, resulting in 178 fatalities. 177,000 people regularly used the Underground shelters at night. During the Blitz nearly 43,000 civilians were killed.

By now it was rare to see a young man out of uniform. Trains were crowded with soldiers carrying rifles and heavy oblong kit-bags, with their identification numbers stamped in big black numbers along the side.

The main roads were full of military trucks, vehicles and open lorries from which high-spirited young soldiers waved and whistled at pretty girls.

I first learned of 'Lord Haw-Haw' when I overheard a small group of women on a street corner laughing and jeering about a voice on the radio the previous evening saying, in menacing tones, 'You've got away with it so far, Hendon, but it is *your* turn next.' I found it puzzling that this ominous statement had caused merriment rather than fear, until Mum explained.

At first, very little information of the war's progress was given out in the media, so people began to tune in to German propaganda broadcasts from Hamburg searching for news. 'Doctor' Goebbels, the propaganda minister, cooperated with the German Foreign Office to plan programmes presenting the war in a favourable light for the German cause, and they tried to undermine British morale by half-truths, twisted truths and blatant untruths.

The British authorities were at first alarmed as to the possible effect these broadcasts would have, but after a while they were seen as harmless entertainment, and were treated with derisive scorn. The newsreaders, obviously English, weren't taken seriously and became a national joke, held in high contempt. ('Lord Haw-Haw' was at first used as a collective nickname for two or three of the readers, but later came to be applied to one man in particular, William Joyce, an Irish-British Fascist who had fled to Germany at the outbreak of war. He became the most hated man of the war after Hitler, and was later captured, accused and convicted of Treason.)

One night we had a very close shave when a bomb landed in the next road. It landed in a clump of laurel bushes so did very little damage, although it made a heck of a thud when it hit the ground. We felt the vibrations within our shelter and were quite convinced we had lost our house. The sense of relief was overwhelming next morning when we saw it still standing.

Supervised by Mum, I was in the bath one evening when the air-raid Alert sounded slightly earlier than we had come to expect. We were about to empty the bath when we heard the dreaded shriek of a descending bomb, followed by the inevitable thud and bump, rattling of windows, and shaking of the very foundations of the house. I don't think anyone could have made it faster from bath to shelter than we did that night.

We heard next morning that a landmine had flattened Colindale Underground Station. There were two trains there at the time, both packed with airmen and nearly all were killed. We were becoming hardened and immune to news of casualties and sudden death, but that event stunned and upset us all, and brought home to us just what great danger we were in. I cannot now but help reflect that an incident like this would be treated as a major disaster in peacetime, but these tragedies were occurring almost every day with barely a two-line mention in the newspaper.

The legendary stoicism of the British was in evidence each morning. A neighbourly nod across a garden hedge would bring forth such pithy one-liners as 'A noisy night, eh?' or, 'Nearer this time!' Sometimes, 'Trying to knock the aerodrome out I suppose.' Defiantly, 'They're not getting me out of *my* home!' Then another nod was exchanged before continuing the day's business.

It was about this time that I asked Mum what would happen to us all if Hitler invaded our country. 'You two girls would be taken for Hitler's breeding programme', (we were too young to understand the implications). 'Michael would be forced to join the Hitler Youth Movement. All Jews, gypsies, the old, crippled, sick and insane would be done away with.' There was no need to continue. To everyone it was becoming increasingly obvious that Hitler was a raving lunatic who just had to be stopped.

One noisy night, knowing we were all awake, Mum called us into her bedroom to see a spectacular sight from her south-facing window. A vast part of central London was on fire. Beyond the stark silhouettes of near-by houses was a huge yellow glow, darkening gradually to bright orange through red to purple. It was barely believable as we all watched awe-struck. The whole sky was aglow. Mum remarked that we were witnessing history; we would remember this sight all our lives, and our grandchildren would read about it in books.

We cuddled together in our dressing-gowns watching for some time, wondering what incidents, tragedies and tales of heroism would be reported in the morning paper; and how much longer we would have to endure this traumatic and frightening state of affairs which had become everyday life for us.

The raids began to slacken off in early November 1940 and families were beginning to regain confidence that they could once more sleep uninterrupted in their own beds. News came of bombings and devastation in Birmingham and Coventry, later Plymouth, and London again in the new year, when Guildhall (not the music school) and St Bride's Church were damaged in a raid on the City.

Winston Churchill appealed to America for help in his 'Give us the tools and we'll finish the job' speech. The fear of invasion was still strong, but it was suspected that Hitler had missed his opportunity. Instead of invading us at the start of the war when we had been so unprepared, he marched into Norway. His armies then turned towards Russia. The nation then breathed a sigh of relief, for an invasion of Britain now seemed unlikely for the present. We prayed that the English Channel, as in the past, would save us yet again.

4

We All Do Our Bit

We rarely saw Dad once he had joined the Royal Marines. I believe that he was first sent to Leigh-on-Sea for initial training, and Mum was allowed to join him there one weekend. He occasionally had a weekend at home while in England and, very rarely, a whole week's leave was granted which usually meant that his unit was due for overseas duty. He was stationed at Portsmouth and Chatham at various times but I was exceedingly vague about his wartime career.

Very little information was given to Mum, still less to us children. Secrecy was paramount. It was constantly drilled into us that we were never to discuss Dad's whereabouts with anyone. Posters on hoardings, in buses and trains warned, 'Ssh – Careless Talk Costs Lives'. It was assumed that Hitler's spies were everywhere.

We never knew in advance when Dad was coming home. The husband of the lady next door was also in the forces. Both she and Mum were awakened one night by the clump, clump, clump of heavy boots getting louder and louder. Each wife lay in her bed wondering whose boots they were. They belonged to Dad whom we hadn't seen for some months. Oh, the excitement that night! He was exhausted after carrying his kit-bag and rifle for many hours, much of it in the dark, but all that was forgotten in the joy of being at home with his family.

Our neighbour never heard her husband's boots again. He died of a fever in Madagascar.

Meanwhile the bombs and raids were having their effect on Nanna and her neighbours in Thornton Heath. Like others without a garden shelter, she felt that the cupboard under the stairs was the safest place during a raid. Once inside her stair cupboard, one neighbour was too frightened to come out even after the All Clear. She only emerged, white-faced and trembling, after much gentle coaxing and encouragement from Nanna, and gradually became a nervous wreck.

Most of the houses in that area suffered from bomb-damage, with some quite badly hit. After a while Nanna and Grandpa could stand no more and decided to move. It seems odd in retrospect, but they moved to Lancing on the south coast near Worthing, renting a two-bedroomed bungalow until their house could be sold. With her usual zest for life she had soon thrown herself into many local activities. Before long she was President of the Women's Institute, learning how to can fruit and make leather goods. In the local drama club she found an outlet for her suppressed acting talent, surprising the family with her emergence as a comedienne. Her portrayal of Grandma Buggins became a local hit. She was a natural, but never understood why she was inevitably cast in that role. She revelled in all the admiration and was at her humorous best when the centre of attention.

Being in possession of exceptionally green fingers, her little garden was soon ablaze with colour, and full of fruit bushes. Gladioli were her speciality and every year she entered a few for flower competitions. Grandpa, much older than his wife, was a very quiet man who spent most of his time sunk into a big armchair reading the *Daily Mail* and smoking his pipe. He had an allotment nearby but it gradually became too much for him and he eventually abandoned it.

In the summer of 1941 when the fear of invasion was still strong, Nanna kept a pitchfork in her shed. One day, adopting an aggressive and threatening stance with it she announced, 'I'm ready for 'em! They won't get past me!' This was typical of the mood of anger and indignation that people felt against anyone who contemplated an invasion of these shores. Any attempt to do so would have been met with total defiance and very bitter resistance.

By now the south and east coasts were forbidden zones, the beaches totally out of bounds, protected by rolls and rolls of barbed-wire to keep people away from the dangers of hidden mines and other protective measures against possible invasion. Along the seashore were placed huge concrete cube blocks to deter enemy tanks from swarming over the beaches.

Before we could visit Nanna we had to apply for a special permit, which was granted because she was a close relative. Conditions of war allowing, each August we children spent three or four weeks in Lancing. Because the pleasures of the sea were denied to us, we turned inland and discovered the delights of the Downs instead. We took picnic lunches to our favourite spot overlooking Lancing and the village of Sompting, a hilly slope with a backdrop of trees and bushes. From there we enjoyed the spectacular view of Brighton and the white cliffs of Beachy Head to our left, across the wide vista of sea to Worthing and Selsey Bill to our right. The trees provided scope for games such as hide-and-seek. We also enjoyed bus rides to Clapham Woods, Arundel Castle, Brighton and Eastbourne; a whole new wonderful world opened up to us away from the confines of poor, sad, bomb-shattered London.

Attached to the rear of the bungalow was a glass conservatory with shelves covered with pot-plants at one end and a healthy thriving vine at the other. We often ate tea of cucumber sandwiches there, accompanied by noisy bluebottles flying around in the hot sun under the glass. Nearly seventy years later the buzz, buzz of a bluebottle still prompts the taste and smell of cucumber.

The large black grapes were delicious. Conveniently for us our bedroom window opened out into that end of the conservatory. I could lie on the upper bunk bed and reach out through the open window to pick as many grapes as conscience allowed. Only one bunch went the first night. As it was not missed, the following night we picked a bunch each. By the end of the week the vine was totally stripped of its grapes. We lay low, waiting for the anger and punishment that surely must follow, but Nanna said nothing. Instead, she guaranteed future protection of the grapes by rearranging the bedrooms!

The same fate soon befell her prize gooseberry bushes. One morning, after preparing pastry for a pie, she went into the garden to pick a bowlful of gooseberries and found the bushes naked. Not only had the lovely soft red ones gone, but the green also. This time her frustration caused a rare burst of anger, followed by silent treatment for two days. That was enough to ensure that we never again robbed her of fruit; but they were the most scrumptious gooseberries I have ever tasted!

After much of the garden in Colindale had been turned over to chickens, it became a constant battle keeping rodents away. One or two were shot, but that did little to control them so it was decided to keep a cat. A tabby joined us, but became ill and died after only eighteen months. Next came Chloe, a beautiful black and white specimen.

To my father cats were a menace, to be tolerated only because of their value in discouraging rats and mice. His main grumble was that they scratched and dug up seedlings and disturbed young plants. We often heard him mutter 'that damn cat!', so it was no surprise that he was very annoyed to learn, during one leave home, that Chloe was pregnant. The thought of even more of the 'damn things' appalled him.

The night before her kittens were due, Chloe had organised herself into a comfortable warm hollow on Bronia's bed, but Mum gently lifted her downstairs into a box filled with straw. Chloe's indignant protests were echoed by both Bronia's and mine, to no avail.

Very early next morning we crept downstairs and were surprised to find Dad leaning over the box, still in his pyjamas, gently stroking Chloe and talking lovingly and soothingly to her. Her very loud purrs could be heard upstairs as she licked each tiny kitten. Dad was not known for displays of tenderness and so, embarrassed at being caught, he dashed upstairs trying to hide his loss of composure by muttering, 'Yes, well … er … I just came down to make a cup of tea.'

Chloe's four kittens grew into the prettiest quartet ever of fluff, fun and frolic. How we all loved and enjoyed those kittens! We brought our school friends home to see them and, when they were old enough, we took the kittens into the garden to play. Neighbours watched from their windows, also enjoying the kittens' mad helter-skelter. Cleo, Blackie, Figaro and Mitzi created a happy diversion from matters of war, and the delight they gave us increased as they grew.

One day I arrived home from school to find a strange stillness in the house. Soon realising the kittens were missing I began a frantic but fruitless search. Mum sorrowfully explained that, as they were getting bigger, she could no longer afford to feed them so she had offered them to the Navy, who planned to take them on board a warship to keep rats at bay.

Silence greeted this unexpected revelation until one of us asked where was Chloe? 'She had to go too so the kittens wouldn't miss her.' It was not long before the obvious truth dawned but I said nothing, preferring to believe that our kittens too, in their own small way, were helping the war effort.

We all missed them.

The nation was at a very low ebb during 1941. Hitler had conquered most of Europe and was now advancing into Russia. Britain and Russia entered into a pact to help each other, and Mrs Churchill started her Aid to Russia fund. Now that Hitler's attention was elsewhere the threat of invasion receded and we all breathed more freely for a while.

Clothes rationing arrived; so did a plague of caterpillars brought on, no doubt, by the thousands of allotments everywhere, with all those inviting cabbages. After the Cabbage White had gorged its way through the depleted vegetation and was fat enough to search for a suitable place to pupate, the great migration began. At Lancing I was confronted by hoards and hoards of caterpillars wriggling across from fields on one side of the road to fences on the other. It was impossible to proceed without treading on them, so I had to pick my way very carefully on tiptoe.

Mum did her best to keep our allotment going when Dad was absent but found it difficult with three youngsters, her Food

Office job and bouts of asthma attacks. We spent a lot of time helping her remove caterpillars from the plants, the quickest method being to grab handfuls to drop into a bucket of salt solution. (I preferred to knock them off the leaves one by one at the end of a very long stick, but was ticked-off for not pulling my weight.)

Apart from cinema and radio there was not much entertainment during the war, which is why the Saturday night dances were so popular. These were held in village or church halls to the records of Henry Hall, Geraldo, Glen Miller, Joe Loss, Jack Payne and their bands. Most of the men were in uniform on leave, relaxing from the tensions of war. I was far too young to attend the dances and envied the older girls who seemed to have such fun.

Cinemas were popular. It was estimated that the total weekly audience was made up of 25–30 million people. Each programme consisted of the main film, a lesser feature or 'B-film', a newsreel depicting the latest events in the war, short documentaries and information films. Once inside the cinema we could sit through the main film again if we wished, as the programmes were continuous.

The Government soon realised the value of cinema to get its message across, so the Ministry of Information produced short features for imparting advice on such issues as raids, allotments, spies, unexploded bombs and healthy eating.

Morale-boosting films appeared which were honest representations of the war, e.g. *In Which We Serve,* the true story of H.M.S. *Kelly.* They were semi-documentary as well as being entertaining. Comedies were thought to be essential for keeping spirits high and were churned out regularly.

There were also Saturday morning cinema clubs for children, containing cartoons, short films and serials based on popular characters from comics. I attended these for a while but found the audiences too noisy, deafening the soundtrack, and I soon lost interest.

A party was once given in our local church

hall for children of absent servicemen. Bronia, Michael and I were invited. I cannot recall if it was Christmas-time but we had paper hats, balloons, a tea party, games, a conjurer and competitions.

We continued knitting scarves for servicemen, and woollen squares for Mum to sew into blankets. More experienced knitters made balaclava helmets, socks and gloves, mostly in khaki for the Army. These were collected by the WVS for distribution where needed, the blankets going to the homeless, air-raid victims, children's homes, casualty needs, Red Cross, and so on.

Our recently widowed neighbour knitted us a doll each, dressed beautifully as soldier, sailor or airman. Michael was given the sailor, me the airman: which proved prophetic in its way, as Michael later joined the Navy for his two years' conscription, and I married an ex-airman.

Mum and her friend at No. 6 conceived the

rather ambitious idea of producing and presenting a concert in the style of one of those pre-war concert parties held at the end of a seafront pier. Proceeds were to go to Mrs Churchill's Aid to Russia fund. The entertainment was provided entirely by the children of our road, and Mum organised sketches, choreographed dance sequences, found suitable songs and choruses and designed the costumes.

All the mothers fully cooperated, pooling their clothing coupons to buy enough bright blue and yellow material to make their own child's Pierrot costume. Each child was dressed in tunic or trousers, topped with a conical hat decorated by large pompoms.

Rehearsals were held in each others' houses with the usual traumas, tantrums, worries and panics, but it all came together eventually. The venture was a success. We gave two performances in a local hall, each attended by a large, appreciative and generous audience. Every one of the eight children had a solo item; singing, tap-dancing, recitation or piano solos, in addition to group items and routines involving the whole company.

It is amazing what children can achieve with enthusiastic coaching, goodwill, co-ordinated effort and cooperation.

Before Christmas in 1941 the Japanese had bombed the American Naval Base at Pearl Harbor and declared war on USA and Britain, prompting President Roosevelt to declare war on Germany and Italy. So at last we had a strong ally on our side and felt more hopeful of a successful outcome eventually, although we had a long way yet to go.

The German armies had reached Moscow, H.M.S. *Ark Royal* had been sunk, the Japanese had overrun Hong Kong, so things were still looking very bleak. In January 1942 they invaded Burma, and by the summer the Germans were in North Africa.

My parents developed a code that Dad used in his letters home to give clues to Mum as to when he was going overseas. His letters usually began 'Dearest', but if he was to be posted abroad he wrote 'Dear Dorothy'.

A letter arrived 'Dear Dorothy' in the spring of 1942. It was a long time before we heard any further news, even longer before we learned where he was, and an eternity before we saw him again.

5

Will It Never End?

As the war dragged on, radio played an increasingly prominent part in the nation's life. Daily news bulletins were a must, and the special record request programmes for the Forces were very popular, containing messages from servicemen overseas for their folks at home. We all hung on to Churchill's every word whenever one of his speeches was broadcast.

Comedians of the day kept us all laughing, raising morale. There were many, but the favourite by far was Tommy Handley whose programme *ITMA ('It's That Man Again')* was so popular it was on three times each week. Meals were served to coincide with his broadcasts so families could eat, chuckle and laugh together. Who can ever forget the much-loved characters of Mrs Mopp ('Can I do you now, Sir?'), Mona Lott, Colonel Chinstrap, Claud and Cecil, Funf (the German spy), Mr Handlebar, Ally Oop and the diver who, descending among gurgly bubbles, always implored, 'Don't forget the diver, Sir, don't forget the diver'?

ITMA was the first programme to introduce the new rapid-fire type of humour, and I therefore suppose it was the forerunner of the *Goon Show.* When Tommy Handley's sudden death was announced not long after the war, the whole nation deeply felt the loss. The BBC was often asked to repeat *ITMA* during the following years but it was explained that the gags and jokes were so topical that a new audience would not have found them funny. They were probably right, but those of us who heard them the first time would have loved a second chance to enjoy them.

Other favourites were Arthur Askey in *Bandwaggon,* Jack (blue pencil) Warner, and dear old Rob Wilton whose monologues in his unhurried lazy drawl always began, 'The day war broke out, my missus said to me, she said, "What are you going to *do* about it?" "About what?" "The *war,* you've got to *do* something",' by which time I was helpless.

The radio regularly broadcast names from the latest casualty lists. It was via one of these programmes that we learned of the death of a grandson of Nanna's cousin. It was a great shock suddenly hearing his name on the list of those killed in action.

Children's Hour was a great favourite for us. We enjoyed listening to 'Uncle Mac' who always ended his programmes with, 'Goodnight children – everywhere'. We found his voice very comforting.

Radio programmes were often linked by a tuning signal based on the three treble notes B-B-C. Also used was the motif from the first movement of Beethoven's fifth symphony. It happened to be the same rhythm as the Morse code signal for the letter V, 'dot dot dot dash' (...-). Beethoven stood for the rights of man, individual freedom and a fair deal for the oppressed, ideas all reflected in much of his music. He would have been very proud to learn that his valiant little rhythmic motif was being used as the 'V for Victory' call throughout Europe.

Along the south coast many of the now empty houses were requisitioned for use by the Army. The soldiers needed canteens, and these were organised and staffed by the WVS. Nanna helped with catering and serving in the canteen on Lancing front. Volunteers worked on a rota-basis, which meant Nanna being involved two afternoons a week, but she baked pies, tarts and cakes at home to take to the canteen.

We often went along with her to help, so got to know several of the soldiers billeted there. I remember one in particular, a sandy-haired reserved youngster named Tommy Swain. Nanna befriended him because he seemed lonely, not given to mixing with the others.

One Christmas (maybe 1942) when our family were together in Lancing, Nanna invited several soldiers and a couple of lasses from the village to share our Christmas dinner and the celebrations afterwards. It was during that afternoon I was introduced to the fun of Postman's Knock, Murder in the Dark, John Brown's Body and other games. I was too young to appreciate their potential for frivolous flirtation and harmless frolics, but the young adults took full advantage of the opportunities, entering into the spirit of the occasion and having a marvellous time.

The soldiers stayed until well past midnight. Tommy had no folks of his own and adopted us as his family, keeping in touch with us for several months. Sadly, we learned that he was killed during bitter fighting on the Continent. We were thankful that he had enjoyed a fun family Christmas at least once in his short unhappy life.

It must have been about this time that Nanna decided to acquire a few ducklings. While they were tiny it was easy to provide them with enough water for swimming. She dug a shallow hole to support a large upturned dustbin lid which contained sufficient water for a little pond. When Nanna wasn't looking we loved to cuddle and nurse the ducklings. I have no idea what later became of them. One supposes that they provided many eggs and a few dinners, but they couldn't have remained happy for long without a larger area of water.

Understandably, the war condition was reflected in the toys of the day. Michael spent hours on the floor directing his mini searchlights onto the ceiling, searching for imaginary planes, and firing tiny shells from realistic anti-aircraft guns at model aeroplanes suspended from the ceiling by string. The guns were adjustable to all angles and swivelled around on a base.

Little grey metal bombs had explosive 'caps' inserted into them before being dropped onto the pavement where they 'exploded' with a sharp crack, a sound which irritated grown-ups when repeated too often! The caps were bought in strips from toy shops and could also be fired in small toy pistols.

There were miniature toy tanks, military trucks, ambulances, lorries, etc. and metal personnel such as soldiers and nurses supported on a circular base and accompanied by props, e.g. stretchers.

Toy parachutes were popular, opening out effectively when dropped from an upstairs window. Michael once tried to make a parachute for himself using an old umbrella, and was preparing to jump out of an upstairs window to test it when Mum prevented him just in time.

Wartime characters, themes and motifs

began to appear on playing cards. Dolls were dressed in uniforms.

Also popular was a board game picturing the faces of leading Nazis around its border, surrounding that of Hitler in the centre. It was hung on a wall, then darts were aimed at it. Scores were gained according to which Nazi was hit. A successful shot at Hitler gained the maximum mark. Goering (Head of the Luftwaffe) and Ribbentrop (Foreign Minister) also had high scores. Goebbels (Propaganda Minister) and Himmler (S.S. leader) scored lower. I think Eichmann was the lowest.

There was another version of this game with rubber rings thrown onto hooks – less dangerous than dart throwing. Such games would be frowned upon now, but at the time they seemed a harmless outlet for our hatred of Hitler, his Nazis and all the evil they represented. Pictures and films of Hitler addressing vast crowds at rallies or reviewing his troops prompted much derision, scorn and laughter. Children took delight in mocking him by marching around with their right arms raised, shouting 'Heil Hitler!', and goosestepping like his army, which we all thought looked ridiculous. All this was good for morale.

During the war all forces' mail was strictly censored to prevent the enemy obtaining clues giving them vital information on troop movements, battle plans, the whereabouts and size of army units and battalions. Although Dad was always careful what he wrote home, so many words had been cut out of some of his letters that they arrived looking like pieces of delicate lace.

Even so, previously arranged codes between Mum and Dad informed us that during the autumn and winter of 1942–43 he was in North Africa, which meant he was now deeply involved in one of the most bitterly fought campaigns of the war. There were long gaps between the arrival of his letters when we had no idea if he was alive or not, but we knew from newspapers and radio that General Montgomery's Eighth Army (the 'Desert Rats') was battling it out with the Germans at El Alamein, eventually winning our first great victory.

After this victory Montgomery was held in very high esteem and affectionately known as 'Monty'.

With the landings of the British and Americans in North Africa and the defeat of Rommel, the war turned at last in our favour. This was a significant victory and there was much rejoicing at home. In January 1943 the Eighth Army captured Tripoli, and in May the Allies finally pushed the Germans out of North Africa.

Meanwhile the Germans had surrendered to Russians at Stalingrad, and there was talk at home of the war surely being over by Christmas. People were impatiently wondering why there was a delay in liberating Europe, and the slogan 'Start the Second Front Now' began to appear everywhere on walls, scrawled in white paint.

Mum procured a large map of Europe and North Africa to fix on to the living room wall, and bought little flags from Woolworths depicting the Union Jack, Stars and Stripes, Hammer and Sickle, Swastika and the flags of Italy and France. They were mounted on pins to stick into the map showing the latest positions of all the relevant armies.

Each morning we listened carefully to the radio news and studied newspaper reports before moving the flags accordingly. Depression set in if the Swastikas gained ground, elation if the Union Jack or Stars and Stripes advanced. Gradually all the Swastikas vanished from North Africa, and the Hammer and Sickles spread westward from Stalingrad. In July 1943 our little flags showed that the British and Americans had landed in Sicily and fully occupied the island one month later. (We learned afterwards that Dad was among the first to land in Sicily, and in Italy in September.)

At home many goods were becoming very

scarce. There was a shortage of petrol, fuel, food and beer. Supplies of petrol were so low that experiments were made to run cars on gas. Huge ugly gas bags appeared on many car roofs. With the shortage of fuel came power cuts and neighbours again had to share ovens for cooking. Nothing was wasted. Clothes and material had been rationed by a points system in June 1941, except for working clothes. This caused enormous problems as children grew. We often wore cut down and adapted adult clothes. Garments were inherited from older girls in the neighbourhood, and in turn handed down to Bronia. We learned to make our own dresses from remnants of material, and alter dresses that had belonged to others.

The WVS helped distribute second-hand clothing among the needy. The Utility trademark on anything new guaranteed good basic design and high standards of workmanship at economic prices. Worn sheets were repaired by the 'sides-to-middle' method. Boy Scouts and Girl Guides helped with the collection and sorting of salvage – anything that could be rescued and used again. Life was very drab. Bright colours were rarely seen. Houses were painted in brown, black or dark green. Even the interiors were dull and cheerless. To this day I hate to see anything wasted. I still have only 6 inches of water in my bath; turn off all lights not in use; remain frugal with my use of gas and electricity; and never buy new if the old will still do. I also still shudder with fear whenever I hear a wailing siren – feelings and habits still deeply entrenched within me and, I suspect, with most people of my generation who lived through the war years.

One of the jobs of council workers was to search for empty houses, or occupied houses with a spare room, which could be requisitioned for the use of US Servicemen. They knocked on our door more than once asking if we could house an airman but Mum had to turn them down.

Michael had a school friend living near Hendon Aerodrome whose family took in two airmen. One of them started courting the beautiful sixteen-year-old at No. 8, other residents in the road following the flowering romance with interest and not just a little envy. Wide-spread consternation followed their engagement ('far too young'), but as soon as the war ended June became one of the thousands of young war brides of American servicemen who settled in the United States, her mother and younger sister later joining her. I often wondered how she fared in her new life.

People were beginning to notice how fit and bonny all the babies were looking. At the start of the war the Ministry of Food had begun to issue concentrated orange juice and cod liver oil, via the welfare clinics, to all children under five to supplement the meagre food rations. It soon made a dramatic difference to children's basic health.

There were long queues at shops for essential foods, but it became an unwritten rule that all the pregnant and elderly be served first, and usually were.

We had a very reliable electric chiming clock in our living room, which had given trouble-free service since the day it was bought soon after Mum and Dad married in 1930. One day it suddenly stopped for no apparent reason. Immediately looking concerned and pale, Mum said, 'Oh no – Daddy's in trouble.'

Not long after, she received official notification that Dad had become seriously ill with malaria, on the very day the clock had stopped, and had been taken from the front line in Italy back to hospital in North Africa. It seemed odd that Mum should link the clock with Dad's welfare, but it was from incidents such as these that we became aware of her uncannily accurate premonitions and highly perceptive sixth sense which rarely let her down.

As soon as he was well enough to travel Dad arrived home on extended sick leave, armed with several bottles of quinine to treat the expected recurring attacks of malaria. He told us of his ordeal and of being so ill;

how he was lying in bed one night soaking in deep pools of perspiration, in a partial coma, when he overheard one nurse whisper to another, 'No need to sponge him down – he'll be dead by morning.'

He remembered thinking 'Oh, will I?', and mustered all his mental energy, determination and stubborn will to survive the night and prove the nurse wrong. It was not his first close shave with death and was not to be his last. His recovery amazed the doctors and, despite all warnings, the malaria never returned. Our clock started again as mysteriously as it had stopped, and was still going strong forty-six years later.

Dad had started the war with thick black wavy hair. He returned from the desert with it nearly all gone. What remained was greyish, thinning and straight, reflecting all the stress and trauma he had been through. He seemed to lead a charmed life while abroad, and had a few tales to tell of near misses, swopped duties and sheer luck saving his life.

In his kit-bag was a badly dented buckle

from his belt. It had saved him when a German charged straight at him with a bayonet. In another incident we would have lost Dad if he had not swopped guard duty with a marine, who was then blown up by a shell while on guard.

We were very proud to learn that Dad had been promoted to Lance Corporal, and were in awe of the stripe sewn onto his jacket. But he later returned it after he had refused to obey an order to place another marine on duty. As the man was very ill at the time Dad refused to do so and he demoted himself. However, he left the service after the war with a report which described his character as 'exemplary' so his transgression was forgiven.

After a few welcome weeks at home regaining his strength, Dad was pronounced fit enough to resume active service. At the end of his leave we all accompanied him to King's Cross station to say our goodbyes. It was the first time we had done this. I was not aware of his immediate destination, but the station platforms were crowded with servicemen kissing wives, children and sweethearts, and the train windows were alive with waving arms and fluttering handkerchiefs.

Once we had returned home Mum said it was suspected that Dad was being sent back to the battlefields, hence the extra lingering and tearful farewell at the station.

6

Here We Go Again

Calls to start the Second Front (allied invasion of the Continent) were becoming increasingly vociferous, but an operation of that magnitude had to be planned with maximum secrecy and meticulous attention to detail, and could not be entered into until all was absolutely ready.

We had noticed that troop movements and

activity were increasing at Lancing and all along the coast. Military convoys and vehicles were clogging up the roads, taking precedence over, and often delaying, civilian traffic. Rumours abounded as we entered 1944. We all knew that the allied invasion to liberate Europe could not be far off, and waited for it with impatience because it would mean the beginning of the end for Hitler and his maniacal policies.

September 1942 had seen the start of my senior education at a girls' grammar school in Hampstead Garden Suburb. The journey to school took an hour, including a forty-minute ride on a trolley-bus which was motivated by wires strung overhead, linked to the bus's roof by a long pole. I had a mountain of homework each evening, which meant bedtime getting later and later, but I soon adjusted to these changes. Bronia joined me one year later.

I was not happy at school. Although I did well academically, I was a failure socially, being too serious and quiet to mix well with the more exuberant self-confident girls, who took a cruel delight in seeing me put down, laughed at or snubbed. They soon tagged me 'Pixie' because of my petite stature. If they expected that to annoy me they were disappointed. I quite liked the name. I was surprised to find I was the only girl in my class with a father young enough to be in military service.

I was too shy to make close friends but I enjoyed singing in the choir (which broadcast once on *Children's Hour*), occasionally performing a piano solo at concerts, and accompanying a talented flautist, which meant visiting her home near the school for rehearsals.

School dinners reflected the austere diet of the day. There was lots of tasteless sponge pudding containing hard stringy dates, and apple pie sprinkled over-generously with cloves. A girl named Eva loved them. After the meal she collected everyone else's cloves and ate them all at once, making us shudder, wince, and turn our puckered faces away in disgust. Tapioca pudding was unpopular and rice was never cooked properly. I cannot remember much about the main course except for the peas. These were invariably hard as pellets, their colour but a pale apology for green. Each serving contained at least two boiled out maggot skins, but we survived, and looked surprisingly healthy on it!

The first few terms at senior school proceeded smoothly without incident. Then the air-raids started again and London groaned. We submitted patiently and with increased fortitude to a further onslaught from above, facing with fearful anticipation all the dreaded consequences.

The raids were sparse at first but gradually increased in frequency and severity. A big difference between these raids and those of 1940 was that all the rescue services were now better organised.

Unexploded bombs became a serious problem. After each was discovered people had to be evacuated from their homes and all surrounding roads roped off. Those marvellously brave and heroic bomb disposal experts then arrived to defuse it. Sometimes a bomb lay undisturbed for weeks, months or even years. Three were uncovered near Dartford nearly fifty years after they were dropped.

It was back to the shelters for everybody. In addition to the Anderson shelters in gardens, there was an indoor type of shelter known as the Morrison. Looking like a large cage with the sides measuring approximately 7 x 5 x 3 ft, it was designed for sleeping in. During one rare visit to my great aunt's home in Chingford, six of us slept in a row inside one of them. (Actually sleep was impossible. We were kept awake by talking, laughing and interpreting all the air-raid noises.) They were considered strong enough to give adequate protection from flying debris, collapsing ceilings and falling masonry. They were not available until February 1941 – too late to have been of use during the 1940 Blitz.

There were no purpose-built shelters at school but there was a large hall and stage under which was a maze of dressing rooms. All girls and staff were herded down there to sit out each raid. The whole of our second year summer exams were held in the makeshift shelters, papers balanced precariously upon our laps. When we weren't taking exams we played paper and pencil games to test our general knowledge and supplement our classwork. By the end of June the raids were so frequent that we spent more time in the shelters than in the classrooms.

It was during our mole-like existence in this concrete labyrinth that my close friendship with Pat grew and flourished. Our surnames were adjacent in the class register so we invariably found ourselves sitting next to each other. We soon discovered that her birthday was the day before mine so it seemed that fate had thrown us together, forming a close bond which was to last fifteen years.

Pat was my saviour, my protector from the taunts and mockery of others, my partner in laughter, my sharer of giggles at all and nothing, to the constant despair of our teachers. She was someone in whom I confided my most private thoughts and with whom I could ride out life's storms.

Her forte was tennis; mine was music. We each admired the other's skill, giving support during visits to the school dentist. In my troubled teen years I don't know how I would have coped without her.

We both detested cookery lessons, which were held in the top floor of the school. Towards the end of the lesson two girls had to carry out a dustbin full of rubbish to empty into huge receptacles behind the school. For most it was a dreaded chore but not for Pat and me. We always volunteered for the job just to get out of the classroom! By the time we had got the dustbin down four flights of stairs, we were helpless with laughter.

We took as long as we could, sitting and chatting at each floor level. The green paint on walls and staircase must have been very badly scored before we were through. Once we deliberately let the dustbin lid roll down on its own to see how far it would go and how much noise it would make. The resulting clatter went beyond our wildest expectations, reverberating around the whole school. Heads popped out of classrooms looking for the cause of the din. We swore it had been an accident and never dared repeat the experiment.

My last four years at school were made more tolerable by our shared fun.

Rumours began to circulate that the Second Front had begun. The skies were filled with the constant drone of planes flying south, giving credence to the rumours. On 6th June 1944 the Allies at last landed on the beaches of Normandy, and so began the last phase of the war. With the Allies now in Rome and Normandy and the Russians advancing towards Germany in the East, the Allied grip was closing in around the Nazis on all fronts.

Hitler was panicking. He had new weapons

up his sleeve and he decided to unleash them in a final attempt to demoralise Londoners and force a surrender. It did not work, but merely increased our anger and determination to see the mad tyrant obliterated.

It was nasty! A new noise arrived above us, which can only be described as a very deep humming drone. This new and frightening object resembled a flying bomb, was pilotless and programmed to end its flight somewhere near London or beyond. The aim seemed haphazard, causing widespread fear and concern.

With experience we learned that we were safe as long as its monotonous bass tones continued overhead, but once its engine became silent we knew it would drop. This sudden quiet was eerie. Panic followed as we ducked under furniture, dived into the nearest shelter, or fell flat on our faces and braced ourselves for whatever the expected crash would bring.

We soon attached nicknames to the horrendous things but 'doodlebug' was the one that stuck. Doodlebugs caused more devastation than bombs dropped from a plane. One, dropped on Edgeware in October, resulted in 5 fatalities and rendered 74 houses uninhabitable. These figure were typical. Over 10,000 of them were launched between June and September 1944, killing 6,184 people.

Emergency services were stretched to the limit. Service engineers worked round the clock to repair damage to gas/electricity/water supplies. Rescue squads, ambulance drivers, the Fire Brigade, police, WVS all sprang into action following each landed bug. By July doodlebugs were travelling north, causing further evacuations of families from London.

The occasional heavily censored letter from Dad gave clues that he was in the thick of it in Northern France, but no details. (He had been in the second wave of landings in Normandy on 6th June.) Paris was liberated amid jubilation in August, Brussels in September. Dad was in Brussels for some time, billeted with a family who had two daughters the same ages as Bronia and I. Marie Elizabeth and Elizabeth Marie were encouraged to start a pen-friendship with us. A few letters were exchanged but contact did not last long because of the language difficulty. A letter arriving later, starting 'Dear Jacqueline, Bronia, Michael and Ann', gave us the clue that Dad had moved on to Antwerp.

Stories began to filter through of horrors uncovered by the liberating armies. In Europe's major cities soldiers found execution rooms and torture chambers, and starving sick Jews in concentration and death camps, with evidence of mass genocide. These stories were met at first with total disbelief. Surely, hopefully, they were mere propaganda? With the proof of photographs, newsreel films and eye-witness reports, incredulity gave way to stunned shock and disgust at such heinous atrocities.

There was intense revulsion that some abominable evil could exist in the twentieth century, that men could stoop so low and become so depraved as to commit such wicked deeds.

There were also reports of a brave but failed attempt on Hitler's life. If successful it would have brought the war to a quicker end, preventing further loss of life.

Hitler's final desperate attempt to break our spirit and cause collapse of morale on the home front occurred in September. Rumours of rockets or rocket shells began to circulate, and became reality in the autumn. The doodlebugs were labelled V1s, and the rockets V2s. They caused new sorts of bangs, huge deep craters, violent earth tremors and high numbers of casualties.

The arrival of the V2s was a new shock, and each one arrived without warning. They were 45 feet long, and 1,043 were launched killing 2,754 civilians, although not all reached their target. London lost 130,000 homes – the damage was extensive. A total of 60,595 civilians were killed during the war.

We learned to live with the fear of sudden

death, constant scenes of chaos, trailing hoses, puddles of water and debris everywhere in the streets. It was not until November that Churchill confirmed that we were being attacked by rockets, although we had suspected it for some weeks.

The Allied advance was checked by strong German resistance during the winter of 1944–45, delaying final victory by some months. That winter was severe and desolate, dragging on like the war itself. Everyone was depressed and fed up as the V2 raids continued. No wonder there was such a release of emotion and wild rapture when victory finally came.

The German offensive in the Ardennes finally collapsed in January and, as the Russians entered Germany, we could sniff victory in the air. But at home potatoes and coal became very scarce, there were further power cuts, and the queues outside ironmongers' stores for paraffin became longer.

By this time I had completely forgotten what it was like to live in a country at peace.

I could not imagine windows without netting or tape, clear peaceful skies, being without fear of death crashing down upon us, shops and streets bright with lights, to see a larder full of unrestricted supplies of food, to have a father living at home, to be able to travel whenever and wherever we wished, to bathe in the sea, to sunbathe on a beach. I tried hard to conceive of such heaven, but my mind was too limited for the task.

Council surveyors began to call on all homes, making note of every crack in walls and ceilings before sending in builders to begin the huge task of repairing all war damage free of charge. Hardly a house had escaped.

The little flags on our wall map were moving towards Germany. Russian flags reached Berlin in the spring, the Union Jacks crossed the Rhine in March. Also in March the last V2 fell, on Orpington in Kent. More details were coming to light of concentration camp horrors. Pictures of wasting bodies of the inmates at Belsen were shocking. The long-awaited Russian-American link up took place in April at the River Elbe. The official end of the blackout came in April although people had already become lax.

Towards the end of the war a very attractive young lady dressed in the Canadian Air Force uniform unexpectedly knocked on the door. She introduced herself as Doris, daughter of Richard Hollings, my grandfather's brother who had emigrated to Canada at the turn of the century. Thus I learned that we had cousins in Canada as well as New Zealand. She was stationed at Odiham in Hampshire and looked us up before returning home. I was thrilled when she left me her bicycle. Being old and somewhat rusty it was not easy to ride but I made great use of it. The children in our road formed a cycling club and enjoyed cycling through London to Richmond Park, or north to Stanmore, once the war was over.

When the danger of invasion had passed,

beaches along the coast reopened one by one as the mines were gradually cleared. We made good use of the one beach at Lancing which had been opened during the last months of the war. Before then, we had swum in the River Adur where it winds its way between the lower slopes of the Downs in the shadow of the tall stately Lancing College Chapel, on its way to the sea at Shoreham. That had been fun, but nothing compared to being allowed now to paddle, splash and swim in the sea.

Our delight knew no bounds. Novelty led us to spend every hour of daylight on the beach, leaving only when hunger beckoned. It took just five minutes to walk from sea to bungalow, dripping with seawater, trailing seaweed and leaving sandy footprints in our wake. Nanna prepared picnics for the beach and, being a strong swimmer, often joined us in the water. Sometimes she made an early morning cup of tea for us, only to find our beds empty. We had already left for the beach, returning an hour later for breakfast absolutely ravenous. She called us her water-babies.

We enjoyed venturing further afield, often walking into Worthing one way or Shoreham the other. Our family had always enjoyed seafood such as prawns, winkles, crabs and shrimps, so one day Bronia suggested that we walk along the beach to hunt for shrimps. Nanna was startled when we returned with a bathing cap full of water and shrimps which Bronia had carefully carried home. Nanna boiled them, but after we watched them trying to jump out of the saucepan in agony, we weren't so keen on eating them.

Gradually the rolls of barbed wire were dismantled and we were able to use the beaches more freely. The enormous concrete blocks remained a while longer, allowing children to play on and around them. The gaps between were just too wide to jump over, except for the very daring and agile like Michael. I never attempted it. Those blissful weeks each year at Lancing were among the happiest of our childhood.

While we were spending some of our Easter holiday there, news came through of the death of President Roosevelt. The nation lost a good friend, and we thought how sad it was that he did not live quite long enough to share in the triumph of victory.

7

It's All Over

When they realised all was lost, Hitler and Goebbels committed suicide, their bodies found in Hitler's bunker in Berlin. The official surrender of the German forces followed on 6th May 1945.

Everyone went absolutely wild with happiness, excitement and relief. Church bells rang out for the first time in nearly six years and people danced in the streets with unrestrained joy, even strangers spontaneously hugging each other. Flags and bunting were strung everywhere. May 8th was declared 'VE Day' – Victory in Europe. Street parties were hurriedly organised and one was held in our small cul-de-sac. Bonfires were lit everywhere.

Accompanied by Bronia, her friend Joan and her mother, I visited Trafalgar Square, a mistake I was never to repeat during times of national celebration. The density of the crowd was frightening. We could not move and were crushed against each other. The only way to reach the tube station was to crawl over the bonnets and roofs of cars jammed to a standstill.

The air of carefree gaiety lasted several days. The whole population was united in its exultant celebrations, like one huge happy family.

After the parties and celebrations were over, a strange thing happened. Suddenly, unbelievably, all the camaraderie, concern for one's neighbour, the caring and sharing, seemingly vanished. Everybody returned home, closed the front door on his own private world and once more assumed the mantle of reticence that is so typically British.

It was all over. People again became strangers. Why does it take a disaster to bring out the inherent goodness of people? We know it lies there under the surface, but we rarely see evidence of it until trouble or tragedy strikes.

Newspaper reports soon reminded us that the war was not yet over in the Far East. Lives were still being lost, battles fought, in the struggle against Japan. It would take the dropping of two atomic bombs to end it, three months later.

It was a long time before life and conditions returned to normal. Food remained scarce and rationing continued. Even five years later bananas were being sold only from under the counter to favourite customers. When Bronia saw her first post-war banana she had to be shown how to peel it.

Each man returning home from military

service was issued with a demob suit, usually badly fitting and of poor quality. After Dad was demobbed he never spoke of the war or his part in it. He casually picked up the threads of his civilian working life in a newspaper office as if the previous six years had never happened. Not for him reminiscences, reunions, or war films ('actors could never portray accurately what we went through'). He drew a curtain across the whole episode.

A corner of the curtain was lifted slightly some years later when Dad boarded No.60 bus. He and the conductor stared at each other in disbelief before breaking out in excited greetings and affectionate back-slapping. The bus was held up for five minutes as the two ex-marines looked back on old times and brought knowledge of each other's life up-to-date.

It was difficult for returning servicemen to resume family life after a few years' absence. Our family also experienced some of the problems of re-adjustment we had been warned to expect. For some months, Dad tried to run our home as if it were a military camp, having strict rules and making out duty rotas. It nearly drove Mum crazy. On Sundays she was to do nothing. We children were to prepare, cook and clear each meal, and complete other household chores as directed. We all hated and resented it, as Dad scrutinised our every move but did very little himself. We eventually rebelled, even Mum.

Gradually, family life settled down to normal. We were aware how lucky we were to have come through those years of upheaval alive and healthy when so many did not, and we gave thanks.

Because there had been no social life for us for many years, I had few clothes other than a school uniform – the need had never arisen. I did not even own a 'best dress', but it became necessary to expand my wardrobe a little as I grew older. We could not afford new clothes, so for years I wore hand-me-downs from two older girls in our road, and these in turn were passed down to Bronia. Jumble sales proved a useful source of supply. There was a lot of making-do, mending, altering and adjusting for many years, with Mum's sewing machine constantly on the go.

During tube journeys into the City I took an impish delight in joining other passengers in peeling the sticky net off the windows bit by stubborn bit. It seemed strange at first to be able to enjoy an unfettered view of the world through clear windows; very strange.

Not long after the end of the war Michael, then aged about ten, wrote to Montgomery to thank him for looking after his father and was thrilled to receive a signed reply in which Monty sent his 'best wishes for the future to you and your family'.

My introduction to politics came at school. Ten of us were seated around the dinner table one day, eating the usual unappetising mish-mash, when the older girl supervising us suddenly asked, 'Who are your parents voting for in the election?' The question prompted a spate of excited chatter, but I had no idea what they were talking about.

She repeated the question to each girl in turn, the replies being either Labour or Conservative, but mostly the former. By the time she came to me, a mental eeny-meeny-miny-mo had come up with an answer. Guffaws, jeers, sniggers and scorn greeted my reply of 'Conservative'. Turning a bright red I sank to the very bottom of the imaginary hole I had quickly dug for myself. 'Why?' everyone asked rather aggressively. I could offer no explanation, so my ignorance and embarrassment prompted more laughter.

I asked Dad about it later. Although he held strong views, he tried to give me a fair unbiased appraisal of the two major parties as he saw them. He pointed out that in times of great national emergency, it was essential that all the main services, fuel supplies, food distribution, industry, farming and the armed forces should come under the rule of Central Government which could organise everything under its control to ensure maximum cooperation, efficiency and united effort, as had been the case during the war. Perhaps also in its aftermath, it would help the country recover and get back on its feet. With this is mind, the Labour Party planned to nationalise all the major services and industries, and expand the welfare state which was started in a small way by Liberals earlier in the century. Higher taxation would pay for all this.

The Conservative view was that complete central control was unnecessary in normal peacetime conditions. There was an instinctive dislike of one's life being controlled by bureaucrats in Whitehall. People were happier and better motivated when they had freedom of choice and individual liberty. Wasn't that what we had been fighting for?

Lower taxation meant more money for individuals to invest in small businesses, creating more work to keep men employed. Healthy competition between smaller firms encouraged efficiency and lower prices. Public money should be spent only on those in true need, e.g. the sick, poor, unemployed and old.

I mulled this over for a while and could see common sense in both viewpoints. Why couldn't we combine the best from both parties? Why couldn't we have the best brains from each party to form the government? Dad had no satisfactory answers to my questions, other than the glib, 'Things aren't done that way.'

Despite the hurt I still felt from the rude and scornful young lefties at school, I thought Labour's policies would probably prove best for the first years of peace during the nation's recovery. There was so much to be done, so much clearing up to do, and massive reorganisation as industry reverted to civil from military production. So I was not very surprised when Labour won the first post-war General Election.

By nature I felt I leaned towards Conservatism for the long term, but I planned to keep an open mind for the future, to wait and see what life had in store. Only experience could gradually shape a viewpoint one way or the other. It would be interesting to await developments, to discover how we would all progress, nationally and individually.

To quote from a recent broadcast: 'Britain won the war. Now she had to win the Peace.'

Postscript

During the years after the war I continued my music training and, after a brief spell of performing, married and settled down to family life in Bristol, later moving to Kent. I have taught music privately as well as in a wide variety of schools. My family includes one daughter, three sons, eight grandchildren and two great-grandchildren. I still teach piano in West Sussex.

Bronia became a cellist and skilled pianist but chose nursing for her career, training at the Middlesex Hospital. She became a district nurse, midwife and health visitor in Berkshire and north London. Now retired from general nursing, she works privately as a carer for the elderly in need.

On leaving school, Michael became a compositor's apprentice at St Clement's Press before starting his career as a printing consultant in sales management. In addition to running his own business near Reading, Berkshire, he is a keen amateur musician. He also has children and grandchildren and is now retired.

Rose (Nanna) lived until 1963, aged eighty-two.

Dorothy (Mum) joined classes in pottery and landscape painting when she was free of family commitments. After retiring, Stanley (Dad) studied classical music composing at Morley College. Both lived to the age of eighty, until 1987 and 1988 respectively.

Jacqueline Hollings, 2009

Thanks are due to:

Joanna Lecuyer for typing the original manuscript.

Sara Watt for her enthusiasm and setting me on the road to publication.

Michael and Patricia Hollings for their encouragement and support.

The publishers hope that this book has given you enjoyable reading. Large Print Books are especially designed to be as easy to see and hold as possible. If you wish a complete list of our books please ask at your local library or write directly to:

Town Gun

Also by Colin Willock

HAZANDA
THE COAST OF LONELINESS
THE ANIMAL CATCHERS

Edited by Colin Willock

THE ABC OF FISHING
THE BEDSIDE WILDFOWLER

Town Gun

COLIN WILLOCK

Illustrated by Rodger McPhail

With an Introduction by
Philip Brown

ANDRÉ DEUTSCH

First published 1973 by
André Deutsch Limited
105 Great Russell Street WC1

Filmset in Photon Times 12 on 13 pt. by
Richard Clay (The Chaucer Press), Ltd, Bungay, Suffolk
and printed in Great Britain by
Fletcher & Son, Ltd, Norwich

ISBN 0 233 96464 9

All the articles in this book were originally
published in *Shooting Times*

Contents

Introduction

I was delighted when I was asked to write an introduction to this book. I have enjoyed the good fortune of being a friend of Colin Willock for many years and not long after I was appointed to the editorship of *Shooting Times & Country Magazine* I asked him if he would write me a regular, fortnightly feature under the title of 'Town Gun'. His first article appeared in the issue of November 18, 1965. A few year's later Town Gun's offering became a weekly one and I hope this happy state of affairs may long continue. This book is made up of a selection of these articles.

If I were asked to sum up the author in two words I think I would describe him as a 'professional enthusiast'. His almost boundless energy and enthusiasm permeate the pages of this book and, inevitably, that enthusiasm rubs off on others, making this wicked world a much better place to live in as a consequence. Whether he is shooting pigeon over decoys or is himself coming under verbal fire when he has to take his turn as field-captain on a motley pheasant shoot; whether he is watching wildlife in Africa or Australia or catching trout at Two Lakes in Hampshire; whether he is flighting duck on his beloved Fenland washes—whatever he is doing, in fact, one realises that the author is always enjoying himself. He also possesses a rich, almost bucolic sense of humour and has the rare ability to extract a lot of fun from misfortune or even near-disaster. It is only necessary to turn to pieces such as 'Night in the Hut', 'Rhino Dodging' or 'Digging Party Forward' for the reader to appreciate my point.

Colin Willock is the head of the Natural History Unit of Anglia Television, the stable in which that remarkable series of 'Survival' films have been bred so successfully over so many years. I know that he has enjoyed this work as much as he has enjoyed anything else to which he has turned his versatile talent but I don't mind saying that I think Anglia TV were fortunate to catch him. As a sportsman-naturalist I rate him second to none. In this book he writes: 'Shooting men and naturalists are often one and the same thing, though only shooting men and naturalists understand how this can happen. The ordinary member of the public simply just doesn't believe it possible.' I think the author might have included hunting and fishing men but otherwise his point is valid. Few writers have done more to blow away the fogs of prejudice that surround field sports and conservation than Colin Willock. This book, I hope, will not only be enjoyed by sportsmen and naturalists but also by many ordinary members of the public. They will probably learn a lot and, in the learning, they will be richly entertained and often highly amused.

It only remains for me to correct one error of fact in the pages that follow. You will discover that the author accuses me of 'conning' him into accompanying me on one of the best hill walks I have ever enjoyed. It is impossible to con Mr Willock into anything. He is much too strong a character to fall for that sort of thing. I wish I could say the same for myself. On that memorable trek through a Highland night and the better part of the next day we took with us a bottle of malt whisky. We had mutually agreed, when we started off at eight o'clock on the long climb up the Llarig Ghru, that we would not touch a drop of this elixir until our forty mile hike was threequarters done. At midnight, however, when we were at 2,700 feet and standing on the summit of the Pass, we (and by 'we' I mean Colin Willock) decided the occasion merited a swig from the bottle. Colin got the taste and subsequently conned me into letting him drink at least two-thirds of the remainder. I am therefore not surprised if he apparently could not see very much when, wending our way beside the Dee, we passed beneath the Devil's Point. Stygian darkness, my foot! I've already warned old Charon to hide the liquor when Colin hails him to be ferried across!

PHILIP BROWN.

PART I

Town Gunnery

Nursery Farm Shoot

By some people's standards, the quality of the shooting a Town Gun enjoys may not be up to much but, by heavens, how one enjoys it. It's the incongruity of the surroundings that does it. That and the fact that the shooting really ought not be there at all.

One of the major pleasures of town gunnery is having a go before departing for the office in the morning. My work does give me one great advantage. I keep rather relaxed hours. I don't catch a train from my outer suburb until just after nine. This gives a fair amount of scope for early morning ballistic exercises.

It was the commuters' train that started it. One station past my usual boarding point, the railway line overlooks one of my nursery farm shoots. I always try to capture a window seat on the farm side of the gangway and then clean the window either with sleeve or newspaper to command a good view of the territory as we rattle and spark past on our electric progress London-wards.

This particular morning, at the start of one of the few frosty spells we have so far had this winter, I looked out from my non-smoker to see a field of what I remembered as young spinach, covered with woodpigeon. I resisted the urge to get out at the next station, perhaps solely because my train doesn't stop there. Next morning would now have to do. Battle, I decided, would commence as soon as daylight broke.

Daylight at this time is not fully with us until around 7.30 am. Over the years I have perfected a form of early morning dressing which, though it appalls my wife, nevertheless has its compensations for her. By spreading my shooting clothes across the bedroom floor in a trail leading to the door, I can grope my way out of bed in the dark when the alarm goes and, by the simple process of treading on things, find each separate item and don it as I go.

This style of dressing requires much the same forethought that is put into planning a car assembly line. In the latter case, it is no good coming to the wheels before the axles are ready to receive them. Likewise, to arrive at trousers before pants would cause delay and confusion, not to say bad language. Get things laid out in the right order and it is surprising how a simple stumble across the bedroom floor can see you safely on the landing wearing everything from wader socks to a Balaclava helmet.

If I'm going to shoot pigeon at seven-thirty, it means that I needn't start at the sock end of my assembly line until at least five minutes past seven—streamlined dressing cuts take-off time to a minimum. However, if I'm going to get up at five-past seven, I might just as well roll out of bed twenty minutes earlier and have a go at the duck also, especially as they flight over the spinach field in question. On this morning I decided to have two for the price of one.

It was cold, windy and very dark when I got the car out. At this hour the streets are still fairly deserted. A few cosy lights are on and you think with pity and a fair amount of scorn about the ignorant folks behind the warm window panes who don't know what they're missing.

The long hedge alongside the field is always a puzzle. The duck can choose any point along its 250 yard length at which to cross. If they're mallard, ten-to-one they'll come out at the top end and go back to the new reservoir. If there are any teal about—and there haven't been many this year for some reason—they'll rocket over the bottom part of the hedge and head back to the old reservoir. Frost like this often brings the teal in.

I hadn't had a teal there all that winter, so the bottom end it had to be.

The ground is so hard that I can drive the car right down the headland almost to my flighting point. This is handy since it means that I won't have to lug pigeon nets and hide stakes far once the duck flight, if any, is over.

By five-past-seven it's getting lighter slowly, clearer gaps showing between the ragged banks of clouds. The sky is beginning to go that watered ink pre-dawn blue when, suddenly, there is a bunch of about fifteen teal up and screaming overhead as if they'd just left Cape Kennedy. Two shots and down comes one, a beautiful little cock, practically unmarked, a regular little jewel. While the spaniel delivers him, two mallard swing over high. A double miss. Oh, well, they *were* going very fast in the gale.

There won't be any more duck. Those four shots will have put them all on the wing, so now out with the pigeon gear. The first thing I find is that I was wrong about the crop. It's not the spinach the pigeon are bashing. It's a field of young turnips and a fair old mess they've already made of them. They've plucked and shredded the leaves until it seems doubtful if the plants can survive.

There's no cover out there and nothing for it but to put the net hide up slap in the middle of the field and hope the birds are really hungry. I've seen them here on turnips before and they seem to get an insatiable appetite for them in hard weather. That appetite and a goodly spread of decoys may do the trick.

The next ten minutes is the zenith of town gunning pleasure. In the midst of this unlikely shooter's world I see the real, that's to say natural, world come to life. It's a rough red dawn, like a battle flag torn to shreds by the gale. Peewits are up and sweeping around the sinister sky like children's kites out of control. Then the gulls begin to flight from the reservoirs, thousands upon thousands of them, all going out to football pitches and flooded meadows, sports grounds and rubbish dumps to spend a delectable, garrulous day foraging for London scraps. They look wild enough against that sky, wild enough for one to imagine they are great skeins of geese.

A couple of mallard that weren't after all disturbed by the shots pass wide of my position. Now, a merganser going high for the reservoirs. Two herons beating out like tired old windjammers tacking in an unfavourable blow. A covey of partridges, only four I note, get up from a night spent among the leeks and zip away low into that rough patch where they often pass the day. A tawny owl says goodbye to the night with one last hoot and there's a kestrel up already, hunting the sewage farm for mice or voles.

The first two pigeon are in and down before I see them. I get one on the ground and the second as he takes off. I want them badly for the decoy build-up. For the next hour they come from all directions, turnip-mad and decoy-happy, from behind, from the sides, swinging into the wind at the last moment, giving the trickiest as well as the easiest of shots.

The irritated and irritating hoot of an electric train reminds me of that other world waiting. I remember that I promised my wife to pick up the good lady who does for us, no later than half-past eight. Can it be that late? It is. Thank heavens I remembered.

I pick up the slain and then pick up our daily help. There's bacon and eggs on the hot-plate at home and twelve pigeon and a cock teal on the back seat of the car. The hide's still up in the turnip field, for I'll be back there tomorrow morning. Meantime there's a whole day's work between me and another early morning session. When I finally pass my farm in the train, the turnip field is grey with pigeon again.

After the Flood

It's an ill flood that flows nobody any good, though some of my friends who found three feet of the Rivers Mole and the Wey in their sitting rooms might not be inclined to agree. My first selfish reaction to the Thames Valley deluge of 1968 was that it would be as ruinous to the duck flighting as it was to the living room furniture. With all those flooded fields to choose from, the duck would, I thought, be spread out pretty thinly on my particular piece of ground.

So, the first night after the waters began to subside, I didn't even bother to go out and look at my suburban nursery farm flight-line. That, as it turned out, was a serious mistake. To tell the truth, I wasn't even going to bother the next night, for the water still shimmered far and wide across the surrounding landscape.

I have often maligned a barrister shooting friend of mine in Town Gun, usually with justification, as for instance when he filled my Land-Rover up with paraffin in his hurry to go wildfowling. One day I shall probably go too far and then he will sue me for holding him up to ridicule, hatred or contempt, or all three.

Against that day, I am now pleased to chalk up one good mark in his favour. It was he who phoned me an hour before dusk, observing that the wind was blowing, that there would be bags of duck about because of the floods and what was I doing sitting at home, anyway?

I repeated my theory about the duck having all of waterlogged Surrey to choose from. To this he replied that he would be round in ten minutes and that I had better be ready.

As we approached the nursery farm, I saw that the water had indeed retreated, except towards the gravel-pit. This was now bank high and overspilling on to a field of lettuce where, only a few weeks before, we had been shooting nice bags of pigeon eating the chickweed. There would be no more pigeon there for a bit and precious little else besides, I fancied.

My friend, who is a man of forceful opinions, gave it as his considered view that the duck would tonight pile into the sewage farm. The sewage beds border the end of the farm directly opposed to the gravel-pit and separated from it by some 400 yards.

Though I didn't agree with his appreciation of the situation, I was happy to let him win the toss. I have a weakness for flooded fields and so, I am certain, have duck. I generously left him the Land-Rover and parted with the suggestion that if he heard a fusillade from my end to come up and join me.

Giving M' Learned Friend the vehicle was, as it turned out, a break of the first magnitude. I was able to approach the flooded lettuces behind a line of trees that took me within forty yards of them. I didn't expect there to be much on this splash beyond the few green plover I could see standing around the edge.

In fifteen years of shooting this particular farm, I can recall no more shattering moments than those that now followed. In fifteen years I had learnt, or so I thought, every quirk and mood of the place. I would have bet that I knew every clod of earth, every furrow, every ditch and hummock. I would also have wagered that I would never see more than ten mallard in the air at any one moment.

As I came round the corner of the last tree, the flooded lettuce patch exploded with mallard. I would guess there were at least 200 of them. I dropped one going away. The duck seemed at least as confused as I was. Some came back and I knocked a drake out of these with my second barrel.

The first duck lay fairly close to the edge of the gravel-pit—I had left the dog behind in case the whole place was under water. I dashed off to pick it and straight away fell into a ditch whose whereabouts and topography under normal conditions I knew intimately. But now it was covered by four feet of water and so, in another split-second was I.

While I stood there shaking the water out of myself and my gun, I saw that some of the duck were circling high. I just had time to reload one barrel and down came number three.

I am used to falling in. I've done a lot of it, from the Medway Estuary to Welney Wash. Somehow I hardly expect it to happen on my own doorstep. But what does a little damp matter compared with three mallard unexpectedly in the bag?

I picked No. 3 duck and then looked around for a more commodious flighting spot than a deep flooded ditch. The edge of the pit seemed the obvious place but where *was* the edge? I reflected that it didn't much matter if I failed precisely to find it. How much wetter could I get? To justify this line of thinking, I straight away stepped off-limits and fell into six feet of water and what was obviously the gravel-pit itself.

I have often watched young dogs panicking about scrabbling back up a steep bank and now I know exactly what they feel. With both waders filled to the straps, it took quite an effort to claw my way into a friendly reed-bed and out on to wet land again.

The first thing I saw on surfacing was that the duck were still milling around, reluctant to leave the area. I blew the water out of my barrels, trusted in IMI and their plastic cartridges to keep my powder dry and sloshed out along what I was certain used to be a track towards a solitary elder, still showing half of itself above the floods.

No sooner had I made use of this piece of back cover than four mallard came planing down the wind, wings half-closed, in a hurry to get back to whatever it was that so attracted them among the lettuce.

I have never made any pretence of being falsely modest. The boy was on form this particular night. I took a right and left out of that lot and added these two to the three duck in my sodden game bag. This was now becoming uncomfortably and unaccustomedly heavy so I hung it by the strap in the branches of the elder. As I turned round, another pair of duck whipped by. I got one shot off and then there were six.

At this point a long-expected sound reached my water-filled ear-drums—that of a Land-Rover being driven at high speed. In a few seconds M' Learned Friend appeared at a collected canter in a cloud of spray and demanded to know where the flighting was thickest.

I directed him to the only other cover, a nettlebed on the edge of a ditch some thirty yards to my right and listened with anticipation for the eventual and inevitable splash that meant that he was settling into position.

Within seconds, we were both engaged again. By the end of the flight we had eleven between us. Lacking a dog, we had to do our own retrieving. We were both well up to field trial standards in the water.

Miraculously, only one duck was lost and that in a very strange fashion indeed. Since I have started out by admitting my lack of modesty, I might as well go on and boast that this night everything, besides the retrieving, went swimmingly. I got nine in nine shots and finished on a right and left.

Having gathered the easy half of the latter, I brought it back stone dead and laid it in the grasses while I took off for the second bird. There was now a strong wind blowing, flattening the flooded grasses and driving quite large waves across the pit. When I returned with my second bird, the first mallard, which had seemed securely anchored, had simply disappeared, blown out on to the darkened waste of the floods.

That Was the Week

To be out is the thing. I suppose many people seeing the title *Town Gun* think: 'Poor old city-dweller. He can't take his gun out of the cupboard much. Poor chap lives within sixteen miles of Piccadilly Circus.' Pity me no more. Here, to put the record straight, is an account of Town Gun's doings this week, a fairly typical one.

Friday: Took a day's holiday due to me, for annual tidal flight with Jeffery Harrison in Medway estuary. Nice late start for a change. The tide is kind this time. Instructions read: 'Be at my house at ten am.' Note with gloom it's a beastly still day. Wife, with right idea after all these years, wishes me goodbye and says: 'Hope the weather turns lousy for you.'

Medway mud is the stickiest in the world. A mile-and-a-half to do. Very soon appalling results of three-month-old oil pollution show up. Creek edges are grimy. Vegetation, much of it food plants for wildfowl, looks as though it has been burned with a flame-gun. How much wildfowl and wader food went with this gift from a German tanker? It hardly bears thinking of.

Effects on the duck population are soon apparent. There should be at least 1,000 wigeon and perhaps 1,500 teal. We count packs totalling around 400 wigeon and 300 teal. Wife's good wishes don't materialise that bad weather for us. With no wind to trouble them, the duck ride the tide all day, both on flow and ebb, and barely flight. I fire five featherless cartridges. Still, it's lovely out there with the tankers riding by, cut off at the superstructure by intervening islands. I love fowling in this place better than anywhere, even when it doesn't work out.

At dusk, Jeffrey gets three teal and a wigeon, but they don't come my way. Plowtering off in the dark is an experience straight from hell. Without a torch and a thumb-stick to prise oneself out of the gutters, I think I'd have sat down and cried.

Saturday: Voluntary promise to wife to miss shooting pheasants this weekend in view of bonus on previous day. First Saturday I've stayed at home this winter. Do odd jobs in the morning. Cut up a tree for logs. Feel so virtuous that in afternoon think I'll take a stroll round local nursery farm. 'I thought you weren't going shooting,' my wife says.

Discover elder son has taken 12-bore for pheasants and friend has borrowed double 20 since his own gun has broken mainspring. Only thing left is son's single 20-bore. Walk into big covey, twelve strong, in leeks almost at once. Miss with first barrel and find to dismay I haven't got a second. End afternoon with two partridges, a snipe and a crazy fool of a woodpigeon that flew directly over my head.

Sunday: After lunch feel virtuous again, having spent all morning taking children to horse riding, fishing and guitar lessons (we do the lot). Decide to have a go at the pigeon. Strange to find them on cabbage when everywhere else in the country they are gorging barley. There isn't much barley in outer London! Still, they won't usually touch our cabbage until the snow or really cold weather comes.

Arrive late on scene and only shoot four. What they're doing to this cabbage won't make them the farmer's favourite bird. They've shredded the smaller plants down for cold slaw and even the bigger ones look as though they've been worked over with a ticket punch. Duty demands that I come out at dawn next morning.

Monday: It's still dark at 7.30 am when I leave home in number one son's taxi. Why taxi? Because, apart from being the ideal student's vehicle (it's cheap, reliable, roomy and slow), son keeps it permanently loaded with pigeon gear, nets, hide stakes, decoys. Check to make sure everything's there and set off. Put out yesterday's birds plus eight rubber decoys. Almost as soon as it's fully light, the first birds come. Don't shoot too well for a strange reason. The field is right against a big house.

Though I'm well within my rights as a crop defender, I have in the back of my mind that the owners may not be too keen on taking breakfast to a twenty-one-gun salute. After three straight misses, feel to-the-devil-with-it and shoot without thinking. Get a number of straight kills as a result.

Tuesday: Home from town to find son with long face. He's been out duck flighting and has bogged the taxi in an onion field. Now he's afraid the farmer may take exception. He may at that, especially as the field isn't exactly ploughed: it's planted with spring onions. So nothing will do but that (*a*) we try to get the taxi out and (*b*) we go and see the farmer to apologise. Better take gun, says son, it's a rough night and there may be rabbits sitting out. Find taxi inextricably sunk in onions, at least until tractor man comes next morning. If a taxi can be said to have plowtered, then this vehicle has done exactly that. But rabbits *are* out. We drive round with headlights raised and windows lowered and shoot a couple.

Wednesday: Out again after pigeon at 7 am. This time reckon I might as well have a crack at duck first. Only two mallard come off and they're well wide of me. Something has gone wrong with the duck this December (1967). Usually we've got a good head of mallard and teal. This year there's flood water everywhere. I reckon that they've got too wide a choice of feeding places.

Thursday: Pigeon again at dawn. Got fewer this time. Shooting is beginning to have an effect. It's incredible the regularity with which the first customers arrive. Half-an-hour after the light begins to turn grey, the skirmishers come sweeping in from over the river. This time of year, pigeon start feeding directly they can see to fly and go to roost very early. Usually they've had all they want by half-past two in the afternoon. Just to show the farmer I've been doing my stuff, I leave a good few breast feathers around among the cabbages.

Friday: Decide to write TV script at home. Fatal mistake as, of course, have pigeon on my mind. Make usual dawn foray and then nip back after lunch just to see if they've returned to cabbage field. They have, so spend happy hour persuading them to go away again. Persuade myself that, when I write at home, I start an hour earlier than in the office. Also, I don't take a lunch hour at home. So maybe this entitles me to an evening flight as well. Wind gets up around 4 pm, so decide I certainly am entitled. Just so long as I finish that script sometime.

Only two duck come in. I get one of them. Feel much better about going back to typewriter. Wife comes in from town and, seeing mallard on hall table, asks me if I've had a successful day's work. 'Yes,' I tell her, 'I've finished the script. I reckon I've earned a day's pheasant shooting tomorrow.' And that's another week gone.

Bus Stop Partridges

This year we have at least four good strong coveys of grey partridges and a few smaller groups—they are not big enough to call coveys—of Frenchmen. Nursery farms like my crazy shoot, sandwiched between rows of four-bedroomed boxes, reservoir banks, sewage farms and even small factory estates, have all held a fine stock of partridges as long as I have lived in the district.

When you think what a hard time the partridge has to survive in the open countryside, its triumphant survival in outer suburbia is all the more surprising. I would hardly have thought that a nursery farm makes an ideal nesting ground for this hard-done-by bird. The economics of growing green stuff for market demand that the ground is seldom allowed to stand idle. There is perpetual disturbance. A crop is either being drilled, weeded or picked. Between times, the land that just surrended a crop of leeks is being immediately spread with sludge to encourage it to push up whatever's coming next.

There may be compensations for the partridge in all this. Market gardeners are not great grubbers out of hedges. They leave odd patches of wasteland on which nothing flourishes

except discarded motor car bodies and battered bathtubs. These wastelands become a tangle of grasses and brambles and pleasant hidey-holes in which to brood a clutch of eggs. We have one such place on my farm, known simply as the dump.

Returning from a morning flight on the river, I often used to put up a pheasant on the dump, though it is now three years since I last shot one there. Maybe I could find one at home tomorrow, but the dump has long become an island in the middle of a fast-growing gravel-pit. This situation has its compensations, too. Not even the wolf-like mongrels who roam the farm will swim across to dump island and I suspect that our partridges know this and nest there. There is another sanctuary in the semi-swamp with its willow saplings which has grown around the ballast tip. Perhaps these two nesting areas between them account for the increase in our partridges. The birds must find safe and undisturbed nesting cover in both these apparently unpromising situations.

I wonder, too, whether a market garden does not supply an especially rich diet of insects for young partridges. There is comparatively little spraying done and this is mainly to defeat the weeds. Sludge from the nearby sewage farm is constantly dumped in great, enriching dollops. I cannot help feeling that this encourages all manner of creepy-crawlies. Whatever the ecological reason, I reckon that we started this season with at least fifty birds on this limited and unlikely ground.

We never shoot our partridges hard. Usually we give them no more than three goes, just enough to sort out a few old and barren birds and to break up the coveys a bit. On our enclosed territory there must be a deplorable amount of inbreeding and would be far more if it were not for our annual stir up.

It has always been tricky to come to terms with these birds. Now, with decreasing acreage, it is even harder. There are factors to be taken into account that certainly never trouble a gun on the Berkshire downs.

If that big covey gets up in the leeks right on the road boundary, will a double-decker bus pass at the crucial moment, compelling us to hold our fire? If they decide to go the wrong way, will they not only swing over the sewage farm but across the mainline railway, too, and if so, will we ever see them back? The safety drill has to be especially rigid. Though there are no footpaths within direct range, spent shot sometimes falls on anglers and lovers sporting on the nearby river bank. It is in vain to persuade an outraged damsel that No. 6 dropping in this way is as harmless as rain.

Four guns is our limit. This year, first time ever, we cleverly worked the two biggest coveys into a large strip of cauliflowers right in the middle of the farm. It had been raining lightly all afternoon but now monsoon clouds were building up fast. We walked the cauliflowers with model stealth. Thirty yards from the end and approaching the point at which there must be a great burst of partridges, we were engulfed in a cloudburst instead. In a second, the sky and ground smoked with rain. In that second, fully twenty birds—we later estimated—rose, though we clearly saw only two, one on either flank, and these fell to shots whose noise was blotted out by the rain. Of the remaining eighteen we neither heard nor saw a feather.

On my nursery farm shoot among the buildings, it is seldom a natural calamity like this that allows our partridges to escape. More often it is a low-flying helicopter, a woman with a baby in a pram, a string of pony club maidens who appear at the wrong moment. The best we have ever done is six brace but worth a hundred in more likely partridge country.

Sewage Farm Duck

My flight-line across the nursery farms and factory estates has behaved in a very odd way this year. The duck have not been running to schedule. Normally, their early morning and evening services are as regular, though, alas, not so numerous, as those provided by the mainline railway that passes close at hand.

The flight takes place between a reservoir and a sewage farm in the evening with a return trip around or just after dawn. In such urban surroundings the flight ought not to take place at all. The miracle and the perpetual fascination is that it does so. I have shot it now for thirteen years, though possibly 'shot' is an overstatement. It would be more accurate to say that I have stood at some point along its course, perhaps three times each week during the past thirteen seasons.

This may sound like criminal over-indulgence but I do not think that it is. My shooting diary tells me that I discharge my piece on not more than one expedition in three; that I seldom fire more than three cartridges on any given flight and quite frequently only one; that the most I have ever fired is eight; that the largest number of duck I have collected to date from one flight is nine; that I put in something like seventy hours per season; that a good bag for the season is between twenty and twenty-five mallard and teal, with an accent on mallard.

Those are the bare statistics. They give no clue to the fact that I have got more joy from this incongruous flight-line than from all the rest of my varied shooting put together. It is the proximity of commuting stockbrokers' bowler hats that makes it what it is—pure secret joy.

I found it originally from the map. I simply joined all likely roosts and feeding stations together with ruled lines, discarded those that crossed quite impossible territory—even I would blush at standing outside a bus station gun in hand—and then visited the remainder at dusk to see what happened.

At one I struck gold first time. Not only did I see eight mallard winking along against the stars, but their course lay across 150 acres of nursery farm. The farmer, good man, rented me his shooting for a nominal shilling, apologising that there was not much about.

It was a great season that first season. I have since discovered that it was a record teal year on my reservoir roost. There has been nothing like it before or since.

At first I stuck to evening flights, trying to intercept the duck as they stormed across the hedge into the filter beds. In those days the sewage farm was a good, old-fashioned, stinking puddle with lovely gooey mud pans rife with wild tomato plants in the early season. There is a reason for these tomato plants which is, perhaps, worth a digression. The human digestive system can break down most things, but not tomato pips. Given a second lease of life and released in such surroundings, the seeds can do nothing but prosper. I do not known whether the duck care for the small red fruits these wild plants produce. But whatever attracted them that first season, the mallard and teal certainly came—and in great numbers.

I began to learn how to come to terms with them. It is some of the most exacting shooting that I know.

At the beginning the sewage beds were unfenced, so that I could easily have got into them and used them as a flight-pond.

Fortunately, for once, I had the good sense to leave well alone. Had I shot inside the farm—leaving aside the illegality of the matter—I should undoubtedly have blown the flight sky-high. I found that, provided I stood out on the market garden and shot as the birds were up and still coming and had not crossed the boundary, the disturbance did not affect them.

These duck come in as though they are fired off launching ramps. Their course from take-off to landing is barely a mile and a half, a kind of sprint race. From the earliest days, it became a point of honour never to drop anything inside the sewage farm, for this meant disturbance, not to say trespass. After a year or two, the local authorities wisely closed the place in, for which I was deeply grateful. By that time the cowboys were beginning to ride our range.

To drop the duck my side of the fence, I found that I had a killing ground in the sky covered by about fifteen degrees of arc. I had to see the birds in time—not easy since sunset and sunrise are in exactly the wrong places for good visibility—and take them at exactly the right spot. Driven partridges coming low over a tall hedge aren't in it.

Then there was—and still is—the length of the boundary to be considered. The hedge is all of 250 yards long and the duck come in at any point they fancy. In this setting many things can influence the flight, factors that you do not meet out on the saltings such as electric train passing at the wrong moment. Add these to the natural vagaries of wind, moon and weather and you practically need a computer. After all this time, and having recorded and logged every freak and fluke of weather and moon in thirteen diaries, I tell myself that I know where to stand for any given combination of circumstances. But, of course, I don't.

After I began to get the hang of evenings, I tried a morning flight at the reservoir end. I did not expect to see much and I was late, hurrying along through a field of leeks in practically full light. Suddenly I heard a sound like the longbowmen's arrows must have made at Agincourt. There, above my head, were a hundred teal, splitting and jinking at the unexpected sight of a human and a gunner at that. I fired a panicky shot that merely stood them on their tails.

As I said, it was a great teal year. For mornings after that I stood behind an oak tree close to the river. On days when it was rough and dark until nearly eight o'clock, they would keep coming in fives and sixes and sometimes twenties and thirties. We get teal now but there has never been anything like that first year since.

The scene has changed. Somehow reservoirs and gravel-pits have opened up round my flight-line now. A large population of mallard and teal use these new roosts. All the same, I do not think that the additional water has incresed the flight. In largely urban surroundings it must be the availability of food that controls the total duck population rather than the area of the daytime roosts.

The season has—or rather, had—settled to a predictable pattern. In early September the main flight is *out* at nights as the young home-bred birds leave to find food. Why they do so beats me, for the filter beds are full of it. Perhaps they are just bored with home-cooking. By October, both mallard and teal are streaming in from the gravel-pits and reservoirs. But this year they have not streamed. You can see them all leave their new reservoir roost against the setting sun but they keep going on into the black hole of the sky to the south. Some nights hundreds and hundreds flight, but very few turn off and make the trip to our filter beds.

As far as I can see these are no less oozy and desirable. The duck have found something else. But what? It cannot be stubble. The little there is in the district has long ago been ploughed in. However, along the river bank towards the by-pass road there are large oak woods and it is a great acorn year. Can this be what has thrown the switch? This week I caught a high fast single, the only one I saw that night, coming back from the river and from quite the wrong direction. When the dog brought him I felt something like a marble in his throat. He was stuffed full of acorns. It does not prove my point but I certainly hope the acorn supply runs out soon and the flight-line returns to normal. There is always something to discover about duck, even when they choose to flight almost along the bus routes.

Cowboy Story

Here on the fringe of Greater London I suppose it is only to bc expected that we get our share of cowboys. Over the years I have had a number of clashes, usually inconclusive, with local lads intent on shooting my partridges and the farmer's notice-boards. I say that the encounters have been inconclusive because I find that there is not much you can do when isolated and outnumbered. For some reason, confrontations always happen when I am on my own and stuck in the middle of a large field with the nearest constable a good two miles away and probably not very interested in poachers anyway.

Lately I have been under the impression that things have improved, though it would be too optimistic to assume that the Armed Trespasses clause is widely recognised, or has even been heard of, among our local marauders.

This week I had the first encounter for some months. It was an unusual one because it was the first time I have had *Shooting Times and Country Magazine* quoted back at me. It happened at flight time the other evening when I was waiting hopefully for a duck on my nursery shoot bordering the sewage farm.

The sewage farm is very properly screened off against intruders by a high wire fence. No one is allowed to shoot there. However, few wire fences are high enough to deter the determined cowboy.

It was still quite light when I heard two shots in quick succession from the direction of the filter beds. A few moments later I saw two youths walking up the beds and heard a third shot. Now, quite apart from it being dangerous to shoot in this particular spot, it is also trespassing—trespassing, what is more, at the expense of the duck who use the place for food and shelter. I hurried over to remonstrate. The conversation went something like this.

Town Gun: 'I suppose you lads realise that you are guilty of armed trespass?'

First Cowboy: 'Good for you then, dad. So what you going to do about it?'

T.G.: 'I, personally, am not going to do anything about it because you are not trespassing on my property. But I think the sewage farm manager might be interested.'

Cowboy: 'Go ahead and tell him then.'

It is at this point that such meetings begin to lose their reality. If you simply say: 'I'm going to do so, right now,' the intruders know that you've got to get your car, drive half a mile and find some official who may or may not be interested in their activities. By which time the invaders have scarpered. So I tried another tack.

'If you shoot up this place,' I said, 'you'll finish the duck for all of us all round here. It's a sanctuary for them.'

'We're not shooting duck, dad. We're shooting snipe.'

A fresh point of attack offered itself 'I suppose you have a game licence, then?'

At this, the more voluble of the intruders walks across, puts his gun down and leans, arms crossed, on the wire fence and says: 'That's just where you reveal the depth of your appalling bloody ignorance, dad.'

'Oh?'

'You don't need a game licence any more.'

'Really?'

'Don't you ever read *Shooting Times*, dad?'

'As a matter of fact, I do.'

'Then you should know that all game and gun licences have been abolished.'

Well, I mean, I suppose one should be pleased that even the

cowboys (who might in time be converted, by reading this journal, into becoming law-abiding shooters) should be numbered among *Shooting Times* readership.

I wish that such characters would learn the elementary fact that you cannot afford to disturb duck on their roosting or night feeding grounds if you wish them to stay around for the sport of all concerned.

Triple Miracle

My younger son, Simon, who is shooting potty, had come home from boarding school for the weekend and duly demanded that I take him out with his 20-bore. For once, I did not have any sport readily at hand. I didn't know of a pigeon situation that needed attention locally. Our wash on the Ouse had so far disappointed and it didn't seem worth making a long journey for a couple of mallard. Nor had we started pheasant shooting on our Sussex farm shoot at that time.

Knowing that Simon would be perfectly happy if he came out with a gun, even if he didn't discharge it, I fell back on a small local farm where there are usually one or two coveys of partridges. At the last minute, my elder boy, Paul, arrived and said that he would like some fresh air, too.

On the way to the farm we speculated on the possibility of sport. I wasn't too optimistic. The cropping there has altered recently and the partridges no longer seem so keen on the place. Anyway, as we all agreed, it was the fresh air and exercise we were after.

As we drove down the farm track, Simon asked me what he did if Teal, the springer, put up a pheasant. He was met with a barrage of scornful comment. One, it was only too obvious what one did. Two, the last pheasant seen, and shot, on the premises had been, I think, in 1965. Small hope of bagging one in 1970.

We walked two or three fields of roots without seeing anything beyond a solitary 'Frenchman' who became airborne long before we could do him any harm. 'Might as well finish by doing the rough,' I said at last.

The 'rough' is a long stretch of weed and rank grass which the partridges have always shunned for some reason. So I confess I wasn't paying much attention. Not expecting anything to happen, I let my concentration lapse. I was just enjoying watching the dog work, though heaven knows what he was getting interested in: field mice or could it be hedgehogs?

A cry from Simon on the left flank. '*Dad!* Did you see *that*?' I told him that I hadn't. 'That,' he explained excitedly, had been a hen pheasant that had got up wild, well ahead, and flown straight down the rough into a small spinney at the end.

'It *can't* have been. There haven't been any pheasants here for at least five years. The local cowboys have got the lot.'

At that moment the springer darted into a thick clump of fat hen and out burst a magnificent cock. I stared at the bird unbelievingly for so long that it was practically out of range by the time I manage to fire my right barrel. The cock folded up.

Teal who is invariably far too quick off the mark was, I think, as surprised as myself. He stood looking at me. 'Hie lost, you cretin.' The terrible thought had struck me that the cock might be a strong runner and that, due to the dog's total lack of preparedness—not mine, of course! we might after all lose the one local pheasant.

Teal came to and took off in his well-known rocket-assisted fashion. The cock was indeed a runner but couldn't outrun the springer sprint champion. I held up the pheasant, as overjoyed as if it was the first I had ever shot.

We reorganised our line and advanced once more. About half a minute later, from a heavy clump of thistles, Teal dislodged a second hen which soared off, climbing fast to give Simon a nice crossing shot with his 20-bore. There was no question about the fatal nature of his discharge. Then hen folded in a cloud of feathers and was duly collected by the ecstatic Teal.

'Right,' I said, 'now we'll get the one that went down in the spinney.' I have made many such confident predictions in my time and have almost invariably been disappointed in the outcome. The bird concerned has usually slipped out down a ditch, broken out through the only gap in the line when flushed, or simply flown straight on past the covert, unseen by the guns.

'This one's mine,' said Paul. I placed him where I thought the bird would fly, fully expecting that, if she was still there, she would take off in the opposite direction. Not having seen pheasants on the ground for so long, no one could guess which she would regard as her home ground.

We put the spaniel in. At first it looked as though the hen had run out up a deep ditch. The dog insisted on taking off, following a strong scent, away from the spinney. At last he came back and disappeared into a tall bank of nettles. Five minutes passed with a good deal of snuffling and back-tracking. Every now and again he would bob out somewhere along the hedge only to be met by a fiercely remonstrating, and far from devoted, master insisting, with main force if necessary, that he get back in there and do some work in return for all the expensive food and shelter provided for him throughout a long summer holiday.

Teal looked reproachful as only spaniels can and then, with the threat of a large gumboot at his rear, sadly returned to the nettle bed. We had got nearly to the end of it when the hen burst out, rising like a VTOL fighter. She turned on course and headed out over Paul with after-burners at full boost. A shot from his single 20 finished her attempt at a breakout.

We all three sat down on a log and roared with laughter. We clapped each other on the back. We laid out our bag of three and admired them as birds have never been admired before. No record bag at a classic covert shoot could have caused more joy or excitement. In just under an hour from leaving home, we had performed what seemed like a triple miracle and for exactly three cartridges.

I suppose it all sounds very silly. All three of us have shot more than our share of pheasants. But it illustrates the old truth that all sport, whether fishing or shooting, is entirely relative to the surroundings in which it takes place. A quarter pound trout from a tiny brook can give as much pleasure as a two pounder from a chalk stream.

I guess we have shot the only three pheasants in the entire built-up neighbourhood, but I feel no conscience about that. Their future could only have been a short one in the circumstances.

Or *were* they the only three? I shall never walk that patch of rough again without paying strict attention. Equally, I know that for all three of us, the occasion will become one to be written in red in our respective shooting diaries.

PART II

Wildfowling

Wild Flight, Tame Flight

In Norfolk they make a charming distinction between real wildfowling carried out below the mean high tide mark and the kind done on inland waters or well-fed flight ponds. East Anglian friends of mine who, as you may judge, don't own well-fed flight ponds, call the real thing a 'wild flight'. By inference, though they never go so far as to say so, they must think of any other sort of duck shooting as a 'tame flight'.

On the whole I go along with this attitude. There can be no doubt that a flight among the *Spartina* and mud is a reward in itself even if it produces an empty, or comparatively empty bag. Let the flight pond men count their slain in tens or even fifties. We wild men are content with two wigeon and a teal, or so we claim.

However, when the opportunity for a really tremendous tame flight comes along, I wouldn't claim that I am either strong-minded or invertedly snobbish enough to resist it. In one twenty-four hours recently, I went both wild and tame. If you want the honest truth, I find it very hard to say which was the more exciting.

To begin with I hit the start of a bleak, blustery, sleety patch of weather. We'd been filming knot for the TV natural history programme, 'Survival', all morning, catching them as they whirled and dissolved and reformed to whirl again like smoke clouds. By afternoon the light had gone, the wind had backed easterly and the tide was making up the harbour. We put away the cameras and got out the guns.

The wigeon didn't wait for either darkness or tide. They

began piling in from the open sea at two in the afternoon. They'd had enough of sitting out there getting seasick. Usually when they do this, they go and squat tantalisingly on the sheltered water in the centre of the harbour. This afternoon they were determined, from the word go, to pitch in the middle of the little salt marsh and to start guzzling samphire seed. There isn't much cover in the little marsh, at least in daylight. It's too near the top of the tide.

At the risk of losing some shooting, I went and fetched a spade and dug myself a shallow pit, giving it a floor of driftwood so that when I lay down I wouldn't be too wet. By now it had come on to snow. The wigeon kept it up until darkness. It was very cold and very wet, in my shallow grave, despite the floorboards. Nor was my fox-hole the ideal situation from which to shoot. No one could call this flight anything but 'wild'. For a wild flight, the bag was, for me at least, something out of the ordinary. I picked them all—eleven wigeon and a mallard.

Evening flight next day was a very different performance. A friend who owns one of the best duck marshes in East Anglia had asked me to occupy one of his hogshead tubs. As we walked out through the tall *phragmites* beds, a bittern got up at our feet and flapped away in outrage that the place he had chosen for a night's rest had been disturbed.

This night, all the stops were out. An easterly gale blew. The sky against the sunset was that livid orange and green that seems to go with very cold dusks. As we got to our flighting area, a great skein of Canadas went honking down the wind well out of range. Then from out beyond the sea-wall came a mighty trumpeting and clear across the eye of the dying sun flew twelve neck-stretching whoopers. What more splendours could the flight have to offer? Did it matter now if we never fired a shot? But this, as I said, was a tame flight plus—if you can call anything that is dressed with bitterns, geese and wild swans 'tame'.

On this fresh marsh there are three or four flighting areas, each one a shallow flooding of water, seldom more than six inches deep and often only two, and each guarded by at least two tubs or reed screen hides. The strange thing is that though the flight ponds seem to be identical, they are almost exclusively patronised by different populations. The mallard like the one farthest inland. Then, perhaps naturally enough, the wigeon tend to dine at the flooded reed patch nearest the sea-wall. Still close to the sea-wall, but farther from the harbour, there is another pond that is beloved by the teal. It was into the hogshead tubs at the teal pond that we lowered ourselves this evening.

The first teal came and went before I had arranged my gear round the edge of my tub. My host, who is possibly opening batsman in any first eleven of wildfowl shots, plucked two out of them while still sitting on the rim of his barrel. When you've got this kind of shooting taking place within fifty yards of your own meagre efforts, you tend to get a bit nervous. So I poked at a low, fast single, missed and killed it in fury with a wild swing with the choke. Sheer annoyance, I find, often makes you swing your gun for the second shot at the speed you should have used for your first.

My host called out 'well done', which seemed to suggest that he was surprised. Right, if that was the way things were, I'd have to show him. So I did—with a double miss at the next bunch of five. Again he took two out of them as they climbed away.

At this particular season of the year, there are seldom fewer than 800 teal on this marsh and maybe more and this night, whipped on by the gale, they all seemed to want our little patch of water. They came from all directions. At times it was like being in the middle of a swarm of very fast-moving bees, or a wind-swirl of autumn leaves with every leaf a bird. In these conditions, you forget that you were ever nervous, forget that there's anyone else shooting with you. You just shoot as fast and as often as you can. You lose count of kills. The best you can do is to try to keep a picture of where any long-droppers fell, though you know the dogs will be along afterwards to do a thorough pick-up.

You begin to worry about ammunition running out, a thing that seldom concerns the wild flighter. You certainly are not concerned with kills per cartridge. The thing is just to see the birds in time as they bore at you out of the half darkness, then to get your gun on to them and through them at a good, crisp speed. The result is that a surprising number of duck fall out of the sky, not a few to rights and lefts. You even manage to knock off a couple that are heading for the stars after they have been missed, unbelievably, with both barrels, by your host. This time he doesn't shout 'well done', very understandably because he's immediately engaged with a fresh bunch.

Looking back on the really hot phases of this fantastic flight, only one clear moment stands out. A single wigeon looked in on the scene, flying medium high and very fast with the wind up its tail. It came to me first. I missed it with both. My companion did the same and then, reloading from the pocket, killed it stone dead with this third shot.

Some of the statistics of this flight are history. They're in the game book. I'm not going to tell you what my ratio of duck to cartridges was. I'll just admit that I got rid of the best part of three boxes.

Some of the statistics are pure conjecture—for instance, that we saw that night at least 300 teal and maybe more.

I don't suppose, in my entire wildfowling life, I'll experience two more exciting flights. So which did I enjoy the more, the wild or the tame? I'll try to be honest. The tame flight was something that comes perhaps once and I'd be a roaring hypocrite if I didn't admit that I revelled in every minute of it. But one of those lasts a very long time. At the back of my mind is still the thought that I hadn't done very much by my own efforts to deserve all those teal flying round my head.

Luxury Fowling

There is no doubt in my mind that one does shoot far better when you are sitting comfortably. I once enjoyed a flight on what must be one of the lushest and plushest inland duck marshes in Britain. Before all you rugged, gutter-pounding wildfowlers accuse me of decadence, let me say that I wouldn't want to take my sport in such luxury all the time: just once or twice in a lifetime is an experience neither to be despised nor missed, however.

I won't tell you where the marsh was beyond saying that it was in East Anglia, close to the coast, in fact so close that you could hear, and sometimes see, the spray pounding at the sea-wall beyond. You can't shoot the marsh any longer. It has now been made a reserve by one of the county Naturalists Trusts, who are interested in it, not so much for the vast numbers of duck it attracts but for the rare waders who visit and nest there in spring and summer.

The speciality of the marsh was teal. In fact, one morning, in a Force Ten gale, my host had shot 109 teal to his own gun between dawn and noon, with several breaks during which he went back for cartridges and phoned his office at the same time to ask his secretary whether anything vital had come up. What sort of business crisis could have interrupted that fantastic storm flight, I leave you to imagine. I would say that only the threat of a take-over bid would have shifted him.

I believe my friend used about 230 cartridges for his big stand. Seeing that the little duck were often doing close on 100 mph downwind, I don't think the shooting can have been too bad.

This marsh's ponds were, of course, fed regularly and generously. The water in them was rarely more than a couple of inches deep and never more than a foot. The ponds were natural ones cut out of the reed beds.

Hides were positive Hiltons. They consisted of a fifty gallon wine barrel complete with lid to keep out the damp and plastic bucket attached to string to remove any unwanted liquid. They were furnished with a comfortable seat. Round the top, above the level of the barrel rim, was a low fence of Norfolk reed with dry wooden shelters on which to lay out cartridges.

On the evening of my invitation it was blowing about Force Four. My friend seldom shot when the wind fell below this strength and he rationed flights strictly. In calm, he never shot more than once a fortnight. But he took the view that a howling gale washed the memory of a cannonade out of the ducks' minds without greatly strengthening their sense of caution. There were a lot of gales on that coast and so he got a fair amount of shooting.

It was a clear night with promise of a deep red sunset that hinted that cold weather was on its way in from the North Sea. There were three of us. I was a little apprehensive, for both my host and his other guest were certainly two of the best all-round shots in East Anglia.

I needn't have worried too much since I was placed in one of the teal ponds all by myself. If I was going to make a hash of things, it would only show up when we came to count our respective bags.

Though it was still fully light, the first bunch of teal came like fighter-bombers before I was properly settled into my tub. They came from behind and were gone in a cork-screwing climbing turn before I could get my gun up. Luckily my host was out of sight on the way to his own pond by then. I knew what would have happened if he had been in my position.

A single teal came next, crossing the pond from left to right, my 'good' or anyway better side. It crashed into the water. Firing had now started from the other two positions, pushing up a spring of about twenty teal that flew straight and level right overhead. The first barrel folded up two and the second was a clean miss as they stood on their little rudders. Oh well, practically a right and left.

Meantime a pair of mallard had had the impudence to land

on the pond twenty yards away (we weren't even using decoys). I clapped them up as if they were pigeon, missed the first easy one and pulled the drake down with the choke barrel at about forty yards.

The next into the bag were a pair of wigeon, going elsewhere but following the water route via the dykes feeding my pond. They both crashed into the tall reeds thirty yards distant. I was halfway out of my tub before I remembered that this was not the sort of marsh where one dashed out and retrieved duck immediately they fell. When the flight was over there would be a stately pick-up by keeper with well-trained labradors.

To that extent it was a tame flight, but there was nothing tame about the duck that were now coming like bats out of the falling dusk.

I tried to exercise some hide discipline, throwing the empties which had scored into my game bag, letting the 'misses' fall on to the bottom of the tub, so that I had some tally of my score. At first, when I had a long one, I placed a cartridge case on the wooden shelf to indicate its direction. It wasn't long before all sense of order was blotted out by the sheer heat and excitement of the action.

I will not say that I ended as well as I had begun. As it grew darker, targets were so fast and frequent that I often became confused, lost my head and scored a double miss. But there were a satisfying number of splashes as well.

The duck were still coming when I heard the keeper and his dogs wading towards me through the reeds. 'Like to leave them alone, sir, while they're still coming in. Doesn't do to paste them too long or too late. . . . Now, how many have you got?'

'Well I should have had a lot more.' The keeper was polite enough not to comment on this. 'About twenty I reckon all told. There's a couple of long ones over there.'

By the time the dogs had finished, we had gathered eighteen teal, two wigeon, three mallard and a gadwall—total twenty-four. Cartridges fired? I had three left out of two boxes of twenty-five. Perhaps not too shameful. Twenty-four for forty-seven. And I hadn't even got my feet wet.

Crazy Like a Coot

At flight the other evening on my gravel-pit, something very odd came over my head, low and flying sort of sideways. It took me by surprise. I think I *could* have fired at it, but that sort of mental check that operates when there is something puzzling you about any shot slowed up my reactions fatally.

Was it a rather inept hen pheasant? If it was, then just as well that I wasn't quick on the draw, for this was the tail end of September. No sooner had the wind of its passing subsided, than I had placed it. A coot, of course. One is rather apt to overlook the fact that those silly coots can get airborne and that, when they do so, they can fly in a most disconcerting fashion—as I once found out to my cost.

The biggest coot shoots took place on Hickling Broad. I say 'took place' because the whole thing stopped, when Hickling became a complete wildfowl sanctuary, several years ago. I'm not sure of the exact date. All I do know is that I was invited to the very last Hickling coot shoot of all.

The Hickling coot shoot, even on this last occasion, had all the ritual of a bullfight. We paraded on a mizzling grey morning at Whiteslea Lodge, a kind of white, rambling summer house quite frequently partially submerged by winter floods. This morning was no exception. We marched to our boats, shepherded by Ted Piggin, who was then warden, across a front lawn one foot deep in water.

Hickling punts are beautiful things to look at but tricky to shoot from. They are light, decked, gunning punts and it behoves you to sit centrally in them. However, for a start we were not to shoot afloat. Tethered behind the warden's motor boat like a string of miniature but elegant coal barges, we set off from the first stand, an archipelago of reed islands somewhere out in the middle of the cold grey vastness.

I drew a stand on the left flank between a distinguished-looking senior military man and a youngster in a seal-skin parka. On our right hand, well out in open water and marooned on butts that grew on lopsided stakes from the bed of the Broad itself, were three Norfolk farmers.

I sniffed the wind, powdered the seed heads of some withered *phragmites* close by my butt and let them fall to gauge its direction and force. I did so knowledgeably, or at least as if I knew what I was doing, and opined to the seal-skin lad that, since the wind was blowing directly to us, we should have the cream of the shooting.

Young though he was, this gun obviously knew a thing or two. He looked extremely doubtful at my optimistic forecast and glanced enviously towards the marooned farmers far out on the watery right flank. Poor chaps, I thought; they'll be lucky if they get a shot.

While all these calculations were going on, the warden was steadily marshalling his beaters, or rather his armada. This procedure follows an historic pattern and the moves are well understood by all concerned, which is perhaps just as well. Once you've got your beating, or possibly boating, force spread over half Hickling Broad, there is very little you can do to get it back into line or 'steady it up there on the left' as lesser land-borne keepers can usually manage to do.

For a long time, nothing happened. This must, I thought, be like one of those gigantic grouse manoeuvres where half the country has to be brought in before the sky over the butts can be blackened with grouse.

Then, suddenly, the military man, who had attended many coot shoots, said: 'It's time the divers came over.' And sure enough, there, two seconds later, they were, pochard, tufted and one or two goldeneye, all with the wind up their shirt-tails.

Both seal-skin and the Army had got two barrels off and three birds down between them by the time I had managed to fire a salute at tail-end Charlotte, a female goldeneye in a good deal of a hurry.

'Bad luck,' said the military man, who had shot two. His voice was kindly, but there was a distinct touch of frostiness, as if to say: 'Didn't I warn you well in advance they were coming. They always do.'

No more divers now, but an occasional mallard. I did manage to get a high one, swinging down the line of guns after one of the farmers had missed it and I began to feel better.

Then, almost at once, the coot started to fly. The boats had

driven them nicely downwind towards us so that, legs trailing, white pates shining, they were at last up and coming.

It looked money for old rope. They seemed so slow. It also looked, just as I had predicted, as though the whole first mob of a hundred birds or more were going to fly directly over us. It seemed as though any moment we left-hand guns must be buried under a heavy fall of dead coots.

Alas, I had overlooked what is apparently the essential quality of a coot, or, at least, of a Hickling coot. Though the bird appears to be coming forward, what it is actually doing—and what it *likes* doing—is to fly slightly sideways, sidling across the wind.

Practically the whole of the first pack swept across our butts just out of range and slid, still progressing sideways, over the three farmers, whose barrels immediately became incandescent with rapid fire and one of whom actually did have to duck every now and again as dead coots, slain by his neighbours' barrage, rained on him.

One solitary bird came forward to us and was unmistakably mine. The other two guns left it with great good manners. Not having worked out the essential 'cootiness' of the target at that stage, I missed it, with both barrels. No one said anything, which made it far worse.

We did a little better when the next lot arose from somewhere down to our left. I seem to recollect that the three of us accounted for about twenty, of which I am ashamed to say that I got five for twice as many cartridges.

There must be a moral to this story. I think it is simply the old one about never over-estimating your own abilities or under-estimating the qualities of the enemy. That and the need for more tolerance, and I confess that when I used to read about those gigantic bags of 1,200 coot, all of which were said to go to a potted meat factory, I was inclined to sneer. 'Slaughter' and 'sitting targets' were terms I had used to myself about the Hickling coot shoots: I just didn't know that the damn birds flew sideways.

Double Act

After a day's pleasant pheasant shooting on a very moderate scale—my host had only just taken over a potentially excellent shoot which he will undoubtedly build up most successfully in a year or two—I was invited to flight his teal pond.

The evening was dead calm, clear-skied and decorated by one of those lovely sunsets that are the bane of serious duck shooters. So I was not expecting very much.

The look of the pond did not particularly reassure me. It was set in the middle of a large, established, mixed woodland with trees tall enough to make any pheasant who topped them, let alone a teal, look small. It did not look like a duck pond to me, though my host assured me that I was wrong. The one thing immediately in its favour was that it was not very far from a well-known south coast estuary.

I privately thought we would be lucky if we saw, let alone shot, half a dozen teal. We arrived as the light was fading in time to watch a single teal get off and depart at high speed. It climbed like a jump-jet and disappeared smartly over the tops of the tall trees that grew right down to the water's edge.

I formed the opinion, rightly as it turned out, that the only way of shooting any teal who came in would be to take them as they went *out*, just as this singleton had done. On such a still night, approaching birds would, I fancied, fly just above the topmost branches and then flip down quickly to the surface of the water. The task of spotting them against the backdrop of trees as they made their descent promised to be well-nigh impossible.

When we came to count ourselves before flight we found we had somehow acquired one extra gun. However, the pond was quite a large one and one of the hides had been built double with a partition in between, rather like side-by-side stalls. I drew for this double effort which didn't please me a great deal.

There is something extraordinarily off-putting for both partners about having to shoot shoulder-to-shoulder. The other chap shoots first, or hesitates, or else you hesitate expecting him to shoot first and the result is too often a miss on a bird which, you tell yourself, you would have killed in great style had you been on your own.

My partner did not seem to suffer similar inhibitions. He was a charming chap who had shot with unvarying inaccuracy all day at pheasants and had confessed most good-naturedly that he was off-form. Moreover, he also confided in me that this was the first time he had been duck flighting.

None of this, as you may judge, cheered me up a great deal. 'Oh well,' I thought, in the beastly way one can't help thinking such things, 'he probably won't see them at all and I shall be able to shoot pretty much as if I was on my own.'

Other things about the set-up were slightly disconcerting. What troubled me most was the height of the cover in front. You not only had to stand up to shoot but even when doing so you couldn't see the water. Vision was restricted to a clear space that began halfway up the trees opposite and ended—thanks to the framing of the branches above the hide—a few feet above tree top height on the far bank. A kind of sky-slit in fact.

Later, I discovered that there was method in this apparent madness. It seemed that the keeper who had built these hides had found that excited guns had a tendency to shoot their colleagues around the pond. The height of the cover did something to curb this exuberance.

While I was reflecting on all these, to me, unfamiliar facets of evening flight, my co-shooter fired. There was a plop and a teal which I hadn't even seen had fallen dead to the water. 'Good shot,' I said and resolved that I wouldn't be caught napping again.

From that moment on, and for the next half hour, the teal came in well-spaced parties of threes and fours. My companion, he who had failed to hit the pheasants during the day, not only saw them as quickly as I did but he shot quicker and far more accurately. Over the wall I could hear him fairly chortling with excitement and delight. And all the time he was banging away and the teal kept splashing down.

Understandably, he shot at some high ones that should have been left to complete a further circle before making their final approach. I told him as gently as I could, and with all the superiority of a veteran flighting expert, that this was not the best course of action and that if he had only waited a little. . . .

Such words of wisdom offered in a spirit of kindly, old-hand to novice, should have done something to restore my rapidly crumbling morale. But I had hardly finished my excerpt from 'Advice to Novice Flighters' before his gun had fired a double and brought down a right and left. After that I decided to shut up and desperately try to score some runs myself. Eventually I dropped a few, perhaps one to his three.

We picked twenty-two teal and three mallard. I don't think any birds were lost, due to the fact that the keeper stood watching with a 'clicker', one of those simple devices that counts for you each time you press a knob. This struck me as a remarkably bright idea that other shoots might like to copy.

My companion was understandably ecstatic. I would say that he had accounted for nearly half the bag. Being an extremely nice man, he was not at all boastful about his successful debut. On the contrary, he simply wondered why he had shot so dismally badly at pheasants all day and yet could hit those flickering shadows of teal. I also got the impression that he was so excited by the flight that he would probably give up pheasant shooting immediately and become a full-time wildfowler.

By then I did not think my own performance—four teal and a mallard for about sixteen shots—entitled me to express an opinion about anything. Nevertheless, I think the explanation is perfectly simple and one well-known to all experienced shooters.

A pheasant gives you time to think and worry, to shoot deliberately, to poke, to miss dreadfully behind. A teal that appears like a will-o-the-wisp is there and gone so quickly that it forces you to employ what army pistol instructors used to call 'instinctive pointing sense'. Instinctive pointing sense, plus swing caused by the need to act quickly, is what kills birds whether they are teal or pheasants. The trouble is that it is not always easy to convince yourself of that fact when you see them coming from far off.

Awash in the Washes

When fowling in the Fens, a place in which, on the whole, I do not expect to drown, I recently nearly did so. All accidents that don't quite turn fatal have their ridiculous side when looked at wryly afterwards. More important, they contain lessons which should be taken very seriously.

The way of it was this. I had met three very convivial fenland fowlers who had picked the same week as I had to stay at my favourite village pub from which I flight the Ouse washes.

At first, I confess, I wasn't very pleased to see them and possibly they felt the same about me. I had really come away to work in the back room which the landlord and his wife kindly set aside for me. My only wildfowling ambition was to break my writing labours by nipping out for morning and evening flight.

These three charming chaps represented a threat that might wreck my routine and weaken my resolve to finish the last 15,000 words of a novel in three short days.

Because they were such nice chaps I quickly found that I couldn't stay aloof. At supper the first night we started discussing fowling. It appeared that they had picked their week for a shooting holiday rather badly.

Their wash, which was several feet lower than my own, was deeply flooded. It was impossible to wade to their flighting points. Fortunately, they had brought a small, and, as it turned out, very shallow freeboarded dinghy. With the aid of this, two of them could motor up the river, land at the only part of their shoot which was wadeable and set up hides there.

The sad part was that this small plot of shootable land wasn't big enough to take more than two guns. So what could I do but suggest that the third gun came with me for morning and evening flight.

There wasn't too much of my own plot above the waves but what there was would certainly house the two of us. I was careful to stress, however, that my real objective was writing and that I should only stay out for morning and evening flight and not a second more.

After the first morning flight it appeared that another calamity had struck my new friends. The outboard motor which they had brought to propel the dinghy refused to do more than start, splutter and stop.

The current in the river which took them to their flighting areas was at least four knots and so they had spent most of their time rowing to beat the dawn, which, as anyone who has tried it will know, simply can't be done.

While I pounded away all day at my typewriter, the sound of oaths, furious yankings on the starting rope, occasional fits of two-stroke coughing and a strong smell of blue smoke told me that they were working flat out to persuade that motor to go. But, at evening flight, the two galley slaves were back at the oars again. This time, the tidal river was with them on the way to flight, but it took them an hour and a half to row back.

Much the same happened on Day Two, though by now they had got the motor to run after a fashion, but only on its test bed in the pub garage. The moment they put it on the transom of the dinghy, it began to sulk again. We have, I imagine, all met motors like that.

That day I wrote even more words than the day before and took out the third member of the party once again to morning and evening flight. We shot one pintail, one jack snipe and two pheasants!

By noon on the third day, my self-imposed marathon was finished. I was ready to be talked into going fowling.

The outboard motor mechanics were still stripping, reassembling, yanking away and cursing. The owner of this recalcitrant lump of metal complaining that the thing had gone perfectly last time he had used it. Freed from my bondage to the typewriter, I now felt that I could take a little interest in his difficulties. 'When was it last used?' I asked. 'About a year ago. I know that the blend of oil and petrol is dead right. It has still got the stuff we mixed so carefully last winter in the tank.'

All that blue smoke! I am not a mechanical genius but it seemed possible that a good deal of the petrol might have evaporated leaving a preponderance of oil in the mixture. We started topping up with neat petrol. After about half a pint and a good deal of stirring, she took off like a teal and purred like a *cicada*.

'Now,' said the triumphant owner, tears of gratitude welling in his eyes, 'you must come out for a flight on our patch. The water has dropped a good deal. If you and John' (the fowler I had taken flighting to my part of the Wash) 'will walk out, we'll go ahead in the boat and set up some hides for you.'

I will digress here to say that I have confessed previously in this column that the building of a satisfactory and not too troublesome hide on these washes has always beaten me. My new chums were old hands at it. With the aid of a pair of garden shears, they cut bundles of *phragmites* reeds. Then they set up a circle of four foot chicken wire on eight stout bamboo canes, stood the *phragmites* upright against the wire, lashing them to the mesh with one surround of binder twine.

The dropping of the floods had changed things dramatically overnight. There had been no snipe around the two previous days. We must have put up 300 jack and common snipe as we floundered out. Moreover they all went over our disembarked companions heads, who did not fire a single cartridge. Later, it turned out, they did not believe in loading for lesser game when they were out for duck, a degree of inflexibility that tried my courtesy as a guest considerably. What a snipe drive we could have given, and actually did give them.

I could hardly complain. They had very nice hides prepared for us and though we did not get many ducks an enjoyable time was had by all. The enjoyment—and nearly everything else, ended when we started to come home. The sailors now suggested that we share the dinghy, and, fool that I was, I agreed.

We were loaded, I fancied, rather too heavily for'ard—two men on the little foredeck, two dogs just amidships, one boatman slightly aft of midships and the other on the engine.

All went well as we nosed with our reborn outboard slow ahead through the reeds. It was only when the Chief Engineer opened up in the middle of that very cold river that the trouble started.

I noticed it first. Water was coming over the bows, to which I had my back, and was pouring over my lap. I turned with considerable horror and saw that the motor had driven our over-laden bows under and we were heading straight for the bottom at full throttle.

When the message to 'Stop both' finally reached the engine room we were all sitting terrified in a freezing bathtub ten yards from shore.

When we made that shore, more by luck than anything found in the Seaman's Manual, I was the first to volunteer to walk home. With waders and wildfowling gear on, we were lucky not to have drowned.

Slough of Despond

Jeffery Harrison said that there were 6,000 duck in and that this was a lot of duck for this estuary at this stage of the season. I said that to me it sounded a lot of duck for any estuary at any time.

'It's East Flevoland,' he explained, 'the Dutch are starting to drain their new polder in the Ijsselmeer. Last time they drained a polder, they deprived a million duck of their home and we got a good many of them. Bring plenty of cartridges. And be here for porridge in the kitchen at 5.30 am sharp.'

As usual before early morning wildfowling departures, I didn't sleep too well. The alarm clock operates perfectly efficiently for 364 days of the year. On this day, a special day, because the wildfowling Jeffery offers can be some of the best in England, would it remember to go off at the set hour of 4 am?

Before I turned the light out, I fiddled nervously with the controls of that wretched clock. Then I woke up to make sure that I hadn't fiddled once too often. Having fiddled again, I dropped into a duck-troubled sleep only to wake at 2 am to make sure that my last fiddling hadn't fiddled the knob to 'off'. This way lies madness.

When the wretched thing did finally explode on the dot of 4 am I was in my first real sleep and leapt out of bed like a teal rising from a gutter. '*Must* you?' asked my wife who knows very well after all these years that I must. She pulled the bedclothes back around her, rather peevishly I fancied.

As I have said before, I dress on the assembly line principle. Having laid my clothes out the night before across bedroom floor, with vest nearest the bed and socks nearest the door, I rush out of bed, dressing as I proceed. By the time I reach the door, I have the lot on. So, by 4.15 am prompt I was on the road.

Hardly had I cleared my own front drive than a police car fell in behind. From the first second I felt that I was likely to become a Z car victim. Sure enough, when I turned on to the dual carriageway of the by-pass, they nosed in front and waved me down.

'Where do you think *you're* going,' a rather young copper asked in a tone that obviously suggested I had the loot in the back. I toyed with one or two sharp replies, reflected that the lads were only doing their duty and that if I gave them any lip I would probably find myself back at the nick talking to Chief Inspector Barlow just when I should be getting ready for morning flight. I settled for something just sufficiently provocative, while still remaining coldly polite. 'I'm going shooting,' I told them.

'At this hour? Where?'

'Wildfowlers quite commonly set out at this hour.' I gave them the name of the estuary.

They obviously still fancied they heard the clink of family silver in my game bag. The boys in blue kept plugging away, frequently repeating their questions to make sure they got the same answers. They did. Finally, convinced that I was a harmless nut, they let me go about my lawful occasions.

Annoying as such encounters are, they are far more beneficial to the public at large than issuing lawful shooters with Shotgun Certificates. It's good to see the cops in their proper role of law enforcement, though one can't help reflecting that their questioning might perhaps be tinged with more of the politeness one expects of the British policeman. Mine was distinctly addressed to a potential, if not actual, criminal.

Despite all this, we reached the sea-wall on time and braced ourselves for what, to me, is the worst walk in the world.

The plod (in deference to the mud I prefer the term 'plowter') out to the island is just over two miles. The first threequarters is a deceptively easy slog, at least it is once you are over the Creek of Despond, a tide-full miniature river in which it is only too easy to slip and fall flat on your back. I have now learnt that this marsh is only really negotiable with the aid of a thumb stick.

You come next to 'Goldeneye Pool', a local name which gives nothing away beyond the fact that someone once shot a goldeneye there. If your host is merciful, you are allowed to catch your breath there. This morning, he wasn't in a merciful mood. Dawn was already rising and so were mallard, wigeon and teal from the creeks along our route.

Jeffery is a master wildfowler, alert for a shot at any time. He makes this appalling journey with his gun at the ready. As a result, he not infrequently bags a duck or two on the walk out.

Made of frailer stuff, I find that I have my work cut out to

stay on my feet when laden down with back pack containing cartridges, Thermos and spare sweaters. My eyes are full of sweat. If I have my gun out of its sleeve it is invariably full of mud. So I leave it encased and slung from the shoulder where it is less encumbrance to my panting movements. This morning was a mild one. I plowtered in shirt sleeves but even so the sweat poured off me.

I remarked that either we should one day die of thrombosis on these muds or else the exertion of the approach march was such that it would save our blood from clotting and our arteries from hardening. As a man who should know about such things, he gave it as his professional opinion that the latter was more likely to prove the case.

The next leg of the journey looks deceptively easy. Not so, at all. You now have to cover a half mile across broken rocks, once part of flood defences. Each rock is carefully picked not to lie flush with its neighbour so that you are continually slipping and sliding at the risk of a broken ankle. The alternative is to slough off into the disgusting ooze at each side of the causeway.

Next something of a respite, solid going along the broken-down grass top of an old sea-wall. Hopes of surviving begin to grow. Skeins of duck against the distant sunrise show up dimly through mists of perspiration.

But the worst is holding itself in reserve for the very last. Now comes half a mile of an obstacle course borrowed from the cauldron of a cold hell. The Devil has poured his most viscous ooze into a series of gutters each one of which lies across the line of march. Thumb stick sinks nearly out of sight—and so do you. Waders attach themselves to the marsh rather than to your person.

You finally make it somehow and making it is well worth while. You think this has been bad? Wait until you come to face the return trip that evening with fifteen duck apiece.

Until recently, I had no conception how either the causeways or the islands of the Medway estuary came into being. Now a kind reader of the *Shooting Times* has written to enlighten me. At least, when I plowter over this loathsome morass in future I shall be able to console myself that I know how it got the way it is.

Fifty years ago, long before we had a Ministry for the

Environment, vast chunks of the Medway saltings were demolished to make Portland Cement. Apparently this vital building commodity wasn't in commercial use until 1840. The main ingredients were chalk and clay and the best clay of all was that dug from the Thames and Medway estuaries.

Thus the trade of 'mudding' sprang up. A 'muddy' was a man of mighty brawn and, apparently, of mighty corresponding thirst. He must have been the same stamp of man that built the banks of the great London reservoirs and indeed the scradge and barrier banks of the fen rivers. Some of the muddies were local men but a good many were as itinerant as gypsies. It seems they drank the local pubs dry. Who can blame them? Their trade was a pretty frightful one.

A muddy earned what was then fairly big money—around £5 a week. They organised themselves into gangs of five or six. The big Thames barges came in on the high tide and anchored close to the edge of the salting to be dug. A full cargo was 150 tons of Medway mud, thus each man was expected to load about twenty-five tons of mud a tide!

The usual routine was to work two tides a day which often meant digging far into the night. I've often come off these selfsame saltings after a late flight stumbling my way down the causeway with a torch.

Now I learned that the muddies did much the same by the light of what they called 'blizzy' (blizzard?) lanterns. The causeways were the narrow necks of saltings which they left intact to enable them to reach the farthest islands. Many are largely eroded now.

My informant has sent me an old cutting showing these hemen at work. They used a wooden spade with a metal cutting edge called a 'fly-tool'. They worked, stripped to the waist, wearing leather thigh boots with canvas leggings and they left behind them one of the most remarkable salt marsh landscapes in Britain.

They also left behind them what are still remarkable—though now controlled shooting—fowling grounds where the wigeon float in on the tide and the teal still arrow up the creeks in large numbers.

Good as the fowling still is, I can't help reflecting how much better it would have been but for the efforts of the muddies. The estuary must have been a wildfowl paradise—and a wildfowler's also—when it was a solid mass of saltings cut by deep tidal creeks. There are such parts still in existence though in private hands. The quality of the fowling there can be second to none in England.

The muddies' digging efforts must be responsible for the horrid viscosity of the mud in the Medway lagoons. I imagine that the iodine-flavoured chocolate mousse we 'plowter' through these days was once covered by four or five feet of solid clay.

Wildfowlers in Scotland

There is a certain hillside in Dumfries where the difference in range to a rising pheasant can vary from ten to fifty yards by the time the thing has flown six feet. It depends, mind you, on whether you are walking at the top of the hill where the bird gets up or standing at the bottom of the precipice over which it takes flight. That is the sort of country it is—and it is country which, at this season of the year, I begin to see in my dreams.

Now, the soaring valleys of Dumfries, with their roe-haunted conifer woods, may not seem the right place for a town gun to be walking, even in his dreams. Nevertheless, it is the country to which at least five town guns, the members of my own syndicate, make an annual end-of-January pilgrimage.

By that time we have shot our thousand acres of Forestry Commission as much as it will stand. We have stood on our semi-suburban flight lines, often described in this column, more than is perhaps good for them. We need a change of air. The air north of the Solway is bracing, pine-scented and snow-scattered. Moreover it supports not only the aforesaid precipitous pheasants but also wigeon, mallard, teal and greylag and Greenland whitefront.

Over the years, this January safari of we city dwellers has become a ritual. It is a ritual that demands that, once you start, you do not stop. For this reason, we drive by night. This leaves the maximum number of flighting hours and walking-up hours and driving hours between 9 am on the Wednesday, when the shooting starts, and morning flight on Saturday when it ends and we all head for home.

The rigours of the excursion can be considerably added to by the weather. Nothing could be more rigorous than 1963.

That year, we started off, five men and five dogs, at eight o'clock on a snowy Tuesday evening from a point fifteen miles south of London. 'You're mad,' our wives said, but then they always say that. This year there was just a chance that they might be right. Shap Fell had been intermittently blocked for the past three weeks.

We had, however, every confidence in our mount—a brand new, diesel-engined mini-bus of a make I will not be uncharitable enough to mention. At the start of the M.1, in a blistering blizzard, the throttle linkage parted. We lifted the engine cover, which was set back inside the cab, and found that it had broken at the point where it joined whatever diesel engines have instead of a carburettor.

Someone then pointed out that a man with a very long arm might just be able to lean down inside the engine and operate the broken control with his fingers. I have very long arms. It was thirty-three miles from the point at which we broke down to the first service station.

The blood ran to my head within the first half-mile. However, whatever I gained in facial heat from this situation was more than offset by the uprush of snow that came straight back off the road through the open cover.

The driver, poor fellow, was entirely at the mercy of the engine room. When he bellowed for more revolutions, I would obediently twist the throttle open. The moment I did so, the exhaust manifold, which was barely a quarter-of-an-inch from the back of my hand—I might add that I have long, slim and, as I like to think, artistic fingers and that these were a must for the job: nothing else would have got in there—the exhaust manifold glowed cherry red and there was an immediate smell of burning skin.

We could not have proceeded thus on any road save a motorway where a constant speed is possible for long stretches except when passing petrol tankers doing fifty, the point at which the smell of scorching epidermis became overpowering. The other passengers paid to some extent, though not in the same measure as myself. When we finally drew into the service station they were all as white as snowmen.

It happened, among other things, to be the coldest night of that pestilential winter. I know it was cold because I then had a very tough springer called Drake. Drake normally never felt the cold. I have seen him come out of the water spangled with ice and positively grin with pleasure. That night even wiped the grin off *his* face.

We drove in one-and-a-half-hour shifts. So that the driver coming off duty could recuperate a little, we had one sleeping bag stretched full-length on the floor among dogs and luggage. When I had finished my stint, which happened to take us over Shap (it was open that night for the first time for days), I found that Drake had already moved into the sleeping bag for comfort. Little wonder. By that time dog and human breath had frozen in a solid glacial film over the entire metal interior of the bus.

Nevertheless we drove into the town of Gatehouse of Fleet, exactly thirty minutes behind schedule. Breakfast had been arranged in the pub for eight o'clock. It was eight-thirty when we sat down and I recall that it was nine-thirty when the first shot was fired at one of those tall mountain pheasants I was talking about just now.

For the next three days we shot screaming cocks in those

snow-covered hills all day, and geese and duck at the loch at morning and evening flight. I have retained more minds-eye scenes from that desperate winter trip than from any similar excursion before or since.

I remember the woodcock that came to a pheasant feed and fastidiously and experimentally took a grain of barley in the tip of its beak.

There was the utter devotion to duty of the two Scottish keepers who never left a bird and one bird in particular. A high cock, gleaming bronze in the reflected snowlight, came soaring down the valley to me, the flanker, on the rocky edge of the river. I hit him hard, watched him climb, trailing feathers like a smoke burst and tower high over the far craggy bank to fall on a miniature mountain peak a quarter of a mile across a stream.

So we all stopped and stood while the keeper forded the very fast and cold spate river, thigh deep, climbed the precipice, clawed his way up where no dog would be willing, or could be asked, to go, picked the cock and made the return trip. All he said when he got back to us was: 'Right, gentlemen. Forward again.'

Then there were the two tufted duck that broke down another valley to rocket past at maximum range and fall to a right and left (not mine) and lie immaculate in the snow side by side.

The pair of Greenland whitefronts that crashed to a right and left (mine this time) so far out on the ice that it seemed we could never dare to send a dog for them. But, while we were debating it, a dog had gone and proved that the ice could bear him.

There was the morning when two of us defied the advice of the keeper to flight the geese on the loch shore and climbed high up into the hills and hid behind a dry stone wall where we had seen the geese grazing the day before. We got four greylag and a mallard for our pains.

But most of all there was the drive back when the mini-bus broke a fuel lead at Scotch Corner and arrived home early the next morning with all four big-ends knocked out. No bad Samaritan garage would help us in that bitter weather. So, what else could five tired men and five even more tired dogs, not to mention a mound of assorted game, do with themselves except keep going?

In Camera

When we six town guns made our end-of-season excursion to Scotland the following year, the weather was far kinder to us than we had any right to expect.

That year, it just blew and rained. The blow at least was very welcome for it brought the geese within range.

Geese are one of the main objectives of this winter holiday to country just north of the Solway. Pheasants in the mountains are another. But pheasants are something we can shoot all season round. Geese are an extra and so here I shall confine myself to them.

I have a personal bag limit of six geese on this trip. This, to some extent, is because I don't want to shoot a larger number of geese. It's also because I tell myself that the great lumbering things are far too easy. My trouble is that even when I talk to myself, about geese anyway, I don't really know what I'm talking about.

Perhaps if I shot geese regularly, they *would* become too easy. But on a once-a-year basis, decidedly not.

The first morning it was pinkfeet. We were invited to shoot on the Solway merse where the pinks are mixed up with odd skeins of barnacles. There is absolutely no cover on this marsh except for the occasional fallen tree trunk. It is as green and as bare as a billiard table.

We strung out well before light along the expected line of flight, lying behind the odd stump, or in any little hole or gully we could find. Two of the party were very occasional wildfowlers though stern men with a tall pheasant. Poor chaps, they had been severely spoken to the previous night about the protection given to barnacles and the unfortunate habit these had of mixing up with parties of pinks. We *afficionados* had tried to make clear that the two species had widely different cries. But perhaps we were not too good at imitations.

I was right-hand man behind my tree trunk. As soon as it got half light, skein after skein of pinkfeet lifted off the saltings a mile or two ahead and, scarcely bothering to climb, headed, gaggling and gowling at the top of their 200 voices, fifty yards out of shot to my left but straight over at least two of my companions.

Not a shot came up to greet the geese, who passed on still arguing about which field to dine in. As it got light, a single goose planed in and pitched 200 yards dead in front of me. I watched him for fully half-an-hour with the glasses, feeding with cautious bolt-uprising of the neck every thirty seconds to make sure no one had any evil intent.

At last, just as I was about to get up and stretch, he took off and flew at nought feet straight down my right barrel. Oh well, what can you do? The first goose of the season. They don't come any easier than that. What was he doing on his own, anyway? I had had a feeling all along that he was a pricked bird. When I went out and collected him, sure enough, he was far thinner on the breast than a healthy bird had any business to be.

The party, as a whole, now crawled out of its trenches as the flight was plainly over. 'That one gave itself up,' said one of the occasional wildfowlers. I thought he spoke a little disparagingly. 'We had a lot of barnacles over us,' said the other. I did not like to tell him they were pinks. Such restraint does not deserve disillusionment. I agree that when in doubt there's nothing else to be done.

Gooseless, the occasional wildfowlers now headed back to the pub for breakfast. Local information said that on a rough day the geese often moved around until mid-morning. The four serious wildfowlers therefore redeployed on to what they hoped might be the flight lines.

My own deployment was an expensive disaster. Just as I was covering a particularly exposed part of the steppe, a big skein of pinks appeared a mile away like a wavering line of crochets in the sky. A hundred yards ahead was a creek. I ran to it, the army valise on my back, in which I always carry cartridges and other gear, bobbing and bouncing on my spine in time with my laboured gasps for breath. I threw myself into the creek, filling one wader, but this was not the worst of it.

As I landed, I heard a splash behind. The valise straps cannot have been fastened. A box of twenty-five cartridges had fallen out. The geese were barely 200 yards distant. The cartridges could take their chance for a few extra seconds. I knelt face down in the mud. The goose talk became deafening. I looked up, saw them high, but in range, above me, picked one, fired twice and missed. Then I put my hand in the creek for the cartridges. They turned out to be my 35 mm camera, all forty quids-worth of it, and full of sand as well as sea-water.

But one can't let a little set-back like that distract one from the main business. I stayed in my creek while two other skeins approached within magnum range.

Now this is what I mean about geese under these conditions being difficult. You've got to stay face down and huddled on your knees until the last instant. Then, when you're certain they're right overhead, you must uncoil and move fast. You look up, pick your goose and fire. The trouble is that when *you* move, so do the geese. They start to slide out on one wing at an appallingly deceptive speed. Worse, your inclination—sorry, *my* inclination—on looking up quickly is to poke. It is very hard to swing in these circumstances.

So I gave up my hideous, shallow creek and hiked over to an extra big tree trunk on the horizon. There I found John Gray, the keenest of our case-hardened wildfowlers, already in possession. What is more, he had two geese.

Very decently, he did not send me away. In fact, there was nowhere else within half-a-mile to go. So, in gratitude, I gave him my emaciated goose and we set all three up as decoys.

We spent the most exciting two hours either of us remember, for the pinks did move all that morning. Often they were very high. Usually they were too wide. Invariably, we were the wrong side of the log and had to crawl round to get away from them. But every now and again we got a chance and what a botch we both made of it.

I like to think that it was something to do with the fact that we were shooting in each other's pockets; that one of us had to give the fire orders; that we seldom moved exactly together; that we were properly concerned about blowing each other's heads off. Some we missed were, admittedly, excusable, being both high and fast. The four that sailed in at forty yards, low and straight for our decoys, were unforgiveable. It was like missing ping-pong balls balanced on a fairground jet of water. Whatever the reason, we missed them. In fact, after a whole morning of creeping and crawling we had not improved our hand. The party's total: four pinks and one camera down in a creek. By the way, if you were to have the bad luck to drop a camera in a salt creek, don't do what I did. Instead, hurry home, immerse the remains in fresh water and keep it immersed until you can get it to a camera mechanic. That way you may just keep the rust from getting at it. Whatever you do, don't stay out on the marsh on the off-chance of getting a goose.

PART III

Pigeon Shooting

Pigeons in the Snow

One way I pay for the shooting given me by kind suburban nursery farm owners is to maintain a dawn patrol during really hard weather on their greenstuff. There is so little apparent choice for our local flocks of woodies that, when the snow clamps down, their targets are easily predictable. We do not grow sprouts or kale or rape along the brick fringe of outer London. So the pigeon settle for young cabbage, spinach and, often, the tops of turnips. Moreover, they start their tuck-in early, just in case the supply runs out or the mob from the woods the other side of the by-pass finds it first. Hence my look-round just after first light.

Despite everything people tell you about the fantastic pigeon shooting to be had in snow, I remain extremely doubtful. The worst thing about it is that you can't decoy. I believe that we have a great deal to learn about woodpigeon. One of the first things that the scientists might try finding out is why a bird with such astonishing eyesight under normal conditions simply cannot see a set of decoys laid out against the glaring white background of a snowy field. The only conclusion I can come to is that pigeon are extremely easily dazzled. Who has not had the experience of walking home from a day's shooting, with the setting sun low on the horizon behind him, only to see a pigeon steaming straight at him on a collision course?

The fact is that my just-out-of-town nursery farms rarely produce a good snow shoot. When it happens the reason, I am pretty sure, is that outer suburbia offers very few alternative feeding grounds under hard weather conditions. They have just got to come in to the one field where the grub is available.

I struck it like this one Saturday morning during that abominable snow span that fell across January and February 1963. Dawn patrol found nothing on the spinach on number one farm where I had expected a heavy concentration. Just outside farm number two, about a mile distant, I came across every pigeon in the district. They were not on the farm itself, but on a tiny smallholding, planted with cabbage, just alongside.

Goodness knows why they had chosen this place. It cannot have been more than fifty yards wide and was all of 150 yards long. It was bordered on two sides by lanes down which a certain amount of traffic was bound to pass. There were huge areas of identical and far more remote cabbage out on the farm itself. There no human or vehicle would come within 200 yards of them the whole day long. But still they choose that narrow strip of allotment.

I put them off and set up a net hide in the hedge. It had now started to blow nicely with a delightful fine dry snow that even settled inside my glasses. Who cared? This, for my neck of what's left of the woods, promised to be a big shoot.

Once I had fired the first few shots, they ceased being suicidal and had a good look round. There were no 'sitty' trees for them to squat in and case the joint with those little built-in field-glasses of theirs. Instead, they made their recce by piling in downwind at full throttle, turning behind me and coming in over the hedge with undercarriage down and flaps set. Either way, they made fine marks, particularly when going downwind. For once I was in good form and could afford to have a go at most of the 'down-winders'.

When I connected, they went rolling down the storm to fall a good seventy yards behind into deep snow. By lunch time I had fired my hundred cartridges and picked sixty-five birds, a good ten remaining buried where they had crashed into deep powdery snow and disappeared without trace.

I packed up and went to see if the local ironmonger had any cartridges. It's the sort of district where ironmongers can sell you a set of plastic duck to go across your wall, but not cartridges. I do this one an injustice. On this occasion he had fifty with rusting primers, which gives you an idea how long they had been in stock.

I gave a thought to domestic relations and returned home for a quick lunch. I was back in that hide an hour after firing my last shot, keyed up and expecting my fifty cartridges to give me not much more than an hour's shooting. I fired three of them all afternoon. Those pigeon cannot have had enough to eat, but they had had enough of being shot at. They were not on the main farm crops either. I never saw them again that day.

This year's snow has brought no worthwhile attack on any of my local crops. I was therefore delighted to get an SOS to assist the Greatest Living Expert on pigeon shooting, otherwise known as Archie Coats, help save a large field of seed rape in Hampshire.

After everything I have said about the effect of snow on pigeon, I suppose I should not have let my heart turn a back-somersault when I saw the strength of the attacking force. In, on and around that rape, sitting in the shelter belts and strips, must have been fully 1,500 pigeon.

A Town Gun finds it impossible to staunch the flow of adrenalin that pumps into the bloodstream when faced with such a prospect. I remarked to the Greatest Living Expert that I doubted whether my 200 cartridges was going to see me very far into the day.

The GLE laughed with the sound of a stone falling into an empty sepulchre. 'We will be lucky,' he said, 'if we get fifty between us.' The GLE does not operate on chance. Shooting pigeon is his business. His intelligence service is impeccable. It pinpoints accurately, and with up-to-the-hour information, every possible target for every pigeon flock within ten miles. There was no worthwhile secondary target for this gang for a good three miles. This rape was right under their noses.

Those pigeon were snow-happy. Once the cannonade started, they did not want it, even though the field was plenty big enough for them to drop well beyond points at which we could trouble them. They came half-heartedly for a bit. Up to mid-day there was a certain amount of high overhead traffic going we could not guess where.

Then they had all vanished. We could not wait for them to come back at dusk, either. This is a big shooting country and the pheasants must be allowed to go up to roost. When we loaded our inadequate bag of forty-seven pigeon into the car, the return flight had started. We shot one, just to show them. Its crop was almost empty. Almost as soon as they had got back to their home wood, they took off again and streamed out, all together, down another valley even though there was barely an hour of feeding light left.

So we looked on our way home and found them clobbering a tiny field of turnips. Do not tell me—and particularly do not tell the Greatest Living Expert—that it's easy to make big bags of pigeon in the snow.

A Disastrous Day?

It was a day when the hail blew across Hampshire so horizontally that it seemed unlikely ever actually to touch the ground. You could see the storms coming, one after the other, like waves of bombers. When they hit you, you built a sort of igloo round yourself, both mentally and physically, and with whatever came to hand: with pigeon nets, pigeon sacks, gun cases, not to mention your own natural fortitude and resilience. Having done so, you trusted that none of the hailstones was big enough, or travelling fast enough, actually to penetrate your waterproof smock. It was that kind of a day.

Despite this, the Greatest Living Expert had been mildly optimistic. After all, they had killed 300 on the same field of clover only a week before and no one had shot it since then. 'Boys,' he said, giving us the benefit of considerable doubt by the mere use of the word, 'I hope you have a fair number of cartridges.'

Further encouragement came from the keeper's son whom we picked up on the way. Only the afternoon before, the clover had been 'blue' with pigeon. He himself had contributed a century to the expert's total of 300 the previous weekend.

Despite all this high-powered intelligence, a shock was in store. When the car wallowed on to the waterlogged stubble, the landscape before us was blue with rain though with very little else and certainly not with pigeon.

In such a situation, and faced with a let-down by natural forces beyond his prediction and control, the GLE is apt to have something close to a seizure. He knows so much about the behaviour and reactions of *Columbia palumbus* in this part of Hampshire (and why not, since he earns his living by outwitting them?) that an occasional illogicality on their part, an unforgivable unpredictability such as a shift from clover long before they've had enough of it, is apt to shake his belief in the general construction and soundness of the Universe itself. The outward sympton is that he roars around the landscape cursing everyone and everything from the greasy furrows that bog his car, to us who sit helplessly and shaking inside it.

'We'll cut our losses,' he announces at the tail end of a particularly horrible stream of oaths. 'They've upped and gone. It's the five per cent exception. No earthly reason for it. They could be on newly sown corn but it's too wet for them. They *should* be here. I don't know where the devil we can go now.'

The twenty-mile drive to the alternative target fills the GLE with gloom. All along the way, small parties of pigeon are busy by the roadside handpicking lumps of grit, presumably with the future object of grinding up some lucky farmer's newly sown corn. 'I don't like to see them spread out like this,' says the GLE. 'It's all *wrong*.' We see small parties of forty or fifty on odd bits of clover but none of the really big concentrations which you have every right to expect in this part of the country. The wind has now risen to around Force Ten. It's hard to see why any pigeon would stand out in the middle of a clover field in weather like this.

At last the GLE puts Andrew and me in a long larch strip where he himself has often killed a 'ton'. There's newly sown corn on either side of the strip. Fifty or more pigeon clap out of the larches as we walk down to our positions. 'It's no good,' opines the expert, 'the picture just isn't right. Still, you *may* get your gun off.'

He leaves Andrew and me to sort things out as best we can and departs on a further reconnaisance that may take in another fifty square miles of country—his operations are conducted on a titanic scale.

Perhaps because we have been warned not to expect much, we are lazy about putting out the fifteen dead birds we have each brought for decoys. We simply lay them on the furrows, not bothering about pegging their heads up. Despite this, a few desperate pigeon come, mostly to Andrew, who is fifty yards along the strip and downhill from me. He shoots rather well, killing almost everything that turns up, which means about ten all told.

Within the hour, GLE returns, crackling like a trail of fulminate of mercury. The keeper has shot the strip the day before and taken one-fifty off it. No wonder we aren't getting much.

Then, alas, he sees my flaccid, head-to-earth decoys. I wish I could record the monologue that follows. It is as rich, earthy and all-plastering as the good Hampshire soil we are supposed to be defending. In essence it says: 'How the devil do you expect to shoot pigeon on a day like this if you don't use every means in your power—you flaming idiot?' All means in your power certainly includes pegging up the heads of all dead birds available. It also means shifting the decoys uphill and a further ten yards out since I have overlooked a single-strand power cable on telegraph poles that runs down parallel with the strip. The pigeon plainly don't like this and won't come to decoys too close to it. So the GLE alters the pattern and is instantly rewarded with what I maintain to be a blinding fluke. For the first time that day a steady trickle of birds starts to come in. What is more, they are now coming to me rather than to Andrew. The expert shrugs: 'See what happens when you trouble to put your decoys out correctly? Now,' he announces, rather grandly, 'I will stay and spot for you. You don't mind, do you? Some damn fools do.'

Naturally, I do mind, but say that I don't. I am so hopping mad with him that I shoot in a state of blind wish to be revenged. The result astonishes me and even mildly shocks him. Every single bird save one—the easiest naturally—joins the now modest bag. However, operations are brought to a sudden stop by a hailstorm of such ferocity that it reduces the entire scene to the consistency of a badly focused television picture. We huddle like survivors on the North Face of the Eiger until it slackens. 'Come on,' says the GLE, 'that's it here. Finish. They won't come back now. We're going to have a look at that clover field where I *wanted* to put you. Not that I believe they'll be there, mind you. I'm practically never wrong when I say that second looks just don't work. If they aren't there first time, they won't be there later.'

So I can't help having a small holiday in the heart when we drive on to the stubble we first thought of to find it blue with pigeon. I now feel better about my laxity with the decoys. It seems that even the Supremo can be wrong just once. 'Now, you two. There's not much time, so get a wriggle on,' says that merciless voice.

We wriggle, building up a thirty-decoy picture, this time with heads well pegged. We erect two net hides, fifty yards apart, against a barbed wire fence.

It is a classical situation, with a big reservoir wood behind us and gale-force wind to carry the sound of our shot into it. I sportingly toss for position. Andrew chooses the upwind hide, which means the pigeon are likely to pass me first. Oh well, there's one born every minute. Now what do you do with a chap who wins the toss and then puts you in to bat on a batsman's wicket? Answer: you clobber him—or rather them. He is a little bitter about this. Leaving a few unshot at, he argues, is a matter of etiquette and natural decency, of which I, apparently, have little. I fail to agree with him but do ease up after I have dropped one full-toss into his hide.

The Greatest Living Expert comes back from a distant wood where he has been stirring them up just as it is getting dark. 'Disaster,' he announces blithely. 'Disastrous day. Everything went wrong, including you two.'

Disastrous day? It's been gorgeous, every hail-stoned, acrimonious, delightful, blistering minute of it.

The Record-Breakers

I had often wondered whether anyone would beat Archie Coats' 1962 record of 550 and, if so, how it would be done.

Within eight short years it has been done. The thing that first caught my notice about Mr Ransford's account was the picture of the new record-holder standing in front of his hide. I saw that it was a bale hide and the final words from Archie's account of his own big day came back to me.

Archie Coats wrote: 'Anyway, I don't want to do it again and good luck to anyone who breaks my score. But I will lay odds that he will have to use a bale hide to do it.'

I thought it would be interesting to find how many other points of similarity there were between the two record bags. There were many. There was also one vast difference. Coats got his big score in January on clover. Ransford's was a harvest shoot on wheat.

All this proves, I suppose, is that pigeon are capable of being damn fools all the year round. And when their foolishness happens to coincide with the presence of a master craftsman with plenty of cartridges at hand, then conditions are all set for a record.

Ransford did not start shooting until 1.30 pm. Coats was in action by eleven. The difference is a reasonable one. Coats had meant to be shooting earlier than that, but had found his first target impractical. A pheasant day was shortly to take place on the beat concerned. One needs to be on the field of battle early in winter. Mid-day is usually plenty early enough at the height of summer.

Despite the fact that both experts found a great many birds using their respective fields, they each took considerable time and trouble in siting their decoys and making their hides comfortable. Comfort as well as camouflage is a vital ingredient of successful shooting as both well knew.

Archie Coats likes to start his decoy picture with at least a dozen dead birds. On that occasion, for some reason, he only had ten. I suspect Mr Ransford had a more formidable total, for he writes that two farm hands helped carry out cartridges and decoys.

Both began in much the same way. Pigeon were over the decoys before they could load their guns. *Guns.* Ransford had a pair, one of them fully choked. Archie shot with his faithful old standard game gun. I suspect that he might have been glad of a second gun, if only because his one weapon became so uncomfortably hot. Ransford got rid of 100 cartridges in the first half hour. Coats' rate of fire was roughly the same.

After the first hot half hour neither bothered much about setting up dead birds. Archie records that he picked up twice and got about 70 birds out, very few on sticks, most simply laid breast-down on the ground.

Both record-breakers had ammunition supply problems. In such circumstances who would not? Who would have the necessary cartridges within reach? Only men used to shooting vast numbers of pigeon. Luckily the cartridges in each case were on hand and willing helpers either found more or brought extra ammo to the hide.

'After setting up the seventy birds,' writes Coats, 'they just came without any lull, from the two main lines of flight mostly; but there really were so many birds in the air over the decoys that I had to keep a tight rein, concentrate and observe a little hide discipline myself.'

Ransford records that nearly every pigeon that came into the field decoyed. 'The continual shooting never deterred them in the slightest degree . . .' Nor were they put off by the number of fallen that lay belly upwards. They were, as in Coats' case, fixated on this particular field and plainly suicidal. The right men were certainly there to oblige them.

Ransford ended with one of the farm men loading. Coats had a keeper friend in the hide during the first part of his shoot, spotting for him.

The new record-holder stopped shooting at around ten to seven in the evening. He'd been in action for six hours twenty minutes. Coats stopped, or rather the pigeon stopped, at about four in the afternoon—a total of five hours. Possibly then the birds were coming even more thickly to the Hampshire pig clover than to Mr Ransford's Shropshire wheat.

Both shooters were dreading the pick-up. Archie had fading daylight to hamper him, so possibly missed quite a few (they only found seven next day). Ransford on the other hand had to compete with standing corn. One is always reluctant to have dogs working this for too long and, as he rightly points out, even experienced dogs often overlook birds in uncut cereals. Coats did not hunt out the strips because pheasants were going up to roost: this particular beat was due for a second time over fairly shortly.

Ransford picked 561 for a total of 699 cartridges. He is fairly confident that he actually killed 600. The ratio of kills to cartridge was therefore of the order of one miss every seven shots, a fantastically accurate performance. Archie fired about 650 for 550. In marksmanship there can have been very little to choose between them.

Flying Decoy

One of my greatest shooting heroes has always been Sir Ralph Payne-Gallwey. Sir Ralph had a boffin's mind and was always experimenting and inventing things. When he wasn't designing crossbows or reconstructing a Roman ballista that was capable of hurling a rock across the Menai Straits, he was hoisting cock pheasants forty yards high on kites to examine the penetration of shot. I fear I cannot aspire to anything as exciting or original as that. Nevertheless, I have been doing a modest bit of inventing myself.

The idea first came to me when shooting pigeon with Archie Coats. It was Archie who, several years back, introduced me to the idea that you could trigger off pigeon that were reluctant to come in to decoys by lobbing a dead bird out of the hide to fall among the slain. The circumstances have to be right, of course. There has to be a 'reservoir' wood full of pigeon within a mile or so, or at least a great many birds trafficking about in the neighbouring sky, before the 'attractor' will pull in the customers. Coats gave it as his opinion that it was 'the flash of falling grey' that did the trick.

The technique is now widely accepted among hide shooters. There is little doubt that, when circumstances are right, the 'thrower' can work the oracle and bring them soaring in once more.

I, personally, always keep a few dead birds in the hide to lob out when a lull occurs. However, I have noticed that the device meets with varying degrees of success even when circumstances *seem* exactly similar.

When I first adopted the Coats ruse I found dead pigeon hard to throw very far. Their wings flopped open and they became an untidy mass in the air. Nevertheless, the 'flash of grey' theory seemed to work about a third of the time, even though these falling bundles, with their wings half open, can have looked very little like the real thing.

So, being tidy-minded, I put stout rubber bands round my throwers to hold their wings tightly to their sides. The dead birds now lobbed a lot farther. But with these I got results about half as frequently. It seemed that, when the wings at least had a chance to fall open, the waiting pigeon reacted more strongly. So what was different about pigeon with half-open wings? The most striking difference is that the flash of grey is then relieved by a remarkably vivid white flash of feather.

Could the feeding signal be not so much the generalised grey blob falling among the decoys, but the flash of the two white wing bars? This seemed very reasonable. For what other purpose had woodpigeon evolved those white wing markings? The birds are flock feeders. It occurred to my unscientific mind that there would be few better signs that grub was up in some corner of a farmer's field than those white wing badges.

Of course, I had discovered nothing new. The ornithologists had been there years before me. I looked up Dr R. K. Murton's monograph on the woodpigeon (which is excellent on everything save shooting!) and found that, in the Pyrenees, pigeon-netters wave *white* implements like table-tennis bats to make migrating birds fly lower.

About those tell-tale feather patches, Dr Murton writes: 'The white wing marks flash when the pigeons alight and serve a signalling function, allowing the whole flock to move as a co-ordinated group.'

I went to a model aeroplane shop and bought a 3 foot strip of 4 inch by $\frac{1}{4}$ inch balsa; also a solid 4 foot length of 1 inch square. This, together with a tube of balsa cement, cost me about 30p.

Taking a dead pigeon as a model, I built a wing in three pieces. The main centre section was 6 inches long and 4 inches wide. The wing tips, raked back pigeon-fashion and cemented on with a slight dihedral angle to give stability in flight, protruded 4 inches farther. I then took a foot of the solid balsa block and, leaving it flat on top, gave it a simple, boat-like fuselage shape, tapering to an upswept point at the tail.

A 1 inch wide fuselage obviously doesn't provide enough 'body' for a plump woodpigeon. I decided to remedy this by cutting an outline profile of the body from the same material which forms the wings and cementing this flat on top of the solid fuselage. Since my flying decoy was only intended to be seen from above, this plan view should, I fancied, be sufficient.

The tail was easy. I simply took a real pigeon tail for pattern and glued the balsa imitation flat on the main fuselage spar.

The pleasant thing about balsa wood is that it is not only ridiculously easy to work, but permits the merest bodger such as myself to achieve a fairly professional finish for very little effort. From first cut to final sand-papering took me exactly an hour.

I had hoped that the dihedral rake on the wing tips would give my glider-decoy sufficient lateral stability. First flight tests, made at short range on to a settee, suggested that this was unlikely. Birds do without rudders very well indeed, but then they have what aircraft designers would describe as 'variable geometry' tail and wing surfaces. The geometry of glued balsa wood is definitely constant.

Reluctantly I gave my wooden pigeon a slender rudder. I also put some weight into its nose by boring a hole into the front of the main fuselage spar and sinking $\frac{1}{4}$ ounce coarse fisherman's barrel lead therein. It now looked remarkably like an early German monoplane fighter of the First World War called, significantly enough, the *Taube*.

Weighting a glider, I recalled from boyhood days, is the most crucial part of the operation. So I played around a good

deal, boring a second hole, sinking another smaller lead in it, then chopping a bit off the original one until my machine flew in a glorious, flat, stable glide.

At this point, my elder son entered the room. Until this moment he has never been really impressed by anything I have ever done. If I had won the Nobel Prize he would just have said 'Oh, good!' Now he appeared genuinely shaken by my skill and dexterity. 'It's better than you'd get in a shop,' he said. I pointed out coldly that you could not get flying pigeon decoys in a shop.

Painting was easy. Basically you need two shades of grey, the darker one for the wings, black for the tail bar, white for the vital wing flashes. Neck flashes, I think, hardly matter. If anything, they are probably a danger signal.

Obviously, there are operating snags. One is the comparative fragility of balsa. But then there are few obstacles in a decoy set-up for the model pigeon to crash into. Flight tests show that you can expect a glide of about fifteen to twenty yards, a bit more with a tail wind. The wind is unlikely to be a head wind in most decoy situations.

My glider-decoy has yet to be field-tested. However, yesterday there were seven woodies sitting in an oak in my garden. I bunged my machine out of a top window and had the gratification of seeing two pigeon peel off and follow it down. I must admit they did not land, perhaps because my model sat there with its wings still open. In a field of twenty or more decoys I doubt whether this will matter much, since incomers usually disregard dead birds lying with their wings outstretched.

Who Needs Enemies?

The local pigeon just had to start some time. The barley was laid and had looked ripe enough for weeks. You could hear them *coo-cooing* in the woods just across the river as if they were discussing when to attack. Four weeks earlier they had made a slight foray against one corner of a barley field. We moved our guns up into position and repulsed this skirmishing attack with the loss of a mere fifteen to the enemy.

Day after day we watched this same barley patch but they never came back to this part of the farm or to any other: all of it was down to wheat or barley. I spent the day before I was due to go for a few days fishing in Wales at home writing one or two pieces that were overdue and endlessly loading and unloading cars to suit the many outdoor whims of my family. I admit that I had had it in mind that I might sneak away for a spell to have a look at those reluctant pigeon.

Family and work kept me at it until five in the afternoon. It had rained so heavily all day that I was not too bitterly resentful at being confined. By five o'clock I just had to get out for an hour or two if my temper was to recover sufficiently to take the whole circus to Mid-Wales on the morrow.

I called in for my barrister shooting friend, Andrew, who was enjoying one of those extraordinary long vacations his profession seem so undeservedly to enjoy every few months. His arm need never be twisted to come shooting. And seeing that he was preparing for a similar family excursion, he, too, was feeling the need for a little light relief.

Neither of us was hopeful. But as we drew near to the field from which we had expected great things for so many weeks, two pigeon fluttered in and 'trod water' with that wing-flapping motion that enables them to stand still in mid-air while deciding exactly where to sit down.

We drove the Land-Rover round the muddy headland with rising hopes. As we came near to the laid barley, more than our hopes rose: about one hundred and fifty pigeon became airborne. Even so, we had seen this before during the past few disappointing weeks. Each time a flock had been spotted and put off the ground it had flown away never to return.

Since time was running short and it threatened to get dark early, we did not make extensive preparations. The decoys were dumped out on the barley without benefit of tall sticks. Some, I suspect, immediately fell off their perches on top of the stalks and dropped from sight. But we had twenty-four to start with and at least half of them must have made the grade.

Nor did we bother much with hides. A couple of stakes and a net apiece, rigged across a deep ditch. Since this seemed to be the only patch of corn in which the birds were interested, we decided to double-bank over one set of decoys and to stand in the ditch barely twenty yards apart.

This time there was no mistaking the birds' intentions. We were hardly back in the ditch before the first birds came in. We saluted them and sent them unharmed on their way.

There are great difficulties, not to say stresses, in shooting side by side. There has to be a system by which each gun knows which bird to shoot, how and when. You can only afford to double-up with someone you know very well and who is as proof as yourself to insult and bad language. It's all very well to say beforehand: 'Let them come right in and then I'll take the left hand one and you take the right and don't fire until I shout.'

What happens in practice is that (*a*) you both shoot at the identical instant at the same bird so that neither is aware the other has fired and each thinks he killed, or (*b*) there is a complete muddle about calling and the bird sails away unshot at, or (*c*) one of you (never me) jumps the gun and fires without warning the other so that the later incoming birds turn away out of range.

Occasionally this produces compensating situations as when the offender misses and the second gun eye-wipes him for hogging the shooting. The opportunities for conflict are enjoyably endless. That is why I say you must know your companion very well indeed. My barrister friend and I delight in the art of abuse and so four-barrelled shooting adds to the joy of the occasion, if not to the skill of the performance. With friends like that . . .

The pigeon on this wet evening were suicidal. I had not seen them pile in to decoys like this outside the best Hampshire pigeon country. This was dormitory London Surrey.

We did not bother to pick up as we shot since the sky was darkening even at that early hour. Most of the birds were falling through the barley stems anyway and were hidden from sight. The day's rain had turned the bottom of the ditch into mud that would have done credit to the Medway estuary. My own feet were stuck fast as in a concrete block. My springer, Teal, sat disconsolately in the mud at the bottom of the ditch, unable to see a thing that was going on above his head and tortured by the cannonade.

To make things more complicated my companion's gun fell to bits—the fore-end bolt came unstuck and the fore-end dropped off in the mud. I sent him home to borrow my 20-bore. He was only absent for ten minutes. In that short time I had the hottest period of all, adding fifteen to the bag. I might have done even better but for the fact that I now had trouble.

A swollen cartridge had jammed in my right chamber so I had to shoot with the choke until my companion returned with the hand extractor.

At about half past seven we sent a bored and reluctant springer out to pick up in pouring rain. A lot of the barley was still standing so we found, I imagine, two-thirds of the bag.

That was how, at midnight, after finally loading the vehicles and making sure everything was ready for a six o'clock family take-off for Wales next morning, I came to be plucking fifty pigeon.

Indoor Pigeon Shoot

I wonder if you have ever had the chance to let off a 12-bore *indoors*? Short of becoming a bank robber the opportunity may not come your way.

The psychiatrists tell us that we all indulge in aggressive fantasies. Maybe yours is firing a shotgun at a glass roof. But have you actually done it, and do you know what happens if you do?

I was not robbing a bank. I had gone, along with four other experienced guns, to eradicate the London pigeons from the pumping station of a well-known South London waterworks. These pigeons were, it seems, befouling the works with their droppings and feathers to such a degree that the pumps were in serious danger of seizing up altogether.

On the basis of try-anything-once, I agreed to join the party, especially as my host assured me that the shooting could be of the hardest. To stand in the yard when the pigeons came in to roost at evenings was, he declared, quite as difficult as trying to knock down pheasants when placed in a very narrow forest ride bordered by tall trees.

The walls on either side of the alleyways in which we were to stand were at least 50 ft. high and there was very little daylight to be seen at the top. The pigeons flighted in from the surrounding squares and parks at dusk. This narrow strip of open sky was where we had to take them.

When this strangest of roosting flights began, I soon found that the red chequers and Greater London descendants of feral racing pigeons and blue rocks certainly lived up to their reputation. In these conditions it was not hard to detect the ancestry of the latter. I think they simply took the towering walls of the water works as something very similar to the sea cliffs beloved of their distant forbears.

I slowly piled up a modest score, missing many more than is my usual average when roosting in natural surroundings. The noise confined within the walls was shattering. To tell the truth, I think the din of the barrage was probably more important than any casualties we inflicted when it came to discouraging roosting pigeons.

While I was engaged in trying to anticipate the most difficult birds of all, the one that appeared from directly behind two tall chimney stacks, I felt a tug at my elbow. A man in dungarees had been standing there for some time watching me miss.

'Do you want to do a bit of good, mister?'

I had obviously been doing little good in his eyes so far.

'This way, mate. They're driving me barmy in here.'

The dungareed operator led the way down the alley and into a large hangar-like building which housed the pumps. At either side were tall, sliding steel doors that reached to the roof. Both sides of the hangar were open.

Above the pumps, at about the height of the average three storey building, stretched a glass roof supported on steel girders. My guide pointed high into the roof, directly above the humming motors of the pumps. 'There!' he said venomously.

I followed his hand. Perched on the girders, quite unmoved by the sounds of firing outside, were five or six red chequers. The man in dungarees gestured at the gleaming, green pump cases. They were liberally spattered with London pigeon guano. 'Shoot the so-and-so's,' he ordered.

I stared hypnotised at the glass roof, imagining the kind of

destruction a load of sixes might produce. I could hear the cascades of crashing glass, the metallic howl of the pumps when they ground to a stop as the fragments fell into their whirling intestines. I could see the water in a million London taps suddenly dwindling to a trickle. My aggressive fantasies played delightedly for a second or two with this picture of destruction and then my better self reasserted itself.

'Impossible,' I said piously.

'Here. Give it to me.'

'Give what?'

'The gun, cock.'

'You'll bring the lot down.'

'Nonsense,' he said, or a word to that effect.

I meekly handed over my 12-bore and watched with the utmost dreamlike detachment while he aimed deliberately at the unsuspecting pigeons and then pulled both triggers in quick succession.

There was, in fact, a heavy fall of pigeons, but not a splinter of glass. The marksman handed back the gun in the manner born, as if to his loader, and ran in like a badly trained spaniel to collect the birds before they became fatally enmesh in the works of his pumps.

When he returned with four pigeon he simply spoke one word: 'reinforced!'

'The glass?'

'Yes, sloping, too, takes the shock, nothing to worry about. You carry on.'

In the next ten minutes, I experienced some of the most bizarre and intriguing shooting of a long and mixed career. The resident birds had, of course, left the steel rafters long since. But now other pigeons, panicked by the fusillade outside, were flying in through the open hangar doors at one end and taking a short cut across the pump house to leave by the doors at the other side.

The noise of a 12-bore fired indoors and confined beneath a glass roof is quite stupendous and immensely satisfying. I don't recommend that anyone other than a hold-up man tries it, unless he has convincing proof that the glass is, in fact, reinforced. I can assure anyone who may get this rare opportunity that it is mighty good for those regrettable and only just buried aggressive impulses.

Back to the more ordinary sort of pigeon. Our nursery farm chickweed festival is still fortunately on. I must have taken a hundred or more birds off the place in the last fortnight. The stock doves that began the event have long since disappeared. It's all woodpigeon now. The interesting thing is to watch how their preferences for certain patches of the weed alter within a comparatively restricted area. On Monday they are hard at it in the middle of a big area of 'shot' lettuces. Three days later they seem only interested in the chickweed among the cauliflowers one hundred yards away. Something to do with the ripeness of the weed, perhaps?

Another thing that appears to have happened as the result of a fortnight of almost continual warfare: they now come in flocks of fifty to sixty, seldom in the hoped for fours and fives or even ones and twos. Result: one bang and you lose the lot for a bit.

One more small discovery to add to the pigeon shooter's armoury and equipment. I don't know about you but, being mean-minded, I always resent wasting a cartridge to put up birds that have settled wide of my decoys. A far cheaper answer, I have found, is a starting pistol.

In the middle of my last shoot, the nursery farmer himself turned up to see how I was getting on. He gave me one for the note-book. Apparently the market gardeners' trade paper has just announced that the only sure defence the nursery grower has against the woodpigeon is the experienced shooter over decoys.

Woodie Watching

There is nowhere to compare with Hyde Park when it comes to studying the feeding and flocking habits of woodpigeon. I have remarked on the astonishing tameness of the species in central London before. I have never seen this better illustrated than during this autumn.

The woodies are feeding on clover and also acorns in parties of up to thirty or forty. They would appear at first sight to be no relation of their wild country cousins.

You can walk within five yards of a single bird, or even through an entire feeding flock, without them doing more than move out of your way like any tame Trafalgar Square feral pigeon. Even when great bounding labradors run in among them, they rarely take to the wing. The dogs seem to recognise the truce, for even gun-trained town dogs take no notice of the pigeons' presence or, apparently, their scent.

It is possible to put them on the wing by clapping loudly, but there is scarcely any panic in their exit. The other evening I amused myself by testing out the effectiveness of the natural 'decoy' pattern. About twenty birds were prospecting for clover on an open piece of sward. Round the fringes, perhaps a hundred yards away, were odder singletons who preferred to dine alone.

I strolled around, approaching these loners to within a yard or two, and then clapping my hands gently to persuade them into the air. Though not one of them rose more than six feet above the ground, since it plainly had little intention of flying more than a few yards, it immediately saw the group of its fellows feeding together. Of ten birds put on the wing in this way, nine planed in to land with the 'decoys' in a way which made the trigger finger itch.

One does not often get a chance to study feeding woodies in close-up. I was struck by how dissimilar the feeding attitude is to that mimicked by most commercial decoys. A woodie, at least a woodie feeding on a low-growing crop such as clover, does not have its head or neck raised.

The body has an almost hunched, curved attitude. The head is well down to the bird's dinner plate. The most characteristic movement, observable from a considerable distance away, is the bobbing and pecking of the head. It is this motion, I am certain, that tells an approaching bird that there is absolutely nothing to worry about and that it is perfectly safe to land and tuck in.

How to imitate this movement? We have decoys on sticks, decoys on springs, decoys on sticks *and* springs. Friends of mine have even built elaborate devices with which to flap the outstretched wings of a dead bird. The latter most surely do work, since the white flash on the extended wings is almost certainly another feeding signal.

But none of these ruses give that all-important head movement of the enthusiastically noshing woodie. Obviously it could be achieved with a sprung head operated by cord from the hide. But how many birds could you manage to work simultaneously in this way? Not more than two, I'll bet.

While watching the Hyde Park birds, I had a crazy thought which I am sure is both uneconomical and impractical, but then some of the most intriguing ideas are just that.

Some time ago, publicans had a craze for exhibiting behind their bars a ridiculous ostrich which dipped its beak in a glass of water, rocked upright and thereafter performed a series of increasingly energetic bows until beak met water once more, whereupon the whole cycle was repeated.

Now I never found out how this worked, though I am sure practically every one of my readers knows the answer. I always assumed it was to do with the cooling action occasioned by the beak reaching the water—or something scientific like that.

The point is: is the idea something that could be built into a pigeon decoy? Would the daft antics of the dipping ostrich when transferred to a pigeon head, produce the all-enticing movement? I'm pretty certain it would. But plainly the difficulties are enormous. Cost for a start. Fragility for a follow-up. Difficulty of transporting the apparatus just to knock the project dead on the head.

Maybe, but as a man who once built a glider for throwing out of the hide so that it circled round, flashing its pigeon-shaped, pigeon-painted wings, I feel that I may be on to something, if only for the amusement of the lunatic fringe like myself.

Blizzard Roost

I'm always hoping for that bonanza day, whether it be when fishing or shooting, when everything goes right, when the opportunities are there due to fortunate accident of wind and weather, and success depends solely on one's ability to take advantage of the good fortune offered by the gods.

In shooting I can think of two such ideal occasions. They both have to do with real hard weather. The first is the opening day of a thaw after a long, hard spell. If you are out on your fresh marsh at the moment the frost unlocks, then you may well see duck beyond your dreams.

Twice this season I have missed that vital moment by a single day—such is the penalty of having to take your outings at the moments when work allows. In each case, companions, who were able to bide their time cashed in on enormous flights barely twenty-four hours later. They had caught the thaw.

The second bonanza needs the reverse in weather conditions. Twice in a shooting lifetime I have had a pigeon roosting flight to remember for all time when a blizzard has suddenly cut loose on the landscape about an hour before normal flighting time.

One of those super flights occurred only last week. The opportunities were there—in vast flocks. I only wish that I had made the very best of them, but then that is the story of my shooting life.

A friend phoned me to say that there were thousands of pigeon coming in to roost in his woods. They had been around for a couple of weeks and he had already shot them twice, picking between thirty and forty each time to his own gun. Would I care to come and help him as he did not know whether they would still be around when the flocks had cleaned up the supply of acorns?

It was a bitter cold afternoon with a heavy leaden sky. I took seventy-five cartridges, expecting to fire a box at the most. I wrapped up in two sweaters and a jacket against the tearing north wind and put a flask of portable central heating in my pocket.

As I drove to the wood, I was greatly encouraged to put up little parties of twenty and thirty pigeon from the roadside verges. Whether they were gritting or looking for stray acorns I could not tell. It was enough to see them about in squadron strength.

There were also plenty of pigeon in the fields, mostly in tight-packed little flocks. These, I guessed, were trying to root clover out of the frost-bitten ground and the light powdering of snow which covered it. These field parties seemed unusually touchy, rising at the passing of the car some twenty yards away.

It was as if the whole pigeon community sensed that something drastic in the way of weather lay ahead of them. They wanted to feed and yet they felt the need of shelter for the night.

We moved into the woods at around a quarter to four. Plenty of birds panicked out as we split up and looked for ideal positions. I choose a stand on the lee-side of the wood, close to some ivy-covered oaks which looked like cosy roosting trees.

Pigeon started to come in at once. The first ones were tempting, but high above the tree tops. No doubt I should have left these until I had played myself in. Over-confident, I opened fire and scored eight straight misses.

This shook my morale badly. So I took a firm hold and forced myself to wait for a reasonably low bird. I scrambled this one down untidily, and knew that I had been lucky to score at all.

The next quarter of an hour was not much better. I knew perfectly well what my trouble was. I was worrying far too much about intervening branches—an old roosting bogey of mine. In the past I have learnt that the only way to shoot beneath trees is to pretend the trees don't exist. You bring down a lot of timber that way, but you do, surprisingly, also bring down a lot of pigeon.

At the end of half an hour I had picked nine birds for—no, I won't tell you how many cartridges. It was at this point that the blizzard broke. Inside the wood you could hardly tell that it was snowing. The flakes were dry and fine. By the time they had penetrated the tree tops the effect at ground level was that of standing in a fine, white, freezing mist.

The pigeon now became suicidal in their determination to get in. There were so many targets that you didn't know which one to pick. Looking up through the tree tops against the snowy sky the birds seemed to be wheeling and diving like bats silhouetted in the mouth of a cave.

I began to score, of course. Who would not, even when off form, in such conditions of plenty? Each time I collected a few birds I made a little pile against the base of a prominent—as I thought—tree. Then the flight line changed, and I would move a few yards in the white-out and take up a fresh stand.

Another small pile of birds and another move. The dog was hard at it now and I had little need of heating, central internal type or external sweater variety. Despite the bitter cold I was panting with the exertion.

The snow added light to the scene and by this light the birds kept coming and coming. It was about twenty minutes before my friend in the adjacent wood stopped shooting that I suddenly realised that I hadn't a bird to show for my entire cannonade, except the one I had just picked. The rest were distributed in neat piles around the wood where I had deposited them against those 'prominent' trees.

I told you that this story was a confession of incompetence. Within a wood perhaps fifteen acres in extent I was now hopelessly lost. I don't suppose the heavy snowfall helped much but I couldn't find a single one of those caches of wood-pigeon.

A bird in the hand is worth several above the tree tops. Pigeon were still milling around up there in the blizzard, and, no doubt, if I kept shooting, I would have got another ten—for I had at last found a sort of form.

I spent the whole of the best few minutes of that extraordinary bonanza flight looking for pigeon dumps.

The spaniel, naturally, found them before I did. Three times I spotted him sitting forlornly in the snow and each time he was parked beside a snow-covered pile of the fallen.

I gathered all the piles in the end but still left at least eight birds unpicked. Altogether, not a very distinguished performance. I collected twenty-eight pigeon in the end. It should have been forty-eight seeing that I had not a single cartridge left.

Perhaps snow does something odd to shooters as well as to pigeon. On the way home I lost my way, taking an hour and a quarter for a normal half hour journey. If only these bonanza occasions were kind enough to coincide with maximum use of my minimum skills.

Delivering the Goods

Pigeon, pigeon, pigeon. The house is full of feathers and the dustman's sacks overflowing with empty cartridge cases. We have certainly shot some pigeon these last few weeks. The deep-freeze is jam-packed. Our local outlet for deep-frozen, oven-ready birds is surfeited. Friends who like pigeon have been supplied and still the birds have kept coming.

I won't shoot if I can't use the slain, or at least see someone else reap the protein benefit. I know that shooting pigeon is largely an extermination operation. Just the same, I cannot abide waste.

So I found myself setting out for the Walton-on-Thames station with a sack full of eighty surplus birds addressed to a game-dealer in Norfolk who would, he assured me, take the birds off me in the feather.

The first shock was that Walton wouldn't take perishables for outward transmission. Apparently it is getting the goods across London—all the way from Waterloo to Liverpool Street—that defeats the system. They recommended that I take my sack, which they had considerately weighed for me (ninety pounds) direct to Waterloo.

It was the first time I have tried getting aboard a full commuter train in the rush hour with ninety pounds of dead pigeon. I doubt whether I shall attempt it again. Eventually I managed to hoist them, with the help of a horror stricken bowler-hatted city gent, out of the passage where they were blocking the gangway and into a luggage rack, where they reposed, Damocles-fashion, over a middle-aged lady's fruit-decorated hat.

Once in similar circumstances, I had a traumatic experience with a dead pike. Despite the fact the pike was in a sack, it persisted in dispensing small gobbets of fish slime on to, in this instance, a man in a flat hat who never, luckily, noticed what was happening to him.

From three seats' distance I now watched my sackful of pigeon in fear that their wounds would suddenly open and release a steady rain of blood. Fortunately no more than a single feather descended all the way from Walton to Waterloo.

At Waterloo I discovered the parcels office to be about quarter of a mile away from the arrival platform. Such a carry was beyond my recently slipped disc. So I gave a porter twenty P to do the carrying for me.

The parcels clerk informed me that he couldn't accept perishable goods of this nature and that the only course open was to take the sack on to Liverpool Street myself. I was less generous with the next porter who bore my sack to the taxi rank. Nevertheless his services knocked a further bird off my profits. The taxi and tip removed another five hard-won woodies from my account.

I should by now have learned that parcels offices at mainline termini are heavily segregated. The one at Liverpool Street is a shortish taxi ride away. The shortest taxi ride and tip can hardly work out at less than two pigeon. For the moment I indulged a terrifying fantasy of paying my drive with two well-shot woodies.

The biggest shock of all was the pigeons' fare to Diss in Norfolk. Their ticket cost me £1·75. At that moment I would have been happy to have got rid of my load at double the price. Nevertheless, just for the record: I had spent the best part of £2·50 from an expected revenue of £6, leaving out the matter of cartridges fired and slipped disc severely strained. The motto 'Waste Not, Want Not' is an admirable one, but there are limits and in this instance I had reached mine.

A few days later, David Home-Gall, who makes his living by taking out keen pigeon shooters, was kind enough to invite me to have a go on his patch.

It is always a revelation to shoot with the real experts and my trip with David certainly opened my eyes to one or two new wrinkles. We can take it as read that David knows all about pigeon. He wouldn't earn his daily bread from them if he didn't know how to outwit them. I have written several times in the past of outings with that other great professional Archie Coats, who operates in Berkshire and Hampshire. The two men have differences in approach which are partly governed by the nature of their respective country—David's is Bedfordshire—but also by their different temperaments.

The absolute common grounds on which they both work is the importance of thorough reconnaissance and the insistence or giving a set-up a fair trial before moving pitch. With David last week I must confess that I didn't think he had got a shoot where he first placed his decoys.

But, as the morning wore on, a steady trickle built up and we finished with seventy or eighty birds, about half of which were, to David's surprise, stock doves.

David Home-Gall's decoys are the best I have seen. They were designed with the help of a taxidermist. The rubber is soft, having a higher latex content than the usual decoy, and is consequently less likely to achieve the tell-tale shine most decoys get after a dozen or so outings.

The paint has been carefully blended to give a dead matt appearance and the detail painting of eye, primaries and white collar is superb. You can argue that such minutiae make little difference to an incoming pigeon. All I can say is that these decoys look more like live birds than anything save a dead one. They are collapsible and inflate by means of a balloon inside.

If I could get twenty or thirty I would change my stock of deeks tomorrow.

Other H-G refinements: excellent cord bird carriers with slip-along plastic collars, each string taking at least two dozen birds. A set of lofting poles that really work without bend or wobble. The lofter is housed in a plastic funnel at the top. A long thin rod sticks down vertically below the decoy, passes through the funnel and into the hollow of the lofting poles. A fixed wire hook behind this rod provides a fulcrum at the exact point of balance for the pigeon to sit naturally in the chosen tree.

David—a man who feels for his victims—has invented a simple humane killer for runners, that penetrates the brain and causes instant death. I particularly liked his patent pigeon packer, a wire self-locking clamp that holds five pigeon for despatch to game dealers. Now, if only I'd had some of those on Waterloo station!

PART IV

My Family and Some Animals

On the Couch

I have long since become reconciled to the fact that my elder son, Paul, has become a better dry-fly fisherman than I am. I suppose I was prepared for the same to happen with shooting. I would not have been surprised if within a year of taking it up he had been knocking them down higher, faster and cleaner. Though it might have niggled me, I suppose at heart I would have been paternally glad. There's something very satisfactory in being bettered by your kids in an activity you fancy yourself to be a moderately dab hand at.

But having paid tribute to his fly-casting and trout-catching, I hope he'll forgive me if I say that there was never any danger of a swift overtake in the ballistic department. When he hit things he did not know how he did it, though, of course, that's a stupid thing to say, for none of us do. If we did, we might start worrying about it and experience a total mental blockage. Far worse was that he didn't know why he was *missing*. He was just aware that whatever he did, things simply flew through the flak unscathed.

So, last week, Dad did exactly what any sensible parent would have done twelve months earlier. He booked a lesson at a shooting school. Now there are many excellent shooting schools. I happen to have a weakness for the West London Shooting Ground. Among its several first-class coaches, my own favourite gun doctor is Percy Stanbury (since retired), so I'll make no pretences at anonymity and just hope all the other fine teachers will excuse my partiality.

From time to time I have taken my own apology for a swing

along to Percy Stanbury, flopped it down in the psychiatrist's consulting room and pleaded with him to do a deep analysis. The metaphor may sound far-fetched but I have chosen it deliberately.

Talking to this man is very close to having a nice lie-down on the analyst's couch. The soothing West Country voice pours over you like syrup. You feel yourself sinking into an almost hypnotic state. From now on, you have nothing to worry about. Doctor will take care of it all. That's the way it always is for me, but then there was no way of telling how the treatment would react on junior.

But the good doctor is at home with patients of all ages and they with him. Junior picks up 12-bore and aims it at doctor's right eye. 'Ah,' says the best psychiatrist in the business, 'there's a bit to straighten out here.' He calls me in, just as if I am an intern on a ward round. 'You can see what his trouble is, can't you?'

I feel that I should diagnose something quickly and brilliantly like: 'Yes, sir, every symptom of a cross-eyed stock psychosis.' In a kindly tone, and perhaps because he can sense that I don't have the faintest idea what is wrong, he explains gently. 'You see. Look at this. . . .' He takes hold of the patient's right shoulder and eases him round rather as if he is demonstrating the lack of traction in a fibrositic joint.

Dr Stanbury explains: 'The poor chap's stance is too closed. It's almost as if he's shooting with a long-bow. He's so closed up on himself that he's made himself left-eyed, when of course his right is his master eye.'

'Thank heavens,' I sigh to myself, like any relieved parent. 'The lad's absolutely normal.'

But now we've moved from the department of psychological medicine into the physiotherapy unit. Remedial exercises are what are needed. Dr Stanbury makes the boy face him with his stance more open, his chest presented in three-quarter profile, rather than in the guarded, boxer's left-foot-forward position of paralytic cramp he has taken up formerly.

After some tension-relieving arm exercises, with and without gun, we move outside to the operating theatre. First, the usual shot tests are taken and recorded on a white-washed plate. The pattern is not too far off centre. There is hope. 'Now, we'll just try the simple going-away ones, first,' doctor says, rather as if he was suggesting to a nervous case that 'this first one won't hurt at all'.

The clay clatters away on its brainless flight. *Bang*. Reaction negative. We give it six more shots. Still no sign that the treatment is taking. But this is an operation under hypnosis. That voice again, gentle, infinitely encouraging, guiding, not hurrying, never flurrying. Doctor doesn't appear at all worried that patient's heart-beat isn't picking up. But unseen to mere observer, something *is* happening. Patient, though still in a coma, is responding somewhere in his deep unconscious.

His movements are quicker, more spontaneous, the position of the limbs better, even the pallor is fading from the cheeks. The moment has come for shock therapy. 'Where did you miss that one?' doctor demands sharply. 'High left,' says patient, without knowing that he's replied from his trance state. Doctor nods and looks at houseman (that's me again). 'First time he's shown any insight.' Patient grins: a good sign.

Doctor Stanbury moves to the next phase. 'Now,' he orders his still hypnotised subject, 'miss this one six inches to the right.' A gasp goes up in the theatre. Instead of scudding away to the boundary, clay dissolves in a puff of black dust. Five out of the next six go the same way. It is time to come round. Dr Stanbury taps patient gently and says: 'There. You *see*!'

Subject, now fully awake and unbelieving, smiles in the way people do, at least on the telly, when they come out of a successful carve-up in the theatre. 'Cor,' says the patient.

But the surgeon knows when it pays to be brutal and force the pace. 'Prepare driven partridges,' he tells the ward sister, who shambles out from behind a safety barrier.

Here, the treatment is repeated, though intensified. At first, the same series of misses. But Doctor Stanbury has his finger on the trouble straight away. 'He's moving the cheek away from the stock too quickly to see if he's hit.' I feel I am expected to make a note. Perhaps 'signs of severe anxiety neurosis' would meet the case. But the neurosis isn't given much chance to settle in.

'Fire your second barrel immediately when you miss with the first.' Patient has no need to do so for the clay flies to bits with the first shot. 'Observe,' the great man explains to me, now cast in the role of the male nurse who will have after-care of the victim. 'He was concentrating so hard on staying there for the second barrel that he never thought about lifting his head.'

Now that the lad has got the feel of what it's like to keep his head down on the gun *and* kill, he's told to remember exactly what it felt like and imitate that feeling. He has a lapse or two but soon he is powdering three out of five driven clays.

At the medium high tower he does even better, disconcertingly better. He's fairly clobbering them. Patient is now confident and conscious enough to murmur appreciatively: 'Gosh, it's like having a flipping radar set with you.'

The great gun doctor smiles. It is the kindly smile of a physican who has saved another life in the early stages of what might later be a fatal and incurable disease.

'Would you like to have a go?' Percy Stanbury says to me. Father misses eight in a row. Once again I experience the deep peace of knowing that I am in safe hands. Gratefully I sink onto the psychiatrist's couch and hear the soft words begin to lap over me.

Ticking in Suburbia

At the time of writing my second son, then thirteen, was a weekly boarder at what he sombrely refers to as 'the local nick'. Recently I received a mid-week letter from him. This was, in itself, a surprise. Even more surprising was the fact that I could decipher the hand-writing. I expected it to contain a demand of some sort but hardly the one that now confronted me. 'Mike,' it said, 'is coming for the day on Saturday. Please take us bird-wotching [*sic*].'

This Mike, I knew from previous experience, was a dedicated thirteen-year-old enthusiast who never moved a step without his Field Guide and powerful binoculars. My son, Simon, had obviously been cracking him up about the wonders of our local, suburban avifauna. Reputations were, I felt, at stake all round. What the devil could I conjure up for the young enthusiasts, to order, and all within sixteen miles of Piccadilly Circus.

The following is a straightforward account of what actually took place on the afternoon on which I found myself the reluctant leader of this formidable expedition.

To start with I insisted that both junior ornithologists should keep lists of every species recorded. At the same time, I explained that I personally was dead against the practice of 'ticking', at least later in adult ornithological life. In case you do not know what I mean by 'ticking', I refer to bird-watchers who rush from sewage farm to reed-bed ticking off their little lists as if just to see a bearded tit or a sedge warbler is enough. Once seen, that particular species can be wiped from the memory.

Bird enthusiasts, no less than other hobbyists, are entitled to pass their time as they choose, of course. I merely wanted to record my personal view to my young followers that ticking does not necessarily stimulate imagination and curiosity to the maximum.

With this thought either absorbed or totally ignored—one can never be quite sure what that glazed stare means: Oh, how I pity schoolmasters—we started right in there ticking.

Without moving out of the garden we got three kinds of tit—blue, coal and great—also starling, blackbird, sparrows (house and hedge), thrushes (song and mistle), robin, jay, magpie, woodpigeon, carrion crow (flying over) and, super bonus, a rare visit from our great spotted woodpecker.

Fifteen species without leaving the premises. Not bad for an opener.

Now we needed something more exotic. I decided on my nursery farm shoot where the gravel company is fast turning a minor partridge manor into useful wetland habitat. During the drive there, one junior spotted a couple of swifts hawking for insects over the high street and dismissed with scorn a counter claim for a flock of racing pigeons. By now a healthy rivalry had developed between the spotters.

No sooner had we got on to the farm than someone shouted

'seagulls'. When this was very properly disallowed by the referee, claimant got to work with binoculars and scored a couple of points with 'black-headed gulls and one black-back'. 'Greater or lesser?' the adjudicator demanded. 'Juvenile lesser.' By common consent we allowed a bonus point for this additional and accurate information.

I'm afraid I got the snipe zipping out of the sewage farm but it was one more for the list. The boys quickly notched up a bunch of eight mallard rocketing around the sky over the gravel works in courting flight, then two green plover tumbling in display, a pied wagtail strutting on a dung heap and a stock dove that rose with a party of five woodies sampling the early chickweed.

The gravel-pit itself did us proud. A heron was prospecting for frogs on the sandy flats exposed by the sinking water level. There were also two moorhens, a coot, two tufted duck and a heavy low-level attack of house martins going to work on a hatch of midges.

I hasten to add that our gravel-pit is in its earliest and least matured stage. Apart from the shallows, there are, as yet, no reed beds or sedges and very little cover, so this could hardly be considered a bad haul of water birds.

On our way across the farm we logged two easy corvids—rook and jackdaw—which brought the total species to date to thirty.

So far we hadn't had to move out of the Land-Rover. This was bird-ticking made far too easy. 'Now you're going to walk,' I told them. 'We'll go to our fishing water and see what we can pick up there.'

We did far better than I had any right to hope on a one-mile stretch of the River Mole. A pair of Canada geese came cackling round a bend and towered just in time to avoid knocking one of the enthusiasts binoculars over bird book. Then a mute swan on the same course flew in creaking majesty past us at eye level. We got a wren hopping into its little cave in the bank and a streak of blue using itself as a flying pick-axe to hollow out a nesting hole. Kingfishers are back on our stream, I'm happy to say.

En route to the second farm where I regularly shoot pigeon, there's a narrow, rutty, gravelly lane bordered with hawthorns that is particularly beloved of finches. There we logged the predictable chaffinches, two goldfinches and a solitary bullfinch. Only a greenfinch was missing but we caught up with a cock almost as soon as we turned into the farm. A skylark, then a cuckoo seen at long range in mid-air and announced by both spotters in the first instance as 'some kind of hawk' made a total of forty species. We got our hawk, or rather falcon, next, a kestrel that dropped out of the top of an oak tree.

It was a sunny afternoon. The one kind of bird I had hoped to be able to find the boys but which had so far eluded us was now making the most of the warmth. Two cock pheasants scrapped in a furrow, while, farther along the hedge, a solitary cock lorded it over five sleek and smug-looking hens.

The boys didn't detect that the first partridge we saw—a singleton—was a Frenchman, but then perhaps I had an unfair advantage. I've known this old boy for a long time. He, or maybe she, never pairs off. We've all tried to come to terms with this barrener for several seasons. He, or she, is far too cunning for us and is remarkably adept at picking a hole in the line or, wisely, just refusing to fly at all.

Maybe the bird is bad for the stock. Possibly someone should bump it off—on the ground if necessary. But I doubt if any of us will have the heart.

When we came home to tea the tally stood at forty-three species, at least a third of which the average householder in commuterville would consider to be unlikely or even impossible neighbours here in the middle of the bricks and mortar. As it was, I am certain that we missed quite a lot. How many blackcaps, whitethroats, chiffchaffs, flycatchers did I overlook? I know I should have had a nuthatch, green woodpecker and, if I'd gone to search a certain conifer wood, a goldcrest. I suppose a really efficient ticker would have chalked up fifty species.

How to File a Ferret

One of the firms in my office building decided to clear out a lot of old equipment. It was thus that I came upon a pile of ancient metal filing boxes lying in the corridor. My personal filing system being fairly chaotic, I thought that these might come in handy to give my correspondence a semblance of order.

These boxes were about eighteen inches long, a foot high and six inches wide. Each had a circular hole one inch in diameter bored in the bottom. It was this hole which revealed to me the true and obvious purpose for such a box. So I took one home.

My wife, who is also my company secretary, greeted the box with great enthusiasm. She, too, reacted at first glance as I had done. She saw the thing as a box file and welcomed it accordingly. I explained gently that this had been my first reaction also, but that a little thought had enabled me to see through such an obvious disguise.

The metal box was quite plainly, I explained patiently, a ferret box. Filled with straw, it would make a very useful enclosure for Fred while he was being transported by car to the scene of operations. Fred is my elder son's very large hob ferret. I have written about his antics previously in this column and pointed out that Fred is a renowned escapologist. However, the heavy hinged metal lid of the box should keep even Fred firmly imprisoned until the moment came to unleash him on an unsuspecting rabbit warren.

My wife rode the punch awfully well. But then she has had a lot of practice. 'I do not suppose,' she said icily, 'there is another human being in Greater London, and possibly in the entire world, who could look at a metal box file and declare it to be an obvious portable home for a ferret.'

Because it seemed the easiest course to take at the time, I agreed with her and left the box standing on the kitchen table.

Half an hour later, my son came home. As luck would have it I was standing by the kitchen table helping my wife with some heavy domestic chore such as opening a bottle of wine. My son's glance fell directly on the metal filing box.

'Dad,' he said with one of those rare flashes of filial gratitude. 'Thanks a lot. You've got me a ferret box.'

Despite the complete destruction of my wife's theories about the number of ferret box recognisers in Greater London, if not the Universe, she was not cast down.

'I don't count *him*,' she said scathingly. 'You've brought him up to be another maniac like yourself.'

There is a very sad sequel to this story and one that hints at the extreme complexity of my family life. The following Sunday, my son took Fred for an outing, housing him in our tin box suitably lined with straw. On the way home, at a traffic lights not far from our house, Fred, the renowned escapologist, did his act once more. He pushed up the lid of the box file and landed with an affectionate, though heart-stopping, thump on my son's neck, just as he was about to pull up.

I suppose even the most seasoned driver might be excused a moment of indecision when finding himself suddenly assaulted in the rear by a ferret. I am awaiting an estimate for beating out a front wing and respraying same at this very moment. Somehow I fancy the rabbits acquired on this expedition will hardly cover the cost.

In such circumstances, even the best of wives cannot be expected to refrain from having the last word. Mine had it. 'I told you it was no sort of place to file a ferret,' she said primly.

Opening Shots

At what age should one start one's sons off using a shotgun? I've heard many theories on this subject and, for once, have expressed none myself. I suppose a great deal depends on the boy himself. I may be wrong but I really do think both my sons are trustworthy in handling firearms. They've both come up through the airgun stage. Parental supervision, and occasionally wrath, has never been lacking at the slightest hint of carelessness or shortage of respect for the sharp end of even an airgun.

Just the same, I've been remarkably loath to hand them a shotgun. This weapon's appallingly lethal nature has perpetually haunted me, particularly where the young are concerned. It is all very well to think a boy is responsible, quite another to ask him to keep his head in the excitement of a cock pheasant exploding at his feet or a partridge covey swinging back through the line. Perhaps, because I have seen what these events can do to even supposedly mature guns, I have held back with my young longer than have some of my friends.

In the good old days in the country I somehow feel that stronger disciplines, and possibly the opportunities for exercising them, existed. Several of my shooting friends when 'young entries'—that curiously outdated and Victorian phrase—were made to walk a whole season with an empty gun. Or so they say; I do not see this happening often these days, although I may be wrong.

One friend at least admits to having been 'sent home' for a 'minor' misdemeanour, though straight away I have to observe that no misdemeanour with a shotgun can ever be minor. One or two shooting friends, reared in well-heeled country setting, were handed over for their apprenticeship to the keeper. All very fine, but I fancy many youngsters come into the shooting game these days who do not have these opportunities—Town Gun's sons, for example.

I held off with my elder son until he was fourteen, then I bought him a single 20-bore with which he still shoots when he can't pinch my twelve. I've never had a single moment's anxiety, nor, as far as I know, has anyone else shooting with him. All of them, quite rightly, would have darn soon told son and then father.

I started my second boy last weekend, one year younger. Why I made an earlier start I cannot think. There was nothing to choose between the two of them as far as apparent responsibility went. Perhaps it was because Number One got so smoothly off the ground that I decided to let Number Two flutter his wings a little sooner. There was also the undoubted pressure that when father and brother are shooting all the time, junior can't imagine why he isn't allowed in on the act.

I launched Number Two in a pigeon hide. I believe this to be quite a sound nursery. Admittedly it does not provide all the distractions of walking up or even standing. What it does permit is close supervision, not only of gun handling but of shooting, provided you, yourself, can forbear to shoot. This takes a bit of restraint when the birds are coming in nicely to decoys and departing with not much more than a bad fright!

Just sit and watch and it is possible to see what junior is doing wrong and offer corrections to fall of shot.

Number Two had ten shots on his own. Though he did not actually connect, he made what I consider to be a most promising start. Under fierce parental orders he learned just how long you must stay still until you move to shoot an incoming bird. Then, having moved, he got up and shot straight away without a moment's hesitation. Hitting will come later. The most important thing, for a beginner, is to get the gun off smartly *without thinking about it*, never mind that he just punches a hole in the sky.

After a time, father had a go, only taking the birds after junior had let drive at them. So there were a few to pick up. It is important to send the boy out to collect these. This is the best way to instil hide discipline. It will be only too easy for him in the first flush of success to rush out to pick up a bird, especially if it is a runner, leaving his gun loaded, propped against the side of the hide, in a position that can only be highly dangerous when he returns.

Nowhere is hide discipline more important than in camouflage nets which show an uncanny desire to catch in top levers, muzzles and toes of butts. So we got that one straight at the outset. Before long, Number Two will be sitting in a hide on his own. When the birds start falling thick and fast for him I want to be quite sure that his gun is unloaded, broken and its muzzles safely turned away from the point of egress and ingress.

Apart from instructing the young, I had an interesting weekend with the pigeons myself, not to say a humbling one. On Saturday I got a call to do duty on a big estate in Hampshire where the woodies were said to be attacking an expensive field of rape. Arrived with companion to find not a bird operating in the area. So drove six miles to alternative farm where a large field of young kale, bordered by two perfect pigeon-holding fir strips, was steadily being reduced by between seven and eight hundred birds.

We began to congratulate ourselves that we had 500 cartridges between us. However, as so often, the birds departed, only to trickle back in ones and twos throughout the day. Unfortunately, we did not know our boundaries on this unfamiliar ground, so did not feel entitled to recce for the new feeding field which the birds must be using.

Companion in a net hide in one fir strip got them coming to his decoys fairly regularly. After three hours had passed and my own total was only four, I decided to move out of my fir strip and rehabilitate a collapsed bale hide on a high crest, level with my partner. Birds missed or scared by him seemed to be departing in this direction.

Once deployed in the bales, my ego received a considerable shot in whatever egos use for an arm. I only got twenty but they were all, save one, high, fast corkers. These birds were leaving the scene at best speed to avoid experiencing again the nasty bang and whoosh of shot past their tails with which my colleague had received them. Even he, a man notably not readily impressed, could scarce forbear to cheer.

Next day, back home on my nursery shoot, I went out just after five in the afternoon to find that a flock of about a hundred stock doves and as many woodies had moved in for their annual chickweed festival.

Being rather pleased with myself on the previous day's form, I took my son's double 20-bore and oh-what-a-fall-was-here. I have always thought of stock doves as rather trusting little birds. Certainly in pairs they can prove to be lacking in all sense of caution. Many a time I've bumped off one only to have its companion come round and offer the second half of the right and left I should have scored first time.

These stock doves were far from tame, and tended to operate in a flock, at least until the shooting broke them up. There was a very stiff north-east wind blowing. Aided by this, they behaved like teal to the ponderous woodies' mallard.

The hide was unavoidably placed in the centre of a large field, without benefit of so much as a wire fence to give it background. This may have made them exceptionally wary. I had only to move a muzzle for them to flick, teal-like, on one wing and jink away. Result: ten shots for one bird in the first hour. Fortunately my companion of the day before was not there to see any downfall.

There is only one thing to do with a bad patch like this and that is to shoot through it. Some sort of form returned towards the end of the engagement, but the best I was able to scrape together was sixteen birds picked and four lost. I am not revealing for how many cartridges.

Two interesting things about the stock doves. They always show up *en masse* in early June and are scarcely in evidence in my part of suburbia for the rest of the year: all were old birds. One stock dove was light brown on wings and body though otherwise bearing standard markings, the type of light plumaged bird known as 'Isabelline'.

Dad under Pressure

A humbling experience does one no harm, though I have to confess I do not enjoy such masochistic exercises. I took Number Two son, Simon, plus newly possessed 20-bore, to that wizard of the human fire control system, Percy Stanbury of the West London Shooting Ground.

Percy has put me through my inaccurate paces on several occasions, straightened out my elder son's shooting kinks and now was destined to face Willock Number Three. (See Page 100.)

He had already killed his first duck, a high cock wigeon, stone dead with his first shot. Before that he had shot more or less inaccurately, but with occasional flashes of unexplained brilliance, at pigeon over decoys. I was inclined, therefore, to include an element of luck in that first wigeon as well as the teal that followed it several cartridges later.

Junior does not look as though he ought to be able to shoot

straight, for he is left-handed and left-shouldered. Terrible visions of cross-eyed stocks came to me.

However, southpaw or not, he *does* shoot off his right eye. So, when I had my 20-bore shortened for him, I asked the gunmakers to take out the cast-off that had been put in it for me and to modify the butt so that it could be lengthened at will.

This way, I fancied, that if I had the inclination to shoot with a light gun from time to time, I might be allowed to 'borrow' the 20-bore which I had given junior for a Christmas present!

To my relief and surprise, the great Stanbury said the gun fitted him like a glove. We walked out to the plate to demonstrate the truth, or otherwise, of this statement. Simon fired at the stationary bird in the middle of the whitewashed plate with convincing accuracy three or four times, smack in the centre of the pattern.

So far so good, but iron partridges do not need much forward swing. Let's see what happens with a simple going-away bird—the one incidentally, which I too often miss. Junior splintered the things into powder. I think, to be accurate, which he damnably was, he missed two out of fifteen. 'Enough of that,' teacher said, 'now we'll try something slightly harder.'

So we went to the low tower and started with singles. True, one or two were missed, but not enough to worry about. By this time, both teacher and father were glowing with pride. Junior's cheeks were almost hotter than his barrels. Was this all there was to it?

Now came the fatal point. Percy suggested that dad would like to have a go? Dad most emphatically would not, after *that* exhibition. Hadn't dad got his gun in the car? Dad said he had not. Junior treacherously said that, oh yes, dad had, for, didn't he recall that they were going on to a duck flight afterwards? So dad walked back to get his weapon and make a fool of himself.

As I walked away I could hear junior banging away behind me and reflected that he's probably powdered a few more singles.

When I eventually returned, plus 12-bore, Percy had a sad face on. Town Gunlet, he said, had suddenly developed an inexplicably warped barrel. 'I knew it couldn't last,' I said smugly and felt better about my own forthcoming exhibition.

I am never at my best under pressure, so I missed the first four singles straight. Junior was patronisingly sympathetic. I could have shot him if I could have been certain, at that moment, of hitting him.

'You're not leading them enough,' teacher told me. I already knew that, but what was the use? 'I hate clay pigeons,' I said weakly, implying that if they had been real birds I would have killed them all.

By iron will and determination I managed to stumble back to a bit of semi-form, killing the last three doubles but never really catching them in the centre of the pattern.

Then it was Simon's turn again. 'What will you give him for a right and left?' Percy asked. I saw them exchange sly glances.

Ten bob a go,' I said generously. 'You're on,' replied my son, rather too quickly.

Well, I'm glad to be able to report that I am not the only member of the family who does not perform at his best under pressure. Junior started by killing the first one cleanly, but never really got on to the second. My money seemed safe.

Coach looked disappointed and surprised. 'Now promise me,' Percy told him 'that you will miss the last one *in front*.' Junior, of course, had never heard that in the entire history of shooting no one has *ever* missed in front. So he clouted three doubles in a row and that was thirty bob gone, though as I well realised, it could have been a great deal more expensive. How much more expensive I only found out when the shoot was over.

Apparently, while I had been away getting my gun, Simon had powdered three doubles in a row and he and Percy had imagined that they were on to easy money.

After this, I am thinking of letting Simon take over Town Gun, but then, on reflection, I have never claimed to be able to hit anything, simply to be able to write about it with a few words that sometimes hit the target.

One Man's Week

As far as the great outdoors is concerned, it has been a fairly varied and hectic week. It started on Saturday with my daughter's demand for a ton of straw. Straw is very hard to get this year, as a good many horse-owners are finding out. The harvest produced a lot of short-stemmed stuff and not too much of that. We had a ton offered, provided we would collect it. So the week began with shifting and stacking that lot.

I returned, muscles protesting, just in time for evening flight. It was a still evening with a beautiful sunset that promised little in the way of duck. But it was nice to sit and contemplate and give my slipped disc a chance to slip back into its rightful position.

One or two mallard moved around, all out of shot. But once again, as I watched little parties come and go, I reflected on the extraordinary urge that makes duck get up and fly when evening comes.

Tonight, some came in, some went out. The out-goers were obviously those who had spent the day on the gravel-pit. Now, if some duck were coming *in*, then presumably there was something for the incomers to eat on the pit.

Then, why did the dayshift find it necessary to go somewhere else when the pit apparently provided all a duck needed? The only answer I could come to is that duck just compulsively move from sheer force of habit when daylight falls to a certain level. They feel uneasy if they aren't moving around, even if conditions are favourable for a night's stay in their present situation.

Obviously there are many occasions when it *is* necessary for duck to flight to other feeding or roosting grounds. But here one could see absolutely no reason for playing general post.

The sheer capriciousness of the creatures was underlined by four mallard sitting out on a sandspit. They'd plainly been there all day and were now getting restive when three mallard flighted in and joined them. Thereupon the day-shift ceased fidgeting and composed themselves for a night's stay along with the new arrivals.

It was a pity I had to risk shattering their calm. At that moment, a single mallard came over and I dropped it well out in the lake. But by then it was too dark for any duck to think of moving. The party on the sandspit just sat there. I have often noticed that when it gets sufficiently dark, the odd shot doesn't put settled duck into the air again.

Next day, Sunday, we were in a hunter trial which means a 6 am start. This wouldn't have worried me, except I not only had to survive the rigours of the day, but return daughter and mount to stables in time to drive to London Airport and catch the night plane to Nairobi for a lightning business trip.

I've heard of swinging safaris, but this one was ridiculous. It lasted exactly three days. Just the same, I did manage to cram in some outdoor adventures in between discussions in Nairobi.

I spent the first night with an old friend, Alan Root, wildlife film-maker *par excellence*, at his home on the shore of Lake Naivasha. Life with the Roots is certainly different. There was a caracal—an African lynx—asleep in the bath. Minnie, their tame striped hyena, nibbled my ankles playfully as I ate lunch. Joan, Alan's wife, was bottle-feeding an infant olive tree squirrel and the otters badly needed some fresh fish.

At the hour at which I'd be thinking of evening flight back home, Alan and I boated out on to Naivasha with a couple of light spinning rods. The otters are particularly partial to the black bass which were introduced to the lake some twenty years ago and have thrived mightily since.

The evening flight was truly spectacular, so much so that I could hardly concentrate on the bass that threw themselves suicidally at our spinning lures. Great skeins of cattle egrets passed across the sun. Garganey, yellow-bills and tree duck confirmed once again that duck all over the world feel the same twilight urge—to move somewhere else, even if they are already on to a good thing where they are. By the time it had fallen dark in that turn-of-a-switch way you find on the equator, we had thirty black bass in the boat, of which we kept half a dozen for our own kitchen and ten for the otter's larder.

Next day we drove down to Mzima Springs in Tsavo National Park. At Mzima, Alan has been making a really sensational film of the life around, and under, the surface of these crystal clear springs. He wanted me to see Mzima for myself and had flown down two days before to set up camp from which he and Joan intended to do a further fortnight's underwater photography among the crocs and hippos.

On the way, Alan explained that an elephant trail ran right through our camp. Since this was the dry season, we might see a few jumbos around, though, in his experience, he had always found elephants far too sensible to tangle with tents.

When we got there, the tents were intact, but the elephants were certainly in occupation of the site and showed little inclination to move out. Since there was only one way into camp, it looked like being something of an impasse. However, it is remarkable how elephants can be persuaded to shift with the exercise of a great deal of patience, helped out with a judiciously lobbed rock every now and again. On the whole, I get the impression they were a good deal easier to drive than partridges.

Nothing much happened the next morning, except that we went out at dawn and got charged simultaneously by two black rhinos, one from either side. The first one we met, in fact, Alan whistled in a rather rude way that rhinos apparently find provocative. He was saying: 'Of course, that's all right provided another one doesn't come belting out of the bush from the other side. . . .' At that moment a second rhino, full of fury, did exactly that. We scraped out by the width of a rhino horn, I reckon.

The week was becoming a bit of a whirl. That night, business finally tied up at a last meeting in Nairobi, I was on an East African Airways Super VC10 on my way home. I arrived back in England, on, let me see, yes, I think it was Thursday.

By now I was properly wound up and couldn't think of sleeping, so when my son suggested an evening flight that night I naturally agreed. We got two duck.

Friday was a day of rest. Back in the office, once more, thank heavens.

But Saturday? Well no week's complete without some contribution to the horse scene, so I spent the day laying the foundations for a new loose-box in the garden that is to be used before shows.

I did get off the hook in the late afternoon. My younger son was home from school and suggested a quick walk round to look for a partridge. We didn't find any partridges, but did fire three shots for three totally unexpected pheasants.

That was the week that was. Anyone know where I can get a nice quiet lie down?

Pigeons on Horseback

I have explained previously that at this season of the year I become the victim of conflicting interests. As a family we are involved in a modest way in the show jumping business. For teenage daughters, who are, of course, the hardcore of the nation's pony clubs, the summer holidays are the crown of the year. This is when all the horse shows take place. And, of course, if you happen to be in a pony club team, then your hooves—and those of the unfortunates who groom and tow you to events—scarcely touch the ground.

Thus I find myself forgoing endless opportunities to defend fields of wheat and barley from the mid-summer mass attacks of pigeon. When I happen to be at a horse show within range of what is obviously a pigeon shooter's bonanza, I find it very hard to keep my cool.

Thus it turned out one afternoon recently when I had been ordered not only by my daughter but by no less a person than the District Commissioner of the Pony Club to be on parade at a certain Surrey riding school at 4.30 pm sharp to attend 'combined training'.

On a normal day I would have been able to get a fair amount of pigeon shooting in during morning and early afternoon. But there are few normal days in my family. In the morning and early afternoon, guess what—we had been jumping in yet another darned show. Our schedule had been worked out to the minute—not by me, you can bet—to get us from our last event to the training session.

It had not been our day. It had rained. A large motor horse box had got itself into the ditch so that we were late on the field of battle. As the result of this we arrived in the ring not on the peak of our possible form, scraped a clear round and then got deservedly knocked out in the jump-off.

Our second event was—well, let's not go into that. Every horse can have an off-day. So can every rider. When the two calamities coincide . . . ! We didn't get eliminated, but we left an awful lot of poles lying around.

All this, of course, you just have to write off to experience. But by then I wasn't in a philosophical mood. It was raining quite hard. It was doubtful whether we would make our training date on time and I seemed likely to have to face the District Commissioner who had rightly I suspect, disapproved of us taking part in a show on that day, anyway.

The very last straw of all was that right next to the showground was a quite sensational pigeon flight with birds pouring in to laid corn all day, oblivious of all the disturbance we were making.

So I arrived, only five minutes late, at the training session, received as I expected a look of disapproval from the DC, and, to crown it all, ran over what turned out to be a far from lucky horseshoe with the Land-Rover's near fore as I drove in at the gate.

Dressage is perhaps not the most exciting equestrian event to watch. I sat on my shooting stick and dimly registered that my offspring seemed to be acquitting herself reasonably well and that her horse was not at all exhausted by his earlier exertions at the show. I was not greatly cheered by this, however, for, what should happen to me again, but that right next door, in the adjoining field of wheat, was another fantastic pigeon flight. This one could easily have been the shoot of a lifetime.

After a time, and only mark you when my daughter had finished her stint—I know my place as groom—I filtered away to inspect the pigeon situation at closer quarters. The wheat field was solid with them. They rose, fluttering, wherever you looked from among fairly ripe but as yet totally unblown corn.

We finished the training session with better than a pass mark. It was then that I looked at the Land-Rover. The horse trailer behind it stood upright enough, but the wretched towing vehicle was notably down by the bows. One of those damned horseshoe nails had punctured a front tyre.

I have nothing but deep affection for the Land-Rover itself. For the quality of the jack with which the makers equip this classic vehicle—or at least all the models I have ever driven—I have nothing but hatred and contempt. It was while sweating to persuade this nasty piece of machinery to raise the injured hoof so that I could reshoe it, that I heard a kindly voice above me and looked up to see the owner of the riding school solicitously offering me his own hydraulic jack.

By the time we were ready for the road again, all the other riders and horses had long taken their trailers and gone home. The good man who had given me his jack in my hour of need, accepted a glass of refreshment (the amount of alcohol one needs to get one through the average day with horses is, I find, phenomenal). We started to chat. I mentioned the pigeon just beyond the boundary of his school's cross-country course.

'You don't mean to say you like shooting pigeon,' he said. I assured him that, when not ministering to horses, this was one of my dearest and keenest passions. 'Then I wish you'd do something about my corn. They're eating it wholesale.' He pointed towards my dream field. 'Come on,' he said, 'if you've got a minute or two, I'll take you up to see the lie of the land.'

My daughter said anxiously: 'We ought to get him home, Dad.' ('Him' being Topper the horse, naturally.) 'He's had a long day.'

'So,' I told her, 'have I.'

And thus it came about that I unexpectedly had full permission to take on a pigeon bonanza. 'Come any time you like,' my kind host invited.

As it turned out, I was unable to shoot until the following Saturday. I knew that the corn wouldn't be cut by then and there seemed absolutely nothing that could alter the situation as it then existed. As we drove away, my daughter said smugly: 'You see, you'd never have got that shooting if it hadn't been for Topper. . . .' 'I'd never have got that puncture either,' I told her.

I was back at the riding school early the following Saturday morning. I should know better by now. Bonanza shoots do not often last. Pigeon find something they like better and move on. There was scarcely a bird in sight when I built my hide and put out the decoys. The corn looked the same, perhaps even riper and more appetising. But the vast majority of those birds had plainly found a crop more to their liking.

Nevertheless it wasn't a blank day. The total score was forty, including about fifteen stock doves who certainly hadn't been feeding on that crop the week before. My jockey was quite right really. I wouldn't have been invited to shoot but for her horse. Next year, if I can slip my head collar long enough to escape from the show ring, I shall be watching the corn around that riding school closely. I do at least know that it has the potential of the shoot of a lifetime.

Topper

For the past few weeks I have to confess I have barely had a gun in my hands. This is partly due to the utter perfidy of my local nursery farmer friends who have suddenly switched over to soft fruit. To my surprise and chagrin, I find that pigeon are not the least interested in raspberries and strawberries. I suppose I might have guessed this. But with the wretched birds addicted to everything that is tasty and the best, I should have thought they'd have been willing to risk a touch of the collywobbles just to enjoy a seasonal snack of these delicacies. Not a bit of it.

That has been only partly the reason for my lay-off (I shall be back in full force once the peas begin to swell in the pod). The main cause of the cease-fire is that my energies have been almost totally drawn off by the Horse.

I have mentioned my connection with horses only fragmentarily in this column. Now I am in the horse business up to the hocks and well above that.

I have spawned one of those daughters who goes into a horse-dive at around five and doesn't pull out, as many girls do, about the sixteen–seventeen year old mark. My filly is a fanatical show-jumper of, so far, middle range. The way things are pointing, I fear it may not always stay at that level.

For many years, in fact for most of my adult life, I resisted the Horse. It crept into my existence via a beautiful half-Connemara pony called Honey who joined our strength some six years ago. Said Honey was one of those naturals who made his rider look good. One tended, with paternal pride, to imagine that the child was winning things by sheer intuitive skill and natural horsemanship.

Some of this may have been true. After all, the Apaches were natural horsemen and never went in much for dressage and I daresay my daughter, who appears to have some Red Indian blood in her, could have had the same kind of luck. One began to think that Wembley was not so far away after all.

Then, two years ago, the inevitable happened. She outgrew her 13.2 pony. Encouraged and excited as the entire family were by our apparent prowess, there was nothing to do but go out and buy a more powerful machine. We looked long and hard and really without the special knowledge that one needs in horse-dealing. We deserved to be fleeced. But by sheer good luck and the charming honesty of the farmer's wife in Wales, who sold us Topper, we weren't.

The lady was a show-jumper herself. She had broken this three-year-old bay gelding, who would make at least 15.2 when he had grown up to be a big boy. He had the nicest possible manners and all the signs of a big jump in him. She didn't really want to sell him. Her husband wished dearly to hunt him. For some reason that I still can't fathom, she liked the way my daughter rode Topper and looked on him and I guess as many horses have been sold for that as for any logical reason.

We got him, I think, reasonably cheap and brought him home in a newly acquired horse-trailer.

It was only then that the enormity of what we had done hit us. Remember we were greener than the grass Topper ate in such alarming quantities—and far more costly food likewise. Even greener than us was the horse himself. He didn't know his left rein from his right, his forelock from his withers and hardly, literally, where to put his feet.

So the bills began. No young girls, however keen, have the knowledge or facilities to school young horses. So we sent Topper to kindergarten.

At what seemed great cost, teacher took him away from his loving owner for a month and taught the beautiful idiot how to walk. Imagine horses not knowing that much! At the third week, they allowed her near him and started to break all the bad habits she had acquired from a pony who knew how to do it all without much assistance from the rider.

In the two years since then, rider and horse have become a team. It has been fascinating to watch and even more fascinating to take part in, even in the role of first groom and payer of bills.

Topper is now full-grown, filling out into a most handsome if not beautiful horse with that big jump just beginning to pop out of him. He's five now and this is the first season in which we can really hope for any results. Even so, next year will be the one when we know if he's genuinely going to come off.

I have become so involved in the entire enterprise that my shooting friends mutter darkly about another good man having gone. They need not fear. I have always found time to fit in many parallel enterprises and fortunately the high peak of horse shows comes at the trough of game shooting. Luckily, too, my wife is an accomplished horse-trailer and is always willing to let me off an occasional show to give the pigeon a going-over. Just the same, I do enjoy those shows. . . .

For me they are one of the best occasions of the spring and summer country scene. The atmosphere is competitive but friendly. The riders themselves—practically all girls, of course, but when you find a boy jumper you can bet he's a real good one—fight to the death in the ring but outside it are always willing to help each other. If there is any rivalry and bitchiness it is invariably from parents who complain to the judges—if they can get at them—or to other parents that their offspring was robbed.

Mostly, though, the prevailing climate is deadly professional and the riding of such high standard that it makes you bite your nails. Round us in Surrey even quite small shows see a turn-out of anything from two to four hundred horses and many of them are red hot; likewise young riders.

I realise now that in buying Topper as a raw recruit we have done it the hard way. Our jockey has had to put in two seasons while both herself and mount learnt the trade together. An easier way would have been to have bought a ready-made jumping machine. It might even have been no more expensive in the end. But I doubt very much whether it would have been nearly so much fun.

Good Show!

Return to England in the spring speedily reminds me that the horse show season is upon us. It's certainly upon me. It arrives with all its attendant pleasures and tensions. The pleasures of meeting some of the most genuine, as well as genuinely com-

petitive people, in the countryside. The tensions caused by horses that go lame and jumping daughters that demand as much service from their humble grooms as does any team of Grand Prix cars from their pit staff. Add to all this the occasional joys of winning, or anyway, being placed.

The first show of the year is our own local show. It gets bigger every year. This season there were well over 400 horses taking part. It's a popular show because it is almost the first of the season. It provides everyone with a welcome warm-up before the bigger stuff begins.

It's a special show for me because I enjoy a brief moment of unmerited glory. I am the commentator in Ring One for the main show-jumping events. This means I have to be on the ground early. No hardship! For years now, when merely competing, I seem to have been first on the ground, and last off. I have arrived towing daughter's horse when the Land-Rover and trailer have been hidden by mist. I have left when the moon has risen in the sky and one needs headlights to pick one's way out of the ground. You have to be keen to last the course in the show-jumping circuit and I'm not talking about the riders!

For those concerned with the paperwork, any horse show starts weeks before the event. I am always amazed at the amount of time and dedication the organisers of such country affairs are prepared to put in for a very moderate profit which, in many cases, goes to charity. There are schedules to be got out, entries to be recorded, mums to be dealt with who enter their young for half-a-dozen classes only to change them at the very last moment. There are jumps and public address systems to be hired. Judges' caravans, ladies' and gents' loos, officials' lunch tents, badges, sponsors, ropes, posts, vets, doctors, ambulance services: none of these essential services gets to the field of battle without intense organisation and follow-up.

The Friday before our show, all those most intimately concerned are ordered to attend the ground. It looks like Agincourt *after* the battle. A collapsed tent, piles of abandoned heraldry, gaily coloured shields. These last two items turn out to be the coloured poles and wings hired at great expense for the three jumping rings. For the first hour, the field of Agincourt suffers from too many Henry Vs and not enough private soldiers. Or are we fighting the battle all over again? One could be pardoned for imagining that there are at least two opposing forces in operation.

Someone devotedly hammered in thirty stakes for ring three, the showing arena, the previous night. Devotion is not enough. These are, it now appears, precisely where the gymkhana events are due to take place. So out they all have to come. There are murmurs but no open signs of mutiny.

I, your erstwhile commentator and star of the morrow, am deputed with a gang of trusting assistants to define the boundaries of the junior jumping ring with metal stakes and a slightly inadequate length of rope. 'When you come to the collecting ring,' the lady in charge bellows, 'dig a trench and bury the rope carefully. It won't take you more than five minutes or so.'

So impressed are we with the importance of the task assigned to us, that we do a really thorough job. No horse, trotting confidently into battle, is going to catch a hoof in our rope. We bury it in a trench at least a foot deep and ten yards wide. The rope runs out when there is only ten yards of the entire ring to go. No matter, we make good by bridging the gap with binder twine, woven cunningly into strands. While this is going on, a second party is enthusiastically erecting jumps to a plan set by the course-builder.

The result looks, if not as formidable as something seen at Wembley, then (apart from the ten yards of twine) nearly as professional. Even the lady in charge of operations looks pleased, or at least relieved. We are not through yet. The judge has arrived. He considers gravely, he walks round judiciously. He paces and repaces. He stands back and surveys.

We mere hirelings recline on the grass, catching our breath

from our recent buryings of rope and 'tumpings' of posts. Here it comes. The judge approaches diffidently. No matter how diffident and charming the manner, the verdict can be seen in his face before he speaks. 'I'm terribly sorry,' he says, 'but I really do think the ring is a bit tight. I'd like to see the two longer sides go out by at least three yards.'

Three miserable yards! It doesn't sound much, but it plays havoc with that carefully buried rope in the collecting ring, not to mention the section of plaited binder twine. Hickstead was never like this—or is it? Perhaps we don't see the groundsmen in action the day before the big occasion there.

I am about to speak sternly to my arm muscles, already atwitch from the last session of post-thumping, when a small girl arrives with a breathless message from yet another of the generals. My services are urgently required at the judges' lunch tent. For a moment hope leaps in my breast as keenly as the winner of tomorrow's 'Open'. Prospects of a largish gin and a ham sandwich present themselves. Then the full horror dawns. The judges' lunch tent! This is a monstrous affair of aluminium poles and irregular shape which defeated the best brains in Surrey for over an hour on a windy hillside only last season. There is just one survivor from that experience on the ground today. *Me!*

Now I am expected to remember how this cross between a wrecked airship and the left-overs of the Crystal Palace fits together. Last year, at least some of the sections were connected together by springs. Whoever dismantled it then wrenched it, literally limb from limb, in understandable fury.

There are only three of us. A computer expert, a shipping man and myself. Three of us outnumbered by approximately twenty different-sized and unrelated pieces of aluminium tubing. We may not be three of the best brains in Surrey where frame tents are concerned, but at least we get it up, facing back to front it's true, in only two and a half hours. By which time, everyone else has left the scene of battle and the pubs are shut.

Next morning, as I wish everyone welcome once again to the show in my best commentator's voice, I reflect that no matter how many mums complain that I got their daughter's name wrong; how many names I *do* actually get wrong; no matter if I eliminate my own daughter as I did on one occasion before the judge had a chance to do it for himself, nothing can be quite as dire as yesterday.

Feather Plucking

I am always slightly astonished when my shooting friends express surprise that I pluck my own birds. 'Why on earth go to all that trouble and mess when the fishmonger or butcher will do the job for you?' If I am entirely honest with myself I have to admit that one of the reasons is that I am basically mean. I really don't see why I should pay good money for a job I can do perfectly well myself or why I should incur unnecessary overheads on an item which I otherwise obtained for 'nothing'. I put the word in quotes because I know equally well that I am kidding myself considerably on this point. Not only do cartridges cost money, but so do shooting rents and subscriptions. No game can be said to be literally for nothing.

Somewhere buried in my devious subconscious is the rationalisation that argues that the pheasant, pigeon or duck was garnered at least technically for nothing. By this I mean that I obtained it by my own skills from the wild. Why, then, should I let some fishmonger or butcher complete the job for me? Let them stick to wopping down codfish on slabs and slicing up best sirloin. What's mine is mine and I intend to keep it that way.

'More fool, you,' my lazier or possibly more opulent friends say. They go on to suggest that if I insist on playing the part of latter-day cave-man, that is my affair. *Their* wives, however, would rather have feather-free kitchens and dustbins innocent of entrails. When I find myself faced with sixty or seventy pigeon after a day's decoying, I come close to seeing their point. However, even that situation has resolved itself. Wood-pigeon in the feather are suddenly greatly in demand, as the advertisements in *Shooting Times* make clear. People at last want to take the surplus off our hands at a worthwhile price. From now on we can keep what we want for the deep-freeze and pack the rest off to market.

As to the other species, I find that I personally seldom have enough pheasants, or, for that matter, duck to make plucking a serious chore. On rare occasions I bag a dozen duck. A dozen duck is a lot to pluck, but shouldn't take more than an hour. If the worst comes to the worst, they can always be split into two sessions. So I remain at heart a personal plucker. I have learned a little from years of removing the outer covering of many different types of quarry. For what it is worth I will pass on my small store of knowledge on the subject.

The most basic rule is that you should wait until your wife has finished with the kitchen. Women and feathers don't mix. Feathers or fur are liable to fly. Moreover, despite the fact that I invariably leave the kitchen immaculate after I have finished, my wife can never bring herself to believe this will be the case so long as she actually witnesses the operation in progress. Work alone, therefore, and wife-free.

The second rule is that a little water cures almost all ills. Partly fill the sink and when in doubt dip the plucking hand into it. Feathers stick marvellously to wet hands and therefore resist the urge that is in all feathers to fly about in a breeze as slight as that caused by the slipstream of a passing cat.

Which brings me to rule number three. Rigorously exclude the cat from the proceedings. We have had generations of cat that instantly cease what they are doing once they sense that plucking is about to begin in our kitchen. I have no idea what cat sense detects this activity. I just know that our cats 'home' from upwards of a hundred yards' range once I go to the game

cupboard. Cats love to flick giblets around with that fastidious upward left-hook they are so proud of. They also like to play with feathers and are capable of shifting them all over the house without apparently having left the room once. Cats, therefore, should be put firmly out.

Dogs, by contrast, evince practically no interest in plucking operations. The spaniel may look curiously round the door to see where the scent of pheasant is coming from. But once he has decided that master is doing his own retrieving and, from the amount of feathers scattered around, seems to be making a pretty hard-mouthed job of it, he invariably retires from the scene.

Lately I have come a little away from the plucking in the moistened sink theory. This is partly because it inevitably means that every month or so I have to clear the U-bend in the pipe, but more so because of the excellent brown paper rubbish disposal bags with which our local hygiene department now supplies us. By standing one of these upright, it is quite possible to pluck *inside* the bag so that few feathers escape. Once again, moistened hands held to keep things under control. I have only one rider to attach to this proposition. Be wary of plucking pigeon into such a bag if you have a heavy head cold. Pigeon feathers are apt to exacerbate such a condition anyway. A sneeze directed into a paper sack three quarters full of pigeon feathers is roughly equivalent to ripping open a bolster with a jack knife directly in front of a large electric fan.

For a long time I started by top-and-tailing my pigeon before plucking them. That is to say I carved off wings, feet and head before de-feathering them. This seemed to be a particularly convenient method when there were two of us at work—the assembly line principle. I quickly discovered, however, that the ball of my right thumb was continally sliced with shallow but extremely painful cuts. These were made by contact with the fractured stub of a previously cut wing bone.

Furthermore, as a weapon of revenge, a dead pigeon has a most effective secondary armament when it comes to fouling up an otherwise clean and tidy kitchen. I refer, of course, to the cargo it carries in its crop. Anyone who has waved a decapitated pigeon around that has up to two ounces of prime clover leaf aboard will know precisely what I mean.

Crop contents are best kept confined, which means leaving the head *in situ* until operations are practically complete. In fact, my firmest advice to novice pluckers is to keep *everything* on, wings, feet and head, until the last feather has been detached from the corpse. Then and only then should these appendages be removed. A small point about removing said appendages: if your wife has a favourite set of kitchen knives, do not risk blunting their edges on wing bones. An old pair of garden secateurs does the initial cracking splendidly. And if your wife (sorry to keep harping on about wives but after all the kitchen and garden are often well within the territory over which they may reasonably be expected to display defensively and occasionally aggressively: and who wants to risk that?). . . . As I was saying, if your wife has favourite rose secateurs well, for heaven's sake get yourself an old pair for stripping dead birds of their accessories.

Two last points: do bury the entrails. I find that wrapping them in newspaper slightly discourages domestic animals from disinterring them at a later date. Lastly, however careful you have been, one or two feathers are bound to have escaped. A moistened, long-handled squeejee mops them up almost perfectly from the kitchen floor.

PART V

Shooting, Rough and Otherwise

Forestry Shoot

Drives on our part-forestry part-farmland shoot occasionally have names given to them by the Forestry Commission or by the Ordnance Survey Map. For the most part we ignore these. We go straight back to what must have been the original style of christening country places. Spinneys and coverts, hedges and rides are named because of what once happened there.

For instance, there's the Captain's Copse which the map dares to call something quite different. This is a long, narrow hazel spinney, running alongside the local single track railway. At one time we didn't own the shooting rights over this desirable wood. It stands on our boundary. Like a defiant outpost, it faces the neighbouring big shoot 400 yards away across the railway, a stubble field and a main road.

The first time we drove it, fourteen pheasants rocketed out. This is pheasant shooting on a scale seldom experienced on our modest manor. We take it in turns to captain each day's operation. This day it was the turn of our senior member and founder of the shoot. He made, as I recall, a serious misjudgment, failing to recognise that any birds temporarily residing in the copse would inevitably be day visitors from the big shoot across the main road.

Perhaps because of the railway line, which we could hardly claim as coming within our boundaries, the captain placed not a single gun between copse and our visitors' home coverts. All fourteen departed at a speed and height which might, in any event, have guaranteed their safety. However, the rise would have been remembered in the annals of our shoot as might in other company, in another county, a spectacular drive from Holkham Clump. We never made that mistake again, but the Captain's Copse it has remained.

Then there's the small triangular patch of hazel, birch and bracken that lies in the apex of two rides. This will be forever known as Hellfire Corner, though the day when cock pheasants rose in wrath and splendour, are long over.

One of the troubles with a forestry shoot is that classic drives are always coming and going as the vegetation goes, but mainly comes. Trees grow up or are felled and brambles hurriedly cover their corpses. Little odd corners, such as Hellfire, become as deserted of birds as they once were full of them. A forest shoot is yet another living example of ecology at work. One really does learn why birds like one place at one time and not another.

Not all the landmarks on our shoot are named after brief moments of glory. Some have their darker aspects. Nothing is darker than the Eighteen Acre, the scene of the only mutiny against captaincy that we have known in eight years of close association.

This disgraceful episode occurred at the end of a long, wet and comparatively birdless day on which the appointed captain had decided 'to do the bits we usually leave alone'. We left them alone for the very good reason that the briars were as thick inside them as in the wall around Sleeping Beauty's castle. It would take more than Prince Charming to awaken any pheasants that happened to be enjoying a long quiet nap inside these places. That afternoon, six sodden guns did not view the captain of the day as a Prince, Charming or otherwise.

'We'll do the eighteen acre,' he announced with a slightly defiant ring. I think it would have been all right if he'd picked himself to lead the wire-cutting assault team. I'll not deny that he had done more than his fair share of ploughing through the rough stuff earlier that day. It is also fair to say that he was probably due for a rest and a chance at a driven bird as one of the standing guns. It was unfortunate, though, that he chose this moment not to lead.

Leaving the captain and two lucky men to line the ride, the remaining four of us set off, mutinously muttering, to the start line some 300 yards distant. As we walked alongside the edge of the wood that we were shortly expected to enter, we glared desperately into its gloomy evergreen depths. Nothing, said one member, short of a flail tank could be expected to get into that stuff. Even if a tank managed to force an entry, it would become immobilised within fifty yards and its crew would never be seen again.

We spaced ourselves out and prepared to go over the top, or rather into the depths. Even my spaniel, who is known to enjoy bathing in brambles and who gets down on his knees and wriggles like a weasel under the thickest entanglements, looked at me as only a spaniel can and pleaded with me not to send him into *that.*

To make matters worse, it was already falling early dark. Nevertheless we set off into the tulgy wood. Within fifteen yards we had lost touch not only with each other but with all sense of direction. Dogs became separated from their masters, a common enough event, but from their sorrowful and desperate whinings appeared to be missing human company in this dismal place.

To make matters worse, a cock rose somewhere and disappeared with a terrified squawk. I bet he never expected to be disturbed in his well chosen fortress. Having heard one bird get up, we should perhaps have felt duty bound to continue the struggle in order to give the standing guns and our captain some sport. Where one bird lurked there might well be others.

But the beaters had had enough. Their only thought now was seeing their wives and children again. As one man they began to fight their way back along the scarcely discernible tracks they had made on entry. It took ten exhausting minutes to reach the ride again.

It was now almost dusk. Surely the standing guns would

have had the good sense to pack it in and make for tea. Someone shouted half-heartedly and received no response from the distant ride. Wet through, torn by wild rose briars, and with a pound of wet pine needles down our necks, we beaters decided we had finished. Tea was now our main thought. We set off at a smart pace back for the cars.

It was half an hour before the captain and his two standing guns joined us. I will not set down the brief speech he made on the subject of loyalty and the high standards of duty expected from all members of the shoot. It was not the sort of address you are likely to hear at the end of a posh covert shoot. But as I have explained, we're certainly not that.

Captain for a Day

On a rough shoot such as ours—1,100 acres of jungle-type forest and two bordering farms totally 400 acres—the enjoyability of any given shooting day is directly proportionate to what the captain puts into it.

We know that we are never going to see great bouquets of beautifully presented pheasants. On the other hand, we do expect one or two pop out of most drives. We try to shoot as few going away as possible. The object is always to give the standing guns one or two really good driven birds.

Captaincy goes by rota. This in itself keeps the thing fresh. When we began to shoot together, eight years ago, only the more experienced guns took it in turns to run the shooting. But now we've brought some of the younger half-guns in, and this has produced some startling, and sometimes surprisingly successful, theories.

When my own first day comes, I always view it with mixed feelings. Uppermost, I suppose, is the fascination of drawing up a plan to meet the new season's conditions. Has the farmer started ploughing-in the stubble above the Beehives and what will have been the effect if he has done this dastardly trick.

Surely it's been too wet for him to get his tractor on to this key piece of acreage? But you can never tell with farmers. They don't run their businesses entirely to suit their shooting tenants.

If the stubble's still standing, it could form the central pivot of about three brilliant manoeuvres. It would be dangerous to bank on it, though.

The last two evenings before D-day are taken up with frantic pourings over the six inch map. The area allotted to me on this particular day includes the better of the farms, not yet shot over, and its neighbouring fringe of forest.

On paper I can't go wrong. This farm was where we put down our stock birds. There has been plenty of cover for them in the shape of a barley field which the farmer somehow forgot to spray for weeds. He has generously left this standing as compensation for some kale he neglected to put in. With luck, and as the result of skilful feeding, our reared birds shouldn't have wandered too far. We have not made the same mistake as last year when we shot them far too early in the season.

Friday night keeps the phone red hot. A last-minute check-up to make sure that everyone is out who said they would be out. Even more important than making a roll call of guns is forming a clear picture of our dog force. The canine strength looks good—four labradors and three spaniels. The spaniels are all-important in some of the thicker beats. We have barbed wire entanglements of nettle and bramble which the best labrador in the business doesn't want to know about.

The phone-round serves more purposes than a mere tally. It enables the master-mind to give some detailed orders in advance. We all know the ground intimately, so if you say to someone: 'I want you to go straight to the end of the clover field and stop it where the cross hedge runs down from the main road,' you've got a good chance of finding a gun in this all-important position when you reach the end of your first blank-in.

Orders given, plans to meet every contingency drawn on the back of two old envelopes, I set out with as light a heart as the circumstances permit. The day is bright. The shedding leaves are red and golden. It's crisp and I feel it is a good scenting day. The guns are on time. Only the stops have not paraded. I trust that they, obedient to orders, are already in position.

The first movement is a long blank-in over four stubble fields, golden and enticing in the cold November sunlight. I line out my walking guns and send two well ahead on the left flank. If anything gets out of the stubbles that's the way it will go, left-handed and at an angle of thirty degrees ahead of the line, back to its home in the forest. I feel like Montgomery before Alamein. I can't possibly lose.

Then the enemy strikes two quick blows. At the far end of the stubbles, 500 yards distant, four maidens on hunters appear. They gallop, line-abreast straight towards us, as if rehearsing a cavalry charge. In fact, they are warming up their beastly mounts. Four cocks and a hen rise in their path and soar back towards the forest, long before our flank men have got into position. We wave frantically. I order a shot fired in the air. The Amazons see us and career out of the farm and back to the road.

Montgomery has only just recovered from this reversal—it is rather like being told that no shells have arrived for the 25-pounders—when a most frightful metallic clanging breaks out. The noise echoes round the valley, down into the forest and is thrown back twice as loud from the far larch woods.

A lieutenant, one of the labrador men known for his optimism, says: 'Don't worry. It isn't on the farm. They're clear-felling a long way off in the forest.' All very well to say 'don't worry', but he's not a pheasant. Nor is he captain. At this moment, every bird within miles must be legging it down a ditch with its wings held over its ears to shut out the appalling din. Besides, far worse, I have a terrible feeling that this noise isn't emanating from the woodlands but from the very centre of the farm, about the spot at which our tame birds were released.

The blanking-in across the stubble starts and, of course, nothing gets up. Doubly assaulted by horsewomen and steam-hammers, the birds have all run or flown. And when we finally get halfway down the stubbles, what do I see but a large shiny hedge-cutter chewing lumps off our best double hedge, the hedge that runs down the aforementioned unsprayed barley field where the bulk of our reared birds should be.

An envoy is dispatched to talk to the hedge-cutter, who very decently agrees to withdraw for the day. By now, the damage is almost certainly done, at least until the afternoon.

But, in fact—and I claim no brilliance for this, merely a desperate sort of flexibility—all turns out well. For as general-in-command I have no choice but to use the rest of the morning doing the woodlands that border and surround the farm. They are very thick, but a commando of spaniels takes care of that. Birds begin to appear, scent is hot. Most people get a shot.

Plans on the backs of envelopes have long ago been torn up. Now frantic improvisation is the only hope. By mid-day there hasn't been a lot of shooting and there are fewer than ten birds in the bag. Completely by good luck rather than by good judgment, capital has been made out of the situation. We've pushed everything out of the woods back on to the farm.

A really determined captain would insist on stops staying out during lunch. But the sun is warm and, with luck, the birds will have found the ground and food denied to them by noise and disturbance during the morning.

And so it turns out. The vital centre has never been known to hold as many birds. The afternoon shooting is all fast, tall stuff.

At tea, everyone says what a fine day it was and how well the plan worked. If only they'd known what the captain was feeling. Oh, well, for the next six weeks I can relax and just go where the captain sends me.

Summer Day's Work

It is my sad experience that resolutions passed at end-of-season shoot shareholders' meetings tend to be merely an expression of goodwill generated in an atmosphere of euphoria left by the happy shooting months that have just passed. After that, the syndicate members disperse to other pleasures, like sailing dinghies, catching fish and even catching up with their wives and families, not to mention the gardening. Goodwill does not necessarily develop into good works.

In view of the many distractions that the summer offers, we have not done so badly. There has been an intensive winged vermin campaign with very marked losses among the opposition, though there are still a sight more jays than I would wish to see chattering derisively and flying ahead in looping flight between the larch plantations. I doubt whether we shall ever fully put paid to them.

Whoever manufactures Warfarin must be highly gratified at the amount we have laid down in old land drains. I hope that the rat population on one farm at least has taken a beating, though I fear that it would need the Pied Piper himself to rid us entirely of this plague.

Foxes we have had to leave mainly to the Forestry, who have gassed fourteen earths. *Fourteen* shows you the size of our problem. I am told that the Commission does not wage quite as total war on the fox as its shooting tenants would like, simply because foxes keep down the various pests—and these include voles—who nibble out their young tree shoots.

Our day-old chicks from the game farm are now well on their way, once again penned on the same self-sacrificing member's back lawn in outer suburbia. This year, our pheasant rearer has not had to contend with as much opposition from his wife, who railed at him last summer in the mistaken belief that her greensward would be ruined for all time. But pheasant guano is nearly as good as that other stuff which comes from the cliff-tops of Peru. I wish to heaven that my grass, which has never held a rearing pen though swallows many hundredweights of expensive proprietary fertiliser, looked one-tenth as healthy.

Though it is delightful to meet a melanistic cock strutting

down the white line in the middle of the road on one's way to the Southern Region commuting depot in the morning, we really can't afford to restock our neighbours' gardens as we did last summer. So this year we have made strict precautions against escape and a landing-net stands handy to retrieve any poult that makes a break when pens are being moved.

But the basis of next year's plan must rely on feeding. In the past we have tried most methods, from metal drums to long trails of straw in the rides, to pyramid hoppers made of six complete straw bales whose centre hollow is filled with grain.

All these work to some extent. The tin cans I like least of all, since they offer the birds the equivalent of slot-machine feeding. Once they've pecked their six-pennorth out of the hopper, there is nothing to keep them around and happy. This kind of bird restaurant lacks the necessary *ambiance.*

Wet is the enemy of the more exposed kinds of feeder. In wet weather, the grain shoots or goes sour. This is just another way, I'm afraid, of saying that there aren't enough birds to eat what we give them. Still, it would be nice to think that we could keep the stuff in fair condition to entice any pheasants that came along.

Allied with the feeder problems is the fact that none of us lives close enough to get round during the week. Feeding has to be done on shooting days. This demands that you (*a*) have some way of keeping your feeder dry and (*b*) have on the spot storage so that a passing gun can scatter whatever is needed on the feeder straw.

Luckily, this year, one of our farming members decided to pull down an old barn with a corrugated roof. So last Sunday we set out in force to put that corrugated to good use; to build roofed-in feeders that will withstand most of the weather.

Working days like this can be the greatest fun. The thing to do is to make them an outing. Children, dogs, wives, particularly if the latter bring the lunch, are welcome.

As much planning as possible needs to be done beforehand. In this case we had got ourselves fairly well organised. Our farming member had put his circular saw to work and cut all the timber needed for the job into the correct lengths. He'd even creosoted it.

We arranged to meet on the shoot at ten o'clock, which means that with luck the last member will turn up by ten-thirty. (Why is it they're seldom late on shooting days?)

Dogs pour out of cars like a pack of foxhounds. It's their day, too. They're delighted to see each other again, delighted to sniff the sniffs and smell the smells of this beloved pleasure ground they had begun to suspect had been barred to them for ever. But the delight must, of course, be kept in hand. We shall not be pleased if some scent-drunk spaniel noses out a sitting hen. Dogs renew old friendships and old enmities.

After an hour or more, a routine becomes established. The lorry goes round the rides dropping supplies and children at strategic points. By mid-day a fine thirst has been achieved and we all begin to feel that we are doing a wonderful and worthwhile job.

The afternoon sees phase B of the operation. There is a bramble thicket known as the 'Beehives' because it still contains some derelict and fortunately unoccupied bee skeps. It also houses pheasants, particularly when lured there by judicious feeding. But the brambles have been growing wilder and wilder so that the birds run about in an impenetrable undergrowth where even the wet nose of a keen dog only persuades them to run faster.

Phase B demands that this bramble tangle be cut down to manageable proportions with rides through it.

There is only one tool for this job, a long-handled slasher with a very keen blade. It's satisfying work, though thirsty, and one from which children and dogs must be excluded. Amateur slashers are not always aware of the path of their forward stroke let alone of their backswing.

At the end of the day we feel we have at least made a start. But there is still much pioneering to be done. Fortunately the local council has recently replaced all our dustbins with paper bags. The next task is to bring these bins down to the shoot and place one alongside each feeder.

In these we shall store our grain for winter feeding. But, before they can go out, the dustbin lids must be drilled and weights attached with wires so that they will not blow off in the strongest gales that our windy heights can hurl at them. Then there's the straw fatigue needed to layer the underside of our corrugated pheasant shanties. Wire stops have to be strung across some of the hedges along which birds *will* run into the next county. Finally, we've at least a dozen more feeders to build. Will it all prove to be worth it in terms of increased bag? I couldn't answer that. All I can vouch for is that it is the greatest fun doing it.

Digging Party Forward!

I shall call this piece: 'Thoughts while Digging a Ditch.' The ditch, of course, is part of the anti-fox protection round yet another pheasant acclimatisation pen. The ditch is there so that the chicken wire can be taken down beneath the surface of the earth and fanned in a slightly outward direction when buried. This is aimed at discouraging the more ambitious foxes from their mining activities.

Over the past ten years, I have dug similar ditches in a good many different locations. They have all had one thing in common. The ground is extremely hard and stony. To get the best out of the situation (and the worst out of me) Nature, or whoever it is who arranges for the distribution of the hard stuff about the earth's surface, invariably manages to embed a good deal of rock or flints just where the shoot Führer has elected that we build our pen.

Today, Nature and Führer have been excelled themselves. They have between them picked a site, three hundred feet up on the Sussex downs, on a slope of around forty degrees, over a bed of solid chalk, covered by, at the best, four inches of topsoil.

How anyone thinks a fox is going to dig down through that lot and have the strength to catch a pheasant at the end of it, beats me. I point this out to our Leader, but he hands me a spade and clinches the situation with the unanswerable argument: 'Well, you chaps are paying for the birds. If you want them all slaughtered just for the sake of avoiding a little hard work. . . .' So we fall to the task, muttering like a rebellious mob in a badly directed crowd scene.

I say 'crowd', but this is an exaggeration. The shoot comes out to perform these hideous chores in carefully allotted details. Perhaps hearing that today is the day for trench-digging, a few have suddenly found that they have had to switch dates. Wiring (next time out) is far easier than wielding a pick-axe at chalk.

Just to encourage us, the Führer now comes round to apologise to the slaves. His brother-in-law, the farmer, was going to have one of his men, an octogenarian, do this task for us. The aged man apparently 'just loved digging'. As unlikely a story as you will find in this column for a long while ahead, and that is saying a great deal.

But the ancient digger took sick and is abed, so has been unable to do the necessary. One is tempted to ask what his condition might have been like had he plodded up to this improbable place and started to assault the downland with spade, mattock and pick-axe. Just walking up the slope has nearly killed Town Gun.

To make things even more frightful, it starts to rain. We've had a clear fortnight of sunny weather, and now the clouds come down low over the downs and a fine mizzle sets in. Chalk is terribly slippery stuff when it gets wet. Moreover, I have no waterproofs.

There is only one thing to do, strip off as much clothing as possible and just let the rain come down. This heightens my sense of suffering and general put-upon-ness and completes the mental image I carry of myself unjustly condemned to hard labour in a concentration camp.

Gradually, as the blisters swell on the hands, one begins to get into a shocked rhythm, or perhaps merely a listless state of defeat. Slowly we creep round the perimeter, a forty-yard side at a time.

When it is my turn for a brief, puffing respite, I sit moodily down on a sopping anthill and wonder whether results will justify the labour. In the past, on several earlier shoots we have made pens, but our reward has not been outstandingly great in terms of reared birds shot. But that was always on Forestry.

This time we are fortunate enough to have a lovely piece of downland with hanging beechwoods. Chalk, for all its disadvantage when it comes to shifting it with a spade, is good land on which to grow pheasants.

The Führer, who has shot here several seasons with his brother-in-law, already assures us that the birds do stay and that previous more modest rearing schemes have yielded a return of which IMI themselves would not be ashamed.

I look down into the beautiful valley below, where the farmhouse appears like a set of toy bricks and wonder why on earth any bird, driven by dog, beater and gunfire off this commanding eminence should ever wish to return here. More than that I wonder how it *manages* to return here. Surely even a pheasant cannot enjoy flying uphill—and such a hill.

This gets me to wondering about what these hills will produce. As far as I can see, almost every bird that takes off from their slopes must be about thirty yards up by the time it has flown ten yards forward. Another ten or twenty yards on its way down the valley and it will surely be practically out of shot.

I can well believe it when they tell me that this shoot offers some of the tallest birds you're likely to see in the land. Next I wonder: will I ever be able to hit them?

I believe the old masters, like Lords Rippon and Walsingham, were telling nothing but the simple truth when they said a high pheasant, flying so fast that there is nothing left for it to do but glide, and with a slight curl on it, was the most difficult shot in the book. It is one that has constantly defeated me on the rare occasions when I have been forced to attempt it.

Yet I have watched a first eleven of crack Norfolk game guns knock these high fliers down stone dead, time after time. Having admired the prowess of one of these Olympians, I once plucked up the courage to ask him how he did it, or at least how he *thought* he did it. Since this gentleman was one of those beautiful natural shots who swing rather than lead, I expected him to say that he just swung a bit faster and pulled as he cleared the bird's beak. Not a bit of it. Here for the record is what he told me: 'I seem to get about fifteen feet in front of it and then at the last moment I give the gun an extra fast chuck back.'

Everyone knows that such subjective estimates of lead are valueless. They are simply what the lead looks like to the individual performer. But I suspect that the value part of the tip was that 'extra chuck' bit. I reckon that if as fine a game shot as my informant felt that he had to give his swing a little extra something, I have virtually got to throw myself over backwards to connect with one of these downhill high fliers.

Anyway, that extra chuck is the mental picture I am going to try to retain and put to good use when the birds start streaming off our downland next November.

Our Leader interrupts my reverie with: 'Just another half hour and we'll call it a day before we all get soaked.' I like that bit. He's remembered to bring waterproofs. He thrusts a mattock into my raw hands.

We do finish the trench. We even get up two sides of the wire. Now there remains—for the light duty party—the rest of the wiring and the covering in at top with fish netting.

By the time I have driven home, feeling fit and virtuous though a trifle stiff, the sun has come out. When she has made me a cup of tea my wife says 'Before you take your dirty clothes off I suppose you wouldn't like to do a bit of weeding.' Too right, I wouldn't, but how can you justify a day's hard digging for pheasants if I'm unwilling to labour a bit in my own—and her—vineyard? Besides, you can reach eighty, it seems, if you *like* digging.

Tall Birds

I don't get too many invitations to covert shoots. When I receive one, I always find myself looking forward keenly to the day. The prospect of having pheasants thrown at me in droves rather than having to hunt for them the hard way; the likelihood of being able to shoot at a procession of driven birds rather than the two or three stormers that a normal Saturday on our own rough patch provides: both these things set my imagination and trigger finger a-tingle. Anti-climax invariably follows, and for a number of reasons. The let-down is so consistent that, at last, after a good many years, I know exactly where I personally stand in relation to game shooting.

At the covert shoot anticipation of the joys to come receives its first blunting at the hands of my own inadequacy. Good driven pheasants *do* go abominably fast. There's no denying it. It quickly becomes very clear to me, often at the first drive, that to hit well-shown driven birds you've got to have a lot of practice at them.

I get my share, I suppose, but my share is nothing like as large as the first-XI men on either side of me. The best of these seem to knock these starling-sized rocketers down as if they were the simplest of clays at a shooting school. It's in vain for me to tell myself that I am a fairly good all-rounder; that I am a demon at decoying pigeon; that I can shoot wigeon with my feet embedded in eighteen inches of marine ooze that holds me so rigid that I might as well be a toy soldier glued to its immobile lead base.

I'd like to be able to console myself with the thought that these tall-bird paragons are superb at just one sort of shooting, that they wouldn't stand a chance at evening flight in a force six nor'-easter. The trouble is that they shoot so darn well that I'm

rather afraid that they would make out fairly favourably under any conditions. 'Oh, well,' I repeat as the third twisting cock goes over me saluted but untouched, 'oh, well, it's simply a matter of having enough practice at this kind of shooting.'

But the real disappointment which I often feel at the end of such a day has comparatively little to do with the number of driven birds missed. It's mainly due to the fact that I have done nothing to contribute to the bag or the day, except to stand there and knock a modest collection out of the sky.

The fact that the birds flew well had nothing to do with me.

Even less had the fact that there was a generous supply of them. I didn't even have to walk more than a quarter-of-a-mile the whole day. A Land-Rover or trailer carried me to the next point of discharge. I might just as well have been a piece of artillery—albeit a piece of not noticeable accuracy—which was dragged to the scene of conflict, sited (but not sighted), and left to put up a barrage when the correct moment in the battle arrived. To none of this had I contributed anything except my presence and my meagre fire-power.

My dog, I know, feels just as deprived. To begin with he wasn't invited, and, if he had been, I doubt whether I would have had the nerve to take him. Such dogs as I saw didn't seem to know what shooting—at least my kind of shooting—was about. Not for them the feverish torpedo run through the brambles on the trail of a fast-moving cock and the joyous moment of temptation—and sometimes of falling into temptation—when the bird explodes into life and air. The dogs at these days behave as zombies, well-trained zombies without doubt, but lacking the dash and spirit that we rough-shooters know. These hounds do not know the partnership which we hedgerow hunters and bramble-bashers share with our labradors and springers.

I believe I can now say, with my hand on my heart, that even if I had £750 a year to spend on a gun in the finest covert syndicate in the kingdom, I wouldn't want to join. I would truly become bored stiff with standing there and knocking them down. Shooting, for my money, is only a sport when you yourself put something into it other than hard cash.

I'm willing to make one exception as far as the big boys are concerned. There is an undeniable pleasure in watching a good shoot well-run by a host or headkeeper who really knows his job: a shoot at which the object is not just an astronomical total in the bag, but tall, testing birds which you're welcome to shoot if you can.

This may be just another heresy on top of the many I have perpetrated already but I have a feeling that there are far too many big bag shoots these days where the bag is made up of indifferent fliers. I'm prepared to be stamped all over with hob-nailed shooting boots for saying so, but it's my notion that easy rearing methods have made big bags fairly easy to come by and that there is now a certain amount of keeping up with the Joneses. 'We got 350 last Saturday,' . . . 'Bad luck, old man, we got four thirty-two.' (But somebody who was present at both battues later reported to me that the birds flew like chickens.)

Yes, a well-run shoot with finely shown birds can be a pleasure as a change from bramble-bashing, even for heretics such as myself. I get invited to about two such shoots in a season. Naturally, if my generous hosts happen to read this, their shoots fall into the spendidly run, magnificently shown class.

Mixed Keepers

During the long drive up to the fens with a guest (who found the whole place frozen solid when we got there!) we started talking about keepers we had known.

Having agreed what an enlightened man and what a good naturalist the present-day keeper almost invariably is, the conversation inevitably turned to the splendid eccentrics we had both known, especially when it came to the question of independence.

I said that I thought that, on the whole, Scottish keepers took the prize for telling guns, be they guests or employers, where they got off. A good many I had known were Highlanders so perhaps this sturdiness of spirit was simply built in as a racial characteristic.

I remember walking a steep valley running down to a fast, rocky river, the far bank of which climbed precipitously to a small fir wood. As it happened I was bottom gun, close to the river bank. I had been both looking forward to and dreading being placed there. It was rather like being longstop to a monstrously fast bowler.

We were walking pheasants, most of whom lay up in the bracken at the very top of the valley. They took off when flushed and launched themselves towards the river. Within very few yards they were doing maximum revs so that further wingbeats were of little use to them. They therefore became that beast of a beauty of a bird, a high curling cock going home at best speed.

The line of guns was staggered slightly forward along the slope in the direction of our drive. It was therefore on the cards that any one of the three guns between myself and the crest would down the things before they reached me. I knew that if this failed to happen I would be on the spot. Everyone on the hill above me would be in a grandstand position to watch my efforts.

We had covered half the hillside without the matter being put to the test. Several hens and a couple of cocks either went forward or were demolished by the intervening guns before they got to me.

While feeling a certain disappointment about this it is fair to say that this was more than compensated for by a deep sensation of relief. We had nearly reached the end of the drive when a perfect Beelzebub of a cock got up with a clatter and a squawk, headed for the river as if he was on fire, left at least three patterns of shot well to his rear and, alas, or maybe hooray, headed straight for me at a height which might just have required oxygen in a lesser bird.

I certainly missed him with my first. I appeared to miss him with my second. I was surprised at neither result. I did not even feel disgraced. Ribald laughter echoed down the glen. I had not even bothered to watch the rest of the bird's progress to the far woods. Nor had my friends. They were too delighted at my failure, for certain wagers had been laid before the drive.

But Laurie the keeper had watched the cock all the way home. 'He's doon,' he announced. 'Where?' I didn't believe it. 'Stop where you are, gentlemen.' We stopped. We stayed stopped for fifteen freezing minutes while Laurie climbed a precipice much as the Highlanders must have scaled the Heights of Abraham and returned triumphant with my cock. 'Mark him, sir, next time,' was all he said.

My guest could easily cap this. He had been shooting on a big pheasant day in Scotland. His host was a very rich man whose keeper successfully reared two thousand birds and took great pride in the way they were shown. He felt, as all good craftsmen should, that the guns should give his birds the courtesy of a good, preferably spectacular, death.

The shooting all day had been fairly indifferent. But things had otherwise gone like clockwork and there was still a good deal of daylight left by the time the final drive was over and the pick-up complete.

As there was no sign of birds even thinking of going to roost yet, the host suggested to his headkeeper that they have one more drive. At this the Scottish keeper stood erect, looked his employer square in the eye and gave his verdict. 'Ye'll do no such thing, sair. If the shooting is the same as it's been all day, I won't have my birds subjected to it.'

Not to be outdone, I recalled a great and justly celebrated East Anglian keeper who was one day loading for a certain noble lord on his home ground when a hare came forward while they were waiting for the drive to start.

Seeing his man was about to dispatch the hare, my friend yelled. 'Don't shoot, sir. Too far.'

The hare was certainly at a goodish range but well within shot. By the time the lord had recovered from his surprise, the hare had loped to safety. He wasn't too pleased about the advice he had received. 'What do you mean, too far?' 'Too damn far for me to carry home, sir.' And that was the end of that conversation.

On another occasion, this same great man was loading for a friend of mine, an exceptional all-round shot, who himself missed a hare. The scene of this encounter was one of the most famous shoots in the land. My keeper friend was so disgusted at the lack of marksmanship that he simply put the second gun to his own shoulder and bowled the hare over at maximum range. 'If you're not going to hit 'em, I suppose I might as well,' was all he said. You have to be a considerable character, or to have known your Gun from childhood, to get away with that kind of eccentricity. This particular keeper satisfied both qualifications.

As the long miles to the fens ticked away, we talked about the other side of the picture. How guns felt about some keepers. We had both had our bad experiences. Keepers whose main ambition seemed to be to prevent their birds from being shot—and not simply on the score that the guns weren't worthy.

Keepers who still had an unenlightened attitude to birds of prey. We agreed that in some parts of the Highlands it would be a long time before the attitude softened towards the golden eagle. We had both met keepers whose dogs were far worse than anything the guns were likely to put into the fray. But on the whole we had met far fewer bad keepers than we had met undesirable guns.

My friend, who, unlike myself, gets around a bit in quite select shooting company, had recently taken part in a big covert shoot where one of the best game shots in the land was performing. Tipping was of the order of £1 per 100 birds. The day had produced over six hundred pheasants which, to say the least, had been indifferently shown.

When it came to rewarding the headkeeper, my friend paid up at the usual rate but the great game shot handed over a single pound note. Not a word passed, not did it need to. The meaning was plain. Not all the independence is on the side of the keepers, it seems. I personally wouldn't have had the nerve.

Those Cunning Cocks

Those stories about how all the pheasants on the South Coast crowed when they heard gunfire from the Western Front during the First World War have always been completely credible to me. Several times when out shooting I have heard a positive barrage of pheasant calling, set off by a deep boom, perhaps made by blasting in a quarry somewhere nearby.

The most vivid demonstration I have ever heard occurred at our farm shoot near Selsey last weekend. We were walking the little marsh—I recently wrote about it, describing how fifty pheasants sneaked out of it in a fog, hedge-hopping past the guns with barely a shot fired. (See page 161.)

This time there were very few birds in the marsh. But there were certainly a great many, particularly cocks, all around it. With a strong south-west wind up Channel, various military, or, more probably, naval booms drift our way from warlike establishments in the general direction of the Isle of Wight.

On this occasion, something like a large calibre naval gun boomed. Immediately the ear, even my ear, which is virtually gun-deaf, was assailed by a crowing of pheasants that made you feel that they must be sitting in every available patch of cover, at least three deep, to mock you. I would not have believed there were as many cocks in Sussex, let alone on our farm.

The gun boomed again and the pheasants repeated the performance only more so. Fascinating enough, but this is only part of the story.

On our first shoot of the year on this farm we had had a fairly evenly balanced bag of pheasants, with, I fear, hens just predominating. On the Day of the Cocks, as I shall always hereafter think of it, we shot about thirty pheasants, only five of which were hens! It was almost as if all the cocks in the vicinity decided to invade us that day, had crowed their defiance and had, unexpectedly, paid the price.

In my experience, cocks on this shoot are very hard to shift at this time of year when there is still a fair amount of cover about. In shooting twenty-five that day, we must have failed to put as many more up. Owing to a Force Eight gale that blew all day, many birds were so fast on the wing that they escaped the barrage. Again, it was noticeable that many of those that did so were cocks.

Why such a high proportion of males? Is this just the way the breeding season went in these parts? If so, it bodes ill for next year. But we have at least done a good deal of our 'cocks only' shooting in November.

I have written about our Selsey shoot before. To my mind it is the ideal rough shoot. Though it is nearly as flat as the fens, the birds fly well, especially if they can be walked away from home and then shown the guns. On this occasion, the Captain of the Day ran things extremely well. He quite rightly elected to give the standing guns the best driven birds possible. In such a wind, they were real corkers. I share his view that on a friendly shoot such as ours, where you walk one drive and, if you are lucky, find yourself standing for the next, one well-shown pheasant is worth ten of what we call *fflutter-fflutter-bang* efforts. The latter are birds scuffed up by the dogs and saluted up the rear end as they attempt to leave the scene.

The really exciting thing about Selsey is that you never know exactly what will turn up. Because it is close to the sea-wall and is criss-crossed with the ditches known in those parts as 'rifes', teal and mallard can always be expected as a bonus. When the fields are wet, snipe *shreep* up from the least expected places. From November onwards, golden plover give unpredictable exciting shooting. Rabbits and, especially, hares abound and we have some of the finest hare-coursing dogs in the Home Counties, alas, as a result.

Fortunately, my own springer is getting too fat to course any more. He just watches the labradors and visibly sneers at their lack of discipline which, in his case, simply means plenitude of girth-inches. In every way, it is the ideal rough shoot with plenty of opportunities for good driven birds.

I'm afraid, as a wildfowl-orientated shooter, I am inclined to think of pheasants as remarkably stupid birds. However, I would make one exception to this sweeping generalisation—the pheasants we get up on the Ouse washes. These are the most sophisticated and educated of birds. Gut-shy trout don't even begin to compete with them when it comes to an inborn instinct for survival and avoidance of human nuisances.

All day they live the life of Reilly on the fen farms, with the pick of the best from the finest agricultural land in England on which to grow fat and wily. When dusk comes, they flight with the duck, over the rivers that separate the washes from the farmland, and cattle down on the marshes for the night.

Long experience has taught them that such few wildfowlers as they meet aren't basically interested in pheasants. They are there for the duck and haven't time to waste pottering round with the dog for the odd long-tail. Anyway most of the fen wildfowlers have got bits of pheasant pottering somewhere else. They may even have real big pheasant shooting. So they rightly put first things first, first things being wigeon, mallard, teal and pintail.

There are times, though, when evening flight is obviously not going to be profitable; when it is dead calm; when the moon's coming up and flight is likely to be very late; when the arrogant and triumphant crowing of cocks becomes too much to bear. Then I am liable to leave my hide or flighting point and set off on a mild foray.

It is very rarely that I succeed in surprising one of these marsh pheasants. The other night was a case in point. I heard several birds crowing up by the river. Since it wasn't more than a hundred yards from my flighting station I decided to go and investigate.

When I reached the bank there was only one possible bit of holding cover that could hide a pheasant, the reedy margin along the river. Teal, my springer, immediately became excited. His rudder began to move and he went straight for the reeds. I stood by to employ the afore-described *fflutter-fflutter-bang* technique.

There was, however, no *fflutter-fflutter*, let alone *bang*. A cock floated up, like a hot air balloon, rising silently out of the reeds, well within shot, and glided across the river as quietly as a barn owl quartering a meadow at dusk.

It gave not a crow, not a rattle of a pinion. A perfect piece of evasive action. While I was marvelling at this suppression of the usual pheasant ebullience, a second cock rose in exactly the same fashion, ten yards farther on, but still well within shot. Once again, I was caught completely flat-footed.

They are, no doubt about it, a race apart, these marsh

pheasants. I catch up with about half a dozen each duck-shooting season, if I am lucky. They are small birds, even the cocks, and very, very spry indeed. I have tried crouching beneath the river bank to flight them as they soar across from the farmland in the gloaming, but they seldom fly straight into the marsh. They land on the broad top of the bank, have a good look round, and, if anything alarms them, promptly fly back across the river. About the smartest thing I have seen was twenty cock pheasants at two in the afternoon, sitting up in a solitary tree on the farmland, looking out on to the washes and deciding whether it was healthy to cross.

Pheasants in a Fog

Our first pheasant day of the year dawned foggy with a certainty that when the sun got to work on the atmosphere it would be shirt-sleeve weather. We'd all heard of how the birds were late and small and weak on the wing and thin on the ground and we were, naturally, expecting the worst.

Our farm behind the sea-wall at Selsey seems to breed pheasants naturally, even though we always put a few down as a token gesture to our neighbours. The soil is light and there are plenty of banks and rifes which afford good nesting cover.

Our shoot captain, who farms this flat, almost fenland soil, was optimistic even as we got out of the cars and peered out into the now patchy and thinning fog. There were a lot of birds about, he said. To prove his point he invited us to look out on to a newly sown field of winter wheat already, in late October, several inches high. Dimly discerned as blobs could be seen at least fifteen remarkably pheasant-like shapes.

It promised well, especially as the farmer now revealed to us that he had two large strips of maize still standing, a completely failed crop which was generously dropping its large yellow grains on to the ground. It was from the maize that the fifteen pheasants had wandered. With a little gentle persuasion they could almost certainly be pushed back inside. There should be quite a few more there waiting to welcome them.

I have never shot pheasants out of maize before though I believe in America, in the Dakotas especially, it is reckoned to be more than the equivalent of a good English field of kale. The birds have to rise vertically to get out of the six feet high stalks and, presumably, once up, keep going.

We drove the maize a strip at a time, which turned out to be a mistake. The first strip was the smaller of the two. Well stopped, it produced perhaps half a dozen birds who rocketed as if celebrating November the Fifth. Four of them came down like spent bonfire-night rockets having given lovely driven shots.

It was not my turn to stand for the second maize drive, unfortunately, for we were all expecting big things. The dogs worked fast, perhaps too fast, for one thing about a crop of maize, or at least about a failed crop of maize—I have no experience of the bumper variety—is that there is little bottom cover. The birds therefore tend to run forward at a great rate. If you have 'keen' dogs like ours, then the canine pace becomes pretty hot also.

However, the strip was well stopped so, although the pheasants might rise as a bouquet rather than in singles and doubles, there should still have been quite a lot for the standing guns to shoot at. The result was most disappointing. About four shots were fired all told and only two birds gathered.

Beyond the maize is a low rushy piece, intersected by rifes, always good for a cock or two as well as a few snipe. It is one of my favourite pieces on the shoot. The guns are sent round to stand on the farm road in front of some cottages and a line of telephone cables. Such birds as come forward *en route* to a cunningly planted patch of artichokes farther on, are liable to fly exceptionally well to clear these obstacles. I was now feeling rather smug that I had driven the second maize patch and was due for a stand on the road.

No sooner had the dogs and walking guns moved into the

first of the rushes than the cry of *foooorwaaard* began to echo through the mist that still hung over the marsh. After three shouts, following which no pheasant had, so far as I had seen, come forward, I happened to look right towards my neighbour in time to see a hen gliding as silently as a barn owl across the road barely three feet above the deck. It departed, naturally enough, unshot at. Was this what had happened to those other birds that were supposed to have come our way?

Now the beaters were getting really enthusiastic. If their warnings could be believed we were about to be bombarded by a continuous salvo of pheasants. And so we most certainly were. Birds got out of that marsh as if it was Holkham Clump. But now we knew where to look for them—at ground level.

They came out of the mist before you had time to see them. They were throttled well back, obviously as blind as bats and very unhappy about being airborne in such conditions. My colleague to the right had several barrels at birds that were disappearing behind—it was far too dangerous to fire at them in front, even when you could see them. But his heart wasn't in it and after a time he gave up saluting these marsh spirits as they merged into the murk like Will-o-the-Wisps.

I was luckier. A few that came directly for the cottages did pour on the coal a bit. They pulled back on the stick and zoomed as any self-respecting pheasant should; I was able to shoot four fairly creditable ones, though robbing myself of a chance at a corking right and left—a rare opportunity on our shoot—by missing a cock with the first barrel and having to kill it with the second.

The gun on my left solved the problem his own way and most impressive it was. Rather than risk crashing head-on into telephone wires, the birds on his side had wisely chosen to sneak out over a hedge and make for the open country. This meant that they were flying faster and more confidently, though still very low. Their course took them past a gap in a hedge perhaps ten yards wide. My left-hand neighbour was snap-shooting them as they flew through the gap in a manner that would have made many a crack snipe-shot envious. He got five by this means and deserved every one of them.

At least sixty pheasants came out of that little patch of marshy rough. For us that is a really big drive. We seldom put more than ten birds out of any one crop. The pick-up? Nine. Most of the low-fliers, those that we actually saw, were allowed to go simply because there would have been no sense in shooting them, even when it was safe to do so.

The explanation of the sudden filling up of the marsh must surely have been that the birds had run forward, because of the ground-level thinness of the maize, sneaking past the standing guns in the mist and legging it alongside the banks of a convenient rife.

I have never considered pheasants as having a high order of avian intelligence. But one would have thought that in conditions of poor visibility they would have found it safer to put a good few yards between themselves and the ground. For a bird that would far rather run than fly I can only suppose that the proximity of *terra firma* is preferable to flying on instruments.

They beat us good and proper. Next time we do that bit I know exactly what will happen. It won't be my turn to stand on the road. Or, if it is, we shall have learned our lesson and stopped the maize properly so that no birds leak out into the marsh.

And if, by some incredible fluke, I do draw a place on the road, then the fog will suddenly come down and it will become bird-walking weather again. In which case I shall abandon my 12-bore and take out a large landing-net. Those fog-blind pheasants were flying so slowly I swear you could have scooped some of them up, lacrosse-fashion, in mid-air.

Monsoon in Sussex

The last day of the pheasant season for me this year was January 22. The South of England appeared to have been struck by a monsoon. Rain came in sheets, laid horizontal across the landscape by a gale force wind. The bitter pill was that it was ideal wildfowling weather. If only it had been our week to shoot the Ouse washes. Unfortunately it was the week assigned to our Norfolk partners.

There were other discouraging factors. Three of the six guns belonging to our farm shoot near Selsey had pressing invitations to shoot cocks elsewhere. On the Friday, our farmer and head of our small group had phoned me to ask whether I thought it would be worth shooting. There would only be three or four of us out.

I like working the hedges and ditches for cocks almost as much as any more formal pheasant exercise, so I said yes: definitely it would be worth it. I thought that he sounded disappointed by my enthusiasm. Only later did I discover that he was scheduled for a hunt ball on the Friday night which meant that he would probably not slip between the sheets until around 5 am.

As a parting shot he told me that his guest couldn't come so there would probably only be three of us. I replied that I would bring a guest and four was a very fine number for cock-bashing.

When Saturday dawned I began to wish that I had not been so keen. On the drive down to Selsey the rain was so heavy that the wipers could barely keep the screen clear.

My guest and I were first on the scene. We sat miserably in the car listening to the tattoo of the Sussex monsoon season rattling on the corrugated iron roof of the barn.

The third gun, David, turned up and remained incarcerated in his vehicle. Should we all go home? Surely no self-respecting pheasant would fly in such weather. Finally our captain drove up. 'Lovely morning,' said the farmer organiser of our activities, 'just what one needs after a hunt ball. Damned glad we came.'

As we slipped on our Solways and waterproof leggings—waterproof? Nothing was going to keep that deluge at bay for very long—he explained that his guest had been able to make it after all. There would be five of us. The reversal of roles was quite extraordinary. All the enthusiasm was on his part now. I can only think that he nursed such a monumental hang-over from the hunt ball, that a day in a blinding rainstorm was his only hope of return to health and sanity.

As it turned out, it was a super day. The weather got, if anything, worse. But the shoot is one which often profits from the foulest conditions. It lies just inside the seawall. Much of it is cut by dykes and drains. The area right against the wall is left as rough grazing and floods easily. There is almost no telling what will appear in front of your barrel, especially under rough conditions.

The cocks were all tucked well down into cover, sometimes in brambles on the almost vertical sides of the ditches. They took an awful lot of shifting. Usually my spaniel had to go right into the bramble and push and push with his nose until the pheasant rose. They rose into the wind and then turned to streak off downwind at, often, I guess, something closer to sixty mph than fifty.

We tried to leave them for guns placed well downwind who would get really snorting, curling shots as a result. A few went wide. Some were inevitably shot not very gracefully as they tried to go forward. But some of those downwinders simply took your breath away.

I had two superb wind-driven cocks. I led them both by what seemed to be three fields and missed them clean with the first barrel. Fury and desperation—I don't claim any skill in the matter—lent speed to the swipe with the second which, in each case, was killed stone dead in a satisfactorily spectacular fashion. I don't often end the pheasant season with a couple of shots like that for, to tell the truth, I am not very clever with really fast, driven pheasants.

But it was the 'various' that made the day. Snipe rose in

wisps from every wet patch of spring wheat and plough. They say that driven snipe are easier than those that get up at your feet. On this day of gales I beg leave to doubt it.

One guest who is an extraordinarily good all-round shot fired ten cartridges at these elusive darts of birds that the walking guns obligingly pushed over him. His return was one snipe.

Then there were the golden plover. There are always great

flocks of goldies to enliven a shooting day on this farm. In the gale they kept low but showed an uncanny skill in picking the holes between guns. When they made a mistake they seemed to spot the gun at the last moment, just before entering effective range. Then they rose, often against the wind, jinking and swerving about in a manner which made the snipe seem almost turgid by comparison.

We walked the flooded meadow close to the sea wall. It was in dream condition for duck. Little sheltered splashes, tucked away well down in the grass, occurred every twenty yards to so.

Teal and mallard in parties of two and three rose from almost every splash. I would like to say that we scored with frequent success. Despite the gale, those duck knew their business. Two of us did the walking. The remaining three guns waited inland behind a bank for any partridges, snipe or duck to hurtle over them.

The mallard simply bored into the wind and beat out to sea, never offering a shot. The teal climbed upwind like kites, turned and hurtled inland in great soaring curves at, I would hazard, something that approached seventy miles per hour. No one had need to feel disgraced that only one came down.

By three in the afternoon, we were all fairly well wet through. The hunt ball survivor and the two guests decided that enough was enough. David and I voted to walk the remaining ditches for a cock or two.

Hen after hen rose under the dog's nose. At the last, in a patch of artichokes, Teal put up a cock. I shot, knowing I was slightly behind but saw it stagger to carry on strongly. David reported that he had seen it start out but had not noticed it continue over the boundary hedge.

Reluctantly we set out to look. In a ditch, 300 yards away, the dog found it stone dead. Last cock of the season and, like the day, one that I shall remember.

PART VI

Foreign Parts

Dutch Treat

I have been watching the Dutch fighting their 400-year-old battle against the sea and winning hands down in a campaign that must, in most respects, resemble what might happen to our own Wash. I watched them holding back the Zuider Zee, or Ijsselmeer as it is now called, and creating huge new farmlands on the former sea bed. It was obvious from what I saw that the wildfowl, at least, need not suffer.

To defeat the sea at its own game, the Dutch conduct a muck-shifting operation that makes the pyramids of Gizeh seem like a pile of stones. First, they build a colossal holding dam, usually between a chain of offshore islands. This is to keep the sea out. What they now have inside this is a vast salt lake which very shortly becomes a vast brackish lake and eventually a freshwater ditto. The change comes about by evaporation, by pumping out the briny and by the replenishment from their rivers.

While this is happening, they construct polders. A polder may easily be the size of a small English county. Essentially, it is an artificial island within the newly formed freshwater lake. You make it by building two parallel walls of boulder clay dredged up from the sea bed miles away; by sinking huge hand-woven rush and hazel mattresses on to the clay; by covering them with rocks (imported from Germany) and then, by using suction dredgers to suck up sand from the sea-bed and squirt, it, as from a huge elephant's trunk, on to the slowly rising clay, rock and mat walls. Then you seal this lot with bitumen.

Finally, you fill in the gap between the two walls with more sand and build a road along the top of it.

When you've enclosed your whole polder which, let us say, is a pentagon whose sides total seventy miles, you begin to pump out the water from inside. Shortly you have a vast expanse of salt mud which has to be leached by weather and by planting huge reed beds, the seed being dropped by air. After a few years, the reeds are felled and ploughed in as humus and you can start to think about grazing.

East Flevoland, the polder I visited, was only started in 1950. Ten years later, there are farms and corn as high as an elephant's eye on about a third of it. The interesting thing is what all this does to birds, and especially to wildfowl.

The first thing that has to be admitted is that the effect can't be all good. The inevitable change from salt to fresh water inside the holding dam must automatically discourage not only many seabirds such as terns but also exotics like avocets and spoonbills. Both the latter would rather forage in brackish water.

On the other hand, there is absolutely nothing to turn away wildfowl, provided that the planning provides for the right sort of shallows and leaves sanctuaries and wetlands within the eventual pattern of farming. The summer flight of mallard from the freshwater sea created by the Ijsselmeer scheme surpassed most flights I have watched during favourable weather in a British winter.

In the initial stages of making a polder, before the farms begin to sprout, the whole place becomes a paradise for all wetland birds. East Flevoland shows the reclamation process stage by stage. About a third is already being farmed, one third is down to grazing, the rest is in the reed bed wilderness state. None of these different sectors is exactly short of birds.

The marsh area is, as you might expect, a bird paradise, though a paradise that will not be allowed to exist for very long. Every hundred yards, as you drive along the road on top of the wall, you see lagoons, still slightly brackish, in which avocets are as common as blackheaded gulls in Britain. Some splashes hold spoonbills. There are garganey, shoveler, teal and mallard galore, of course. Plough into the reed beds on foot and you are assailed by a cloudburst of bearded tits. I watched three marsh harriers quartering quite a small area.

Stage two, the grazing land, is dyke and drain intersected, as is most land in Holland. This, of course, is ideal wader, heron and duck country.

Stage three, considering the short time that has passed since the project was started, is the most astonishing of all. Huge fields of wheat, oats, barley and roots reach for the horizon with a stretch that makes fen fields seem like handkerchiefs. It was not the right time for seeing pheasants, yet more broods scuttled along dyke edges and roadside verges than, I warrant, you could see in Lincolnshire. This plainly is game country to match, or even exceed, our own flat shires. There must also be an abundance of small rodents. Buzzards, rather surprisingly in this flat and thermal-less country, patrol the ditches with obviously more than hope behind their hooked beaks.

When the corn is cut it is not difficult to imagine what kind of stubble flight of mallard the polder farmlands will offer.

Towards the end of the trip round East Flevoland, even my fears about the terns were partly allayed. Among the cranes and caravans of a construction site, on an ideal sand and shingle bed that had previously been the bottom of the sea, at least 1,000 common terns had nested and reared young. Moreover the old birds were fishing perfectly happily and successfully in the newly created freshwater.

So what does this hold out for us? I suppose, in time, the barrage schemes on the Wash and elsewhere are bound to come. If so, there seems absolutely no reason why we shouldn't keep, or even increase, our present wildfowl population, provided the National Environment Research Council, the Wildfowl Trust and WAGBI have a say in the planning. The only real fear must be for the wading birds who must surely be deprived of their muddy foreshore.

America Takes Refuge

I have reported on several negative aspects of the sporting and wildlife scene in the United States and especially on the general gun-happiness of hunters there. Now I'd like to adjust the balance by writing about what is good and even better than good—brilliant.

Under the heading 'brilliant' you can place the Americans' handling of any kind of reserve or national park. I suppose it is true to say that the natural resources of the United States, unimaginably vast when the Pilgrim Fathers landed, have been run down at a rate that seems impossible. A rate that has certainly not been equalled by any other nation or land on earth.

All this was true until fifty or sixty years ago. Then along came President Teddy Roosevelt, a keen hunting man, and the trend was put into reverse almost equally fast. Of course, the damage of the previous 300 years was so colossal that nothing could be done about a lot of it.

You couldn't resurrect 600 million acres of slaughtered forest. You couldn't restore the bison and pronghorn herds, or the passenger pigeon, or the Labrador duck, especially the last two for they had vanished altogether. You could, however, and Teddy Roosevelt did, start a system of National Parks and Monuments and Wildlife Refuges that has been growing in scope and size ever since.

The first thing that strikes the visitor to any of these places is how beautifully and efficiently they are run. Not all contain wildlife. Many National Monuments simply preserve nature, a scenic marvel like Walnut Canyon, home of cliff-dwelling Indians; the Petrified Forest; the last stand of giant Saguaro cacti in the United States. It doesn't matter whether the subject is animate or inanimate, the treatment is equally effective.

You drive straight to the visitors' centre. This is a one-storey building, built of local stone and timber, architect-designed almost to disappear into the surrounding landscape. You soon learn that you cannot afford to miss these out. They are museums in the most modern manner with the complete history, geology, zoology of the monument or park displayed and explained in the most fascinating and visually exciting way. Sometimes, as in the case of the Desert Museum outside Tucson, Arizona, most of the exhibits—snakes, birds, mammals—are live and in their natural setting.

Even if you turn up off-season, there are rangers on duty to explain it all to you. If you wish, you can watch a ten minute colour film show about the area. I thought that I was proof against swallowing large doses of tabloid information. I soon became converted. I was there to learn as much about the South West as possible. I found that half an hour in the visitors' centre sent me out with a good chance of knowing what I was looking at and how it got to be that way.

Some months ago I was complaining in this column that our British national parks, such as they are, make no attempt to arrest or interest the traveller. I argued that in some parks or nature reserves, in the Highlands for example, it would be perfectly easy for the warden to maintain a collection of the animals that lived on his forests or in his glens, animals that the casual driver-through would be unlikely to spot for himself.

I further suggested that there should be coloured identification drawings of the birds of the area, perhaps even a plantation of the most typical and interesting trees and other flora. I added that I was perfectly certain my suggestion would never be taken up. All this costs money, not much money, but money all the same. Money is the one thing we are not willing, or cannot afford, to spend on such frivolities.

The difference is that the Americans do not consider them frivolities. It's easy to laugh at the USA's big-talk of a 'great national heritage'. I got the impression during my travels that the sense of owning this heritage was very real.

Another thing that was admirable was the rigidity with which they deal with even the mildest vandalism. Nothing, but nothing, not a stick, stone, leaf or berry, is allowed to be taken away as a souvenir. In the Petrified Forest visitors' centre lies a heap of petrified tree, in fragments varying from a few ounces to a hundredweight. A notice says that this was taken away by rangers from visitors' cars as they left the Monument. The resulting fines during the last twelve months totalled close on 2,000 dollars. The signs warn: 'Leave nothing behind but your footprints. Take nothing away but photographs'—and they mean it.

Parks and Monuments are mainly for tourists. Wildlife Refuges are for animals and naturalists, though tourists are quite welcome if they stick to the rules.

The USA has 280 Refuges covering seventeen million acres. They occur from the Florida Keys to the Aleutians. They are, alas, oases in a continent that is very largely a wildlife desert, at least compared with its natural abundance and fertility of only 150 years ago. But what green oases these refuges turn out to be. According to habitat, they shelter a huge variety of endangered creatures from Texas Longhorns in Wichita to the few surviving whooping cranes in Texas.

Many of the finest refuges, readers of this journal will be delighted to know, are for waterfowl. I visited two of them.

Wildfowl refuges are essential in the States because of the vast distances migrating fowl fly and because of the hunting pressure along the routes. There are four main flyways, the Eastern, Central and Western and Pacific. The first refuge I visited, Bosque del Apache in New Mexico, was quite small by American standards, about 57,000 acres in all. As we drove into it, we began to see all kinds of small birds, in fact, almost on the scale you would expect to see, and would take for granted, in Britain.

Red-shouldered blackbirds picked at the seeds in the reedmace heads. American sparrowhawks, a bird much more akin to our kestrel, lined up along the telegraph posts. The magnificent buzzard-like, red-tailed hawk wheeled in the sky. Loggerheaded shrikes, not unlike our great grey, prospected for prey on fence wires. There were flocks of bluebirds on their way north. I saw birds totally unfamiliar to me like the towhe, phainopeppla and, where the swamps from the Rio Grande began, clouds of killdeers, an American wader close to our own ringed plover.

It was good to see birds in quantity again. The reasons were plain to see. Here was properly provided and managed habitat, and, more important, habitat protected from the ravages of the gun-happy.

The Refuge Manager, a lad with a dream of a Texan accent, gladly took us round. Like all the American rangers I met, he took a real pride and joy in showing his wildlife treasures to anyone who was really interested.

Most of his 5,000 sandhill cranes had moved out north, but there were still fifty or sixty of these handsome and oriental-looking birds standing in an aloof group on their own mudflat. A hundred yards apart, on another mud bank, about the same number of snowgeese were eyeing the bright, hot, blue New Mexico sky and talking among themselves, possibly discussing whether this fair spring day was a suitable one on which to begin their 3,000-mile flight up to the Arctic tundra. It looked good enough to me.

The whole scene with its skeins of mallard, teal and pintail flighting off against the backdrop of the jagged, blue mountains was something I had always hoped to set eyes upon since I viewed my first Duck's Unlimited films.

Bosque del Apache almost seemed too exotic a setting for duck, at least American duck, but then, I kept reminding myself, I was practically on the Mexican border. The very water in the lagoons came from the legendary Rio Grande.

There were other guests on the refuge besides waterfowl. A fine herd of mule deer lay peacefully munching in the tall grass of an island marsh and roadrunners lived up to their name by legging it down the tracks ahead of us. The spring sunshine had woken up the turtles. Two or three soft-shelled turtles lay with their strange, beaky, prehistoric-looking heads out of the water. Their bodies were propped up at an angle of forty-five degrees on partly-submerged roots and logs, their rear-ends still well below the surface.

They looked like small boats, either ready for launching or not pulled quite far enough above the tideline. The Refuge Manager said that launching was nearer to the truth. When the turtles lay half out of the water like this, ready to resume their aquatic life, it was a sure sign that spring was here.

In another dyke, the water was building up behind a small, rudimentary dam. I did not like to voice my suspicion that this was the work of a beaver in case I made a fool of myself. Beavers, to me, have always been creatures of the mountain streams and northern woods, not baskers in the lazy, torrid, desert air. Surely New Mexico was no place for a beaver to be busy in.

But this was a beaver all right, the Refuge Manager said. It was a solitary old male who was building himself a little dam as compulsively as beavers will and must. That old beaver, he said, was causing a bit of a problem. The trouble was he was so darn good at dam building that he kept cutting off the water supply to one of the duck marshes.

Instead of flowing as the management plan intended, the water backed up behind the dam and flooded out over a wide area of good timber—as the beaver intended. One reason that beavers build dams is to make a larger area of edible timber accessible to them for cutting and easy towing through water.

The trouble with this beaver was that he just didn't appreciate that this was a waterfowl reserve. The Manager was quite willing to persevere for a bit with breaking down the dam, but the trouble was that the beaver built it up faster than he could demolish it. One time, the Manager said, he'd tried leaving out lamps at nights to stop beavers working. They'd seemed to appreciate the extra illumination until dawn broke. Then they'd simply taken the oil lamps and built them in as part of the dam. In the end, if he didn't mend his ways faster than he mended the dam, that particular beaver would have to go.

But the main pride of Bosque del Apache was its Mexican duck. These duck are on the danger list, at least as far as America goes, and are responsible for what, at first seemed to me, to be a very strange hunting situation on this Refuge.

Hunters were allowed to shoot their full limit of snowgeese, yet were forbidden to shoot mallard, of which there was obviously an enormous surplus. The reason, I soon found out, was that no one can tell the difference in flight between a Mexican duck, male or female, and a female mallard.

When I saw a rearing-pen full of Mexican duck, I appreciated the justice of this statement. I couldn't tell the difference when they were on the ground at six-feet range, at least not until the Manager pointed it out. The main difference is a slightly lighter bill and head. The Mexican, like the black duck, is very closely related to the mallard.

While we were standing by the rearing-pen, a large, peregrine-sized hawk made a brief appearance in the sky. The Manager identified this fine bird as a Cooper's hawk. The hawk was after sparrows, he explained. Three times recently he had watched it swoop in at full speed and take one. No, not the sparrows that were happily hopping around in the grass, but the sparrows that lived on the food inside the rearing cages. You would think, he added, that these birds had every reason to fancy themselves secure from hawks. But not where the Cooper's hawk was concerned.

The mesh of the cage was one-inch chicken wire. Often the sparrows fluttered close to the roof of the cage. When they did, the hawk made its approach along the line of the roof, reached out with a talon and grabbed a sparrow inside the wire, pulling it out and flying away with it without even checking in its flight.

I would have given a good price to have seen this happen and an even better one to have captured it on film.

In the United States every sort of law enforcement officer carries a six-gun, often in an elaborately embossed western

holster and gunbelt. One of the most flamboyant I saw belonged to a Navajo Indian Reserve ranger who stopped his pick-up truck in the middle of the Painted Desert in order to discover whether we were taking petrified wood or anything else away.

In such matters the American attitude to conservation of environment is superb. Nothing is permitted to be removed, plant, animal or stone, from a national park, national monument or reserve.

The ranger was charm and politeness itself. When he

discovered that we were filming the tracks of desert animals, he was eager and willing to help. His knowledge was considerable. But then he was as red as his redoubtable ancestors who fought the US cavalry to a standstill in these parts a mere hundred years ago. The name on his jacket, 'R. Redsteer', and the six-shooter at his waist reminded one that the West is still the West.

High-powered personal armament is all very well in the case of responsible citizen R. Redsteer, full-blooded Navajo. Perhaps it's not so good when the pioneer spirit and its built-in right to tote a gun is preserved in the more slap-happy ordinary citizen and hunter.

As illustration of this freedom to squeeze a trigger when, where and how you like, I will cite the instance of our arrival in a small town along the Apache Trail. We pulled into this hamlet for gas (see how easily the jargon possesses one) on the very day that the javelina season opened.

Javelina, by the way, is Spanish for peccary, America's only wild pig. These fierce little brutes inhabit much of the scrub and desert country of Arizona and New Mexico.

We intended to visit a marvellously scenic canyon called Chiricahua, the hang-out of that greatest of Apache leaders, Cochise. It was from this impregnable fortress of eroded sandstone, each of whose million pinnacles resembles a fantastically carved, exotic chess piece, that Cochise raided the Mexican settlements and the ranches to the south.

To reach the canyon we aimed to take a short cut by dirt road across the mountains, in fact along the old Apache Trail which the pony soldiers used when they built Fort Bowie to fight the old man and his indomitable warriors.

'You don't want to go thataway,' the attendant at the filling station told us. He sounded so grave about it that one could be pardoned for fancying that the news had just hit town that the Apaches were off the reservation once again. Or was it, perhaps, because the road was so bad that it would knock the bottom out of our Chevvy station wagon?

The attendant quickly cleared the matter up. 'It's those goddam hunters,' he said. 'First day of the peccary season, they all go up in the hills and get high and, man, then they're likely to shoot at anything that moves.'

We took off for the hills, regardless. A hundred miles saved is worth the chance of a little stray lead.

In the event, we need not have worried. We saw hunters' caravans parked among the cacti. We even saw hunters, conspicuous to us, if not to the peccaries, in red hats or red jackets. All seemed sober and well behaved. No bullets came our way. But once again, the roadside signs had not escaped. The first we passed had twenty-three bullet holes in it. All of them were freshly minted, the edges of their wounds bright and fresh. The term 'cowboy', it seems, applies equally in its true land of origin.

Vultures in Spain

In all my born days I'd never fished in such freezing water. The stuff that came roaring and pounding down the rocky bed of the Rio Ara in the Spanish Pyrénées was on more than nodding terms with the snow that still lay in patches on the seven-thousand-foot peaks below which the Willock family caravan had finally rested in the valley of Ordesa.

Because a caravan holiday demands that you travel light, I had no waders with me. Gym shoes and bathing shorts are not the best possible insulation against the temperature of a mountain river, even when you fish it in August.

I've fished some spectacular places in my day and seen a good many others, but the valley in which the Spanish Parque Nacional de Ordesa lies takes a lot of beating.

The Grand Canyon is the only thing I have seen which can top it, and then only because there is more of the Canyon. This Spanish valley could easily be a part of that mile-deep American wonder. At Ordesa the escarpments soar vertically on either side of the river for three thousand feet. The rock is eroded into pinnacles and towers that match most scenery you can find in Arizona or Utah and that's saying everything.

In two respects, both very near to my own heart, Ordesa differs greatly from the American South West which it otherwise greatly resembles.

The first difference is the abundance of birds of prey in the Pyrénées. At first you don't see very much in the sky over Ordesa and you begin to think that Spanish raptors are suffering from the same threats as their American and northern European counterparts—an excess of shotgun lead and chemical sprays.

But then, one afternoon, you are lying on your back succumbing to the Spanish habit of the siesta, just dreaming among the alpine flowers outside the caravan. You stare absently at the bright blue sky far beyond the peaks. Banks of cumulus are building up and the hot air from the rocks below is wafting up the towering cliffsides and over the battlements at their top. As you look idly upwards enjoying the pattern of white cloud over rock, you notice for the first time specks unimaginably high above your head.

Until this moment, I had expected to find my Spanish birds of prey soaring actually along and below the escarpments. Given that the tops of our particular peaks were between six and eight thousand feet high, then these specks must be all of four thousand beyond that. Once you grasp this fact, the afternoon sky is never empty of interest as the glasses bring these stratospheric bird gliders into focus.

The bunch of dots tumbling and falling slightly lower than the rest are ravens, enjoying as ravens will, aerobatics and free-fall parachute displays on the cushions of thermal supporting them. For them it's a kind of aerial trampoline.

Next a great dark bird, longer wing-spanned than an eagle, surely, spirals upwards from behind a distant peak, attains full cruising height, and, without a wing flap, makes off down the valley on a gentle gradient of air along which it appears to be moving at jet-plane speed.

The slight dihedral to the wing tips makes the bird almost certainly a griffon or a black vulture. Or could it be a lappet-faced? We'll never know, for he is soon out of sight. We prefer to believe that we have seen a black vulture.

Before the argument has exhausted itself and the participants, a new star has appeared in our firmament. We get to know this character quite well. He comes over as regularly each afternoon as one of the high-altitude recce planes one remembers from earlier sky-watching.

This golden eagle has a primary or two missing from each wing, so he's easily identified. Sometimes he comes—or is it she?—with a mate. They usually operate lower than the vul-

tures and swing in tighter circles. Sometimes, when the day is cloudy, they are only fifteen hundred feet above our heads.

The eagles are cordially hated by the valley's resident falcons. Peregrines and kestrels nest along the cliff walls and we have managed to pinpoint two of their eyries. No sooner have the eagles arrived overhead than the falcon fighter squadrons are scrambled.

At the height at which the battle takes place—one almost expects to see vapour trails—it is hard to tell which species of falcon is doing the attacking. They are all pretty courageous and the eagle's behaviour is little short of downright cowardly. Usually he or she only stands it for about five minutes and then lopes off to a quieter piece of the sky.

Sometimes the battle is really spectacular. It must be the peregrines who press home their attack in such a ruthless and reckless manner. They climb to a hundred feet or more above the great birds and come in like fighters, only standing off at the last second, passing so close that the eagle has to flip on to his side to take avoiding action.

But our star turn is a pair of Egyptian vultures who live on the cliff about eight hundred feet above our caravan. Every morning at eight they leave to go hunting as the sun touches their roost for the first time. We don't see them until around five in the afternoon when first one arrives at enormous height and makes a cautious recce.

Usually he lands on part of the cliff well removed from his roosting ledge and waits for his partner to come in sight. Then, as if to signal the coast is clear, he takes off, rises on a thermal to meet his mate and they both soar in to perch for the night together. The ritual is unvaried and you can almost set your watch by it. Not every holidaymaker has vultures for breakfast and tea.

I started on the trout fishing and there I must come full circle and end. There is no doubt that our Rio Ara, typical of many in the Pyrénées, possesses rough stream trouting of a very high order, especially where the stream grows smaller and quieter high up in the Parque Nacional itself. Indeed, we caught some of those delicious bright silver trout on dry-fly to prove it.

But the same thing that protects all those Spanish birds of prey, mercifully, seems also to protect the fishing, unmercifully. It is hard to be sure or just about one's hosts in a country where you do not have the language. But bureaucracy and fear of doing anything that the next chap above you, or the policeman outside your door, hasn't approved or won't approve of, seems to pervade the citizens. This works fine when the natives are dead scared of breaking the hunting laws, but not so well when it works against friendly visitors trying to get legitimate permits to fish.

I wish to go on record as saying that I have never found it harder anywhere in the world to evoke the spirit that usually exists between brother anglers. I have never found it harder to get a permit, or got less co-operation. Finally I was told that my permit had run out after six days.

It may have been the language barrier that defeated us. Indeed I would like to think that it was. At present I feel that I may well go back to watch eagles and vultures but certainly shan't bother to take my trout rod with me again.

Fishing for Tigers

The strange mechanism I have previously referred to in this column that cancels out all desire to shoot whenever I go to Africa, does not, by some inconsistency of personality and attitude which I fail to understand, seem to apply to fishing.

So when, in March, I found myself setting out to make a wildlife film on the shores of Lake Rudolf in the wild country in the north of Kenya's Rift Valley, I packed my rods but left my gun behind.

Rudolf's fishing has always been a legend as far as I am concerned. It is said that you can walk across this mighty inland sea on the backs of Nile perch. I suspect this is an exaggeration though not too much of one. However, it was not the Nile perch *Lates albertianus*, that interested me so much. I had caught those before in the Victoria Nile in the whirlpool below Murchison Falls. What intrigued me was the possibility of catching Rudolf's tiger fish on a fly.

Tigers are named for their side stripes, I believe, though I prefer to think the label is in honour of their nature and their dentition. Both are quite formidable, especially the teeth.

The whole of their upper and lower jaws are armed with a set of very long sharp 'canine' teeth, rather like the holding teeth of a pike, except that the tiger sharpens his at the edges as well.

Why they consider it necessary to carry these teeth is something of a mystery. They appear to spend their entire lives making things hot for the vast shoals of fry that inhabit Rudolf. They slash into these like a lot of blood-crazy sharks. The quarry is so small that they must presumably wolf it down whole. Never mind, nature gave them these terrible teeth and the teeth give the angler his first problem.

Tigers are usually caught on a small spinner. I wanted to see if they could be outsmarted on a fly. Spinners are commonly attached to fine trace wire. Flies are commonly attached to fine nylon. Tigers think less than nothing of nylon, fine or coarse. They simply bite it straight through.

There's no reason why you shouldn't tie a fly direct to trace wire except for the fact that the finest is usually pretty stiff stuff and doesn't lend itself to the suppleness required of a fly-cast unfolding in the air. But I had a lucky break.

A few days before I was due to fly out to Kenya I wandered into Carter's tackle shop in South Moulton Street, London W1, to find, to my regret, that they were having a closing down sale. Included in that sale was some of the finest trace wire I am ever likely to see. The spool had a lion on it and the legend *Au Lion d'or*.

I took this as a very good omen in view of my destination. In fact, I was so delighted at this find that I bought a ten foot reservoir fibre-glass fly rod I really did not need and some large (sale price) tandem lake lures, which I did.

Having no idea what lures tiger fish preferred, but fancying that their tastes would be based on quantity rather than quality, I put a handful of home-tied Polystickles into my fly box and caught the East African Airways Super VC10 to Nairobi where a small aeroplane was waiting to fly me over some of the most intimidating country in Africa, north to Rudolf.

At first, the Rudolf tigers beat me all ends up. No matter how quickly I put the fly down near a rise, they ignored it. After one evening rise frustratingly spent in water boiling with fish, I decided that tigers moved rather more quickly and erratically than lake trout. With the latter, it is often a question of working out their cruising circle, spotting the last rise and judging where the next one will occur on the circumference of their feeding beat.

With tigers, there's just no telling. I discovered that the only way to make contact was to work out quickly which way the whole shoal seemed to be charging and then get in at least six feet ahead of it.

Contact was about all I did make. They bumped the lure, gave it a tug, but wouldn't take hold firmly. The fly I was fishing was a big tandem demon with twin silver bodies that seemed closely to resemble the tiny fry the fish were chasing. I had discarded Polystickles, as they looked far bigger than any of the food fish the tigers were after.

The moment I put on a Polystickle, however, things started to happen. A tiger of around two pounds took me first chuck and hung on. The fight was vivid and lively, but not really as active as for a trout of similar weight. The fish fought until it was right on to the sand and then suddenly gave in. When I put it back in the water, it didn't look as though it was going to revive and eventually sank away into the depths no doubt to become croc carrion. Subsequent fish played themselves out and practically succumbed to exhaustion or shock, once landed.

I had caught my first tiger and was staggered at its beauty. Aft of the admittedly hideous teeth, the fish was bright silver, marked rather like a grey mullet, as streamlined as a grayling and decorated with an elegant forked tail, the lower lobe of which was bright yellow. A tiger burning bright, indeed.

Thereafter the Polystickle worked the trick time after time. The only snag was that I had a limited supply of these lures. I am glad I don't fish for tigers all that often, for it is strictly a lure-a-fish proposition. What you get back after a tiger has taken you is a hook shank decorated with a few fragments of the original dressing. At the current price of lake lures, this could be expensive fishing, even forgetting the air fare to Rudolf.

On my last afternoon—my mission was filming, remember, and I couldn't fish *all* the time—I caught thirty fish, and was caught myself in a sandstorm that buried my tackle bag and filled my reels so solid that I had to strip them and wash them in the lake before I could continue fishing.

Strangely enough it wasn't the tigers of Lake Rudolf or the large, though not very lively, Nile perch that gave me my biggest angling surprise on this trip. It was a modest food fish called a *tilapia*.

Tilapia are the tastiest freshwater fish I have ever eaten. But I had never thought of them as a sporting quarry. They are chubby little bream-like characters who feed mostly on the bottom. That no doubt is how a pound and a half *tilapia* came to take a fly I had allowed to sink too deeply.

That ten-foot reservoir rod tip went down into Lake Rudolf in an arc that not even the biggest tiger had made it assume. The *tilapia* fought in a way that would have put a chalkstream trout to shame.

Some time ago, there was talk of introducing this species to the warm water outlets of British power stations. If they ever do, take my tip—don't go all the way to the Rift Valley. Take your fly rod, some small wet flies and hurry to your nearest atomic cooling towers.

Once in a Lifetime

It was without doubt the greatest wildlife sight I have ever seen. It happened in the Rift Valley of Ethiopia, where I was doing the research for a 'Survival' TV film about great white pelicans. The pelicans were impressive enough, but this story has nothing to do with pelicans, apart from the fact that I was on my way to their feeding grounds early one African morning when it happened.

Our cameraman Dieter Plage and I were driving along a small muddy stream that connects two lakes in the Ethiopian Rift Valley. On our side of the stream was a mile or two of typical open savanna dotted with acacia bushes. Suddenly, against the far mountains, something like a very big bunch of teal appeared and then behind them another party and above them and beyond again endless more parties of anything from thirty to two hundred strong.

We stopped the Land Rover and watched. Instead of making for the water these first flocks circled and pitched half a mile back on the grassland. But now there were more coming and many more behind them. We stood with our mouths falling open while the build-up continued. At the end of forty minutes, the entire savanna, from half a mile back to within a hundred yards of the stream where we stood, was bright golden with sandgrouse.

We still did not realise that we were standing on top of the objective of this fantastic gathering. At our feet, the stream widened into a little muddy beach, the sort of place waders usually patronise. The beach was no bigger than a tennis court.

The flight had begun in earnest. The calls of the first airborne parties triggered off the rest. Squadron after squadron took off, weaving intricate formation patterns against each other, often through each other. The whole gathering was going to drink at that one little beach.

The first parties to land there numbered hundreds, but these were soon pushed forward towards the water by the pressure of thousands, and tens of thousands, behind them. It appeared that very few of the grouse could actually get a drink though closer observation, and later examination of the film, showed that all *did* drink.

Some parties went round for a second or third time and came in again. Mostly, though, no matter how far back an individual bird landed from the water, he progressed forward in an orderly fashion, shoulder to shoulder with his fellows in the same rank until he could actually dip his beak.

At the height of the flight, the process of pouring in and pouring out was continuous. It was like a jet engine sucking in air and spewing it out, only this was not air but a solid cloud of bright yellow birds. The noise at the high point of activity was literally frightening.

The time from first bird coming in to last party leaving for the desert and arid scrubland all around us was exactly six and a half minutes.

When that first flight was over we caught our breath and compared notes. All the birds we had observed were chestnut bellied sandgrouse. We had both seen one single bird of another species—the yellow-throated—flying in with one of the earlier parties to drink. There may, of course, have been other odd birds out in that huge concourse, but this specimen stood out so clearly by darker markings and larger size that I seriously doubt it.

We had both counted the sips of water taken by individuals. We agreed that the average was four sips, the least three, and the most seven. Seeing that many of the birds must have flown anything from ten to fifty miles from the surrounding country to get that drink, it seemed a small enough reward for all their hard work.

We filmed this fantastic sight for five mornings running until we had covered every aspect of it, including the assembly on the savanna. On the fourth morning we were lucky to have Leslie Brown, one of the most eminent ornithologists in Africa, along with us. He had shown proper doubt at my estimate of 50,000, but even Leslie admitted to 'at least 40,000 birds and the biggest concentration I have ever seen'.

From Leslie we learnt some fascinating facts about the species. It seems that the use of an assembly area is their usual method of approaching the water. It is inbred caution that makes them act in this way. In the breeding season, the males open up their specially adapted breast feathers when they drink to trap droplets of water which they carry back to the young in the nest.

Although they seem to be sipping the water they are, in fact, sucking in a good deep draught. I have read somewhere that scientists in America have demonstrated that mourning doves can make up a quarter of their body weight with this kind of drinking. It seems reasonable that the sandgrouse, a similar sized bird, should do the same.

Sandgrouse are, of course, a prime sporting bird in hot countries. They are, I can vouch, delicious to eat. However, no pigeon shooter or wildfowler worthy of the name would have wanted to fire into those vast aggregations. You could hardly have avoided knocking down a dozen to fifty at a shot. But when the flight was nearly over there were a few high, fast singles that would have made worthy marks.

There was a sudden end to this story. On the sixth day, when we planned to make sound recordings, it rained hard just before dawn. That morning only two thousand birds came in. The next morning it rained even harder. There were none. The sandgrouse were getting their drink elsewhere and with less trouble.

I imagine that the scale of what we had seen was possibly a once-in-a-lifetime phenomenon. I certainly shall never forget it at least not until the day when all the 39,000 wigeon on the Ouse washes flight into my pool within the space of five minutes. Then I'll have game, set and match.

Rhino Dodging

It feels as though I have been away for a year. In fact, the time lag is a mere six weeks. During that interval I have flown 35,000 miles in twelve different aircraft; driven 5,000 miles by road and track through some of the wildest and grandest scenery in the world including the Snowy Mountains of Australia, the Drakensberg Mountains of South Africa, the Etosha Pan National Park and the Namib desert in South-West Africa. All of which, I hasten to add, was in the cause of business. Film business. Natural history film business, and some of it to do with the problems of rhinos, both black and white.

Rhinos, alas, are in short supply wherever they still occur throughout the world. It is their considerable misfortune that they carry on the end of their snouts a couple of sharp spikes, made, incidentally, of compressed and compacted hair, which the ignorant and impotent regard when ground into a fine powder as a certain cure for failing sexual prowess.

If it were not for this ridiculous fallacy, no rhino would be in danger of imminent death from poachers. My most recent encounter with rhinos occurred in the Hluhluwe Game Reserve of Natal. (If you find difficulty in pronouncing the name, take heart. Zulu is a very hard language to master. The nearest I can come to Hluhluwe phonetically is *sher-sch-Loooo-ee.*)

I have had quite a bit to do with rhinos, both black and white. My first contact with them was in 1961 when we went to Uganda to make a film about capturing the remains of a scattered population of white rhinos in order to move them to Murchison Falls National Park—where they have since thrived.

Prior to that encounter I had been told by those who ought to have known that white rhinos differ considerably from their distant relative, the black rhinos. White rhinos, I was assured, were of a docile disposition and never charged on sight, as do their black and irascible cousins. This is undoubtedly true. However, since the only method of catching them in those days was to lasso them from a fast-moving truck, and since the first one we caught weighed three and a half tons, the resulting encounter showed a new side to the white rhino's character. I have seldom been so frightened in my life as when that huge animal, incensed by finding itself on the end of an inch manilla hawser, proceeded to take our truck apart.

There are plenty of white rhino in Hluhluwe. In fact, by one of those freaks of human persecution coupled with natural distribution, there are far too many white rhino in the Zululand reserves whereas they barely exist in other parts of Africa. There are also a great many black rhino there and, for some reason that defies rational explanation, these are fiercer and more aggressive than any other black rhino in Africa. The Hluhluwe blacks are legendary terrors as I found out when I made a foot safari with ranger John Forrest.

Though John knew that we were not entirely innocent in the ways of these unpredictable animals, he was careful to brief my wife and I afresh before we set out.

'There is,' he said, 'no honour among those of us who regularly have to make foot patrols through this stuff.' He pointed at the thick, low scrub which makes up a great deal of the reserve. 'You often can't see a rhino at ten yards, so what I mean is: it's every man for himself. You can be walking through the bush with what you imagine to be three loyal and trusted companions and suddenly you look round and they've gone. They haven't told you that they're going, but, if you look carefully, you will find them all safely up trees. In which case, if there's still time, the only thing left to do is to get up a tree yourself.' My wife pointed out, reasonably enough, that it was some time since she had climbed a tree—a thought which more or less matched my own sentiments. 'Don't worry,' said John, 'if the moment comes you'll remember how.'

He had, he went on to tell us, quite recently been charged by four black rhinos at one time, each one coming from a different direction. Then there was one black rhino on the reserve who wasn't content with treeing its victim. The brute propped himself upright on his stubby front legs against the trunk and slashed away upwards into the branches with his horn. One Zulu ranger, who wasn't aware of this characteristic, had failed to climb quite high enough and had been lucky that the rhino had done no more than hook a horn into a trouser pocket, ripping his shorts half off.

What was it that made the Hluhluwe rhino so outlandishly aggressive? John couldn't answer this one since at Umfolozi, the sister reserve connected by a corridor through the bush several miles long, the same species was reasonably docile. One explanation might be that it was the nature of the thick bush that made the Hluhluwe variety so touchy. At Umfolozi, the country was far more open so, possibly, the rhinos had more time to size up the opposition and make up their minds whether human intrusion constituted a threat to their well-being. John confessed that he had become distinctly sensitive about the possibility of being skewered by a black rhino. He claimed, and I fully believe him, that he could not only smell, hear and see rhino before they spotted him, but could sense their presence. The development of special senses was vital to personal survival. Rhinos made him distinctly jumpy.

By the time we set off I was a fair way towards becoming jumpy myself. My wife in the middle of the file seemed comparatively relaxed. We crept and crouched beneath the tangled foliage towards the banks of a small overhung river where John hoped to show us some large crocs. He made a careful personal recce to ensure that there were no buffalo, or for that matter rhino, lying in wait for us and then, parting the branches, revealed a twelve foot croc not more than five yards away.

It was while we were admiring this reptile that there suddenly came an almighty crashing from a dense clump of bushes. I, as I have admitted in this column several times, am partly deaf as the result of firing too many 12-bore cartridges. So I didn't hear John Forrest hiss 'Run!' There is no honour in the Hluhluwe bush. Not even family honour. When I looked again, my wife had disappeared. I realised suddenly that it was time that I looked for a suitable tree. At that instant, the cause of the disturbance came crashing out of the scrub—a magnificent kudu bull.

When the other two returned, I fancied they looked a bit shamefaced. 'Just a kudu,' I said rather grandly. Fortunately John didn't know I am partly deaf and my wife was too breathless to tell him!

Duck Down Under

What timing! I left England on a business trip to Australia a few days after our own duck season ended to find that in New South Wales and Victoria it was just at that moment opening. Although one of the bosses of the New South Wales National

Parks in Sydney offered to fix me a licence, I found that, as usual, I had no urge to shoot in foreign parts. Funny, but this is a universal sensation I get all over the world. For me, wildfowling is inseparable from the frozen, blustery British winter. I'm prepared to give the rest of the globe's duck and geese a safe conduct, though perhaps if I lived overseas, I might think differently.

My business was mainly in the cities and there was the whole of Australia just waiting to be eaten up with the outdoor eye. The truth is that you could drive for a whole year and not make more than a set of tyre tracks in the red dirt of this immense continent.

In the end I settled for hiring a car and driving from Sydney to the next state capital, Melbourne. There were sanctuaries and national parks on the way, plenty of them according to the latest maps, so perhaps there would be something to be seen and learnt. There most certainly was.

When we last made films in Australia five years ago, conservation was a word hardly thought of, let alone spoken or acted upon. In these past five years, there has been a tremendous change, at least in the two states I toured and I rather think everywhere else. Huge new state national parks are being set up, especially in virgin forest areas.

Kangaroo control is run by New South Wales rather on the lines of the Red Deer Commission in Scotland. All 'roos are protected there and can only be cropped under licence and then only where a grazier or landowner can show that he is suffering economic loss.

There are schedules for protected birds and mammals, at least as comprehensive as our own and the fines, if anything, are heavier. To the British eyes, there are some odd things on the unprotected list, including sulphur-crested cockatoos. Beautiful as they are, I imagine a gang of these splendid birds can play hell with a fruit crop. Conservation has to be practical but I don't myself much fancy a day's cockatoo decoying.

Though it was a day or two after the opening of the duck

season when I started my thousand-mile drive, I soon spotted my first duck hunter. He was bedecked with badges, carried an over-and-under and wore his licence in his hat.

He was proudly carrying a brace of black duck, a bird very akin to our own mallard. He looked what my friends in Norfolk call a 'tradesman'. In short, he was no amateur but a man who knew his stuff. Even so, he was well short of his bag limit—twenty duck on opening day and ten a day thereafter, but if he was a true tradesman, then I don't suppose he was too worried.

Not all Australian shooters are like this man, however, especially on opening day which can be, I have been told, very much like the start of the deer hunting season in some of the Eastern States of America. In the USA, farmers have been known to paint COW on the flanks of their livestock. In some parts of New South Wales and Victoria, pelicans, ibises and commorants on opening day would be well-advised to fire off their recognition signals at regular intervals to avoid catching the flak of the trigger-happy irregular shooters.

On this point things are improving. Bill Steel of the New South Wales National Parks told me he used twenty wardens on the first day of the duck season, plus a helicopter, in an attempt to check indiscriminate enthusiasm. To exert maximum control on the Australian 'cowboy', the States have recently brought their opening dates into line so that they can communally keep an eye on the ungodly.

But it is not mainly in the area of the trigger-happy that Australia faces a duck problem. 'Cowboys' are nuisances rather than a serious hazard to the waterbird population. Australia's wildfowl are up against much the same threat that the duck of America faced from the Twenties onwards—destruction of wetland nesting habitat.

At one time it was believed that over-shooting was responsible for the American decline. Then the State, Federal and private organisations like Ducks Unlimited began to research the problem and discovered the real cause was environmental—destruction of habitat. The wetlands and potholes of the prairie provinces of Canada had undergone large scale drainage and filling in as a result of a grow more wheat policy. Those same wetlands were found to be the 'duck factory' for the whole of North America. Without the nesting grounds there could no longer be the vast numbers of waterfowl on the US flyways. So, when it was almost too late, a policy of restoration was successfully begun.

Australia started in somewhat the same position, except that this is a continent not yet despoiled, and in which technological progress has happily arrived at the same moment as environmental awareness. And this is the first time in history that these two forces have had a chance to meet in a virtually virgin land.

So far as Australia's waterfowl are concerned, the parallel is very close indeed to that of the prairie provinces. Almost all Australian duck breed in the south-east in the Murray-Darling rivers region. These rivers and their tributaries form the largest drainage system on the continent and take care of the run-off from no less than 414,000 square miles.

In the old days these waterways periodically produced flooding over a large area, replenishing marshes, swamps and billabongs. When the floods came, the duck, by that special duck magic, knew all about it and flocked in to breed. Unfortunately, this corner of Australia is the one most suitable for immediate development and its coastal strip supports a very large section of industry and the urban population.

To quote the New South Wales wildlife authorities: 'wild duck populations in Australia are declining. This decline was inevitable when, in the interests of agriculture the first swamps were drained and rivers dammed and domestic animals began to trample the edges of the billabongs. The time has come to take serious stock of the waterfowl situation and for active conservation measures to be instituted if wild duck are to remain reasonably common. . . .'

Well, those are sound and pious words, and one is tempted to say that one has heard it all before. All too often pious sentiments don't stand up against the engineering ambitions of the hydro-electric authorities and state or private industry.

I'd be tempted to shrug in this case except that everywhere I've been in Australia I've met with intances of conservation and pro-environment forces showing their muscles and forcing old bully technology to back down.

In one case it was an unsightly and polluting factory given nine years to pack its bags and get out of town, 'town' being a beautiful estuary. Meantime, it must cut out pollution or close down far quicker than that. In another case it was a bunch of private citizens who simply told the municipal authorities that if they destroyed a particularly beautiful bay just to make a waterskiers' paradise they'd blow up the sea-walls.

Final word to the New South Wales National Parks Panel on the subject of duck: 'there is little doubt that if farm authorities were consulted during the planting stages of water conservation works, with little effort many of the structures could be adapted to increase waterfowl population rather than destroy them.' British drainage engineers and conservation bodies please copy.

PART VII

The Ouse Washes

Introducing the Washes

The pleasure of taking an appreciative audience for a first view of something that you, yourself, consider utterly wonderful is often the next best thing to seeing it all again for the first time oneself.

Thus, it was with great joy that my fowling partner and myself took two friends, who normally count their duck in twos and threes, to our own small portion of the last remaining segment of the Great Fens—the Ouse Washes.

I have seen this magnificent landscape with wildfowl on many, many dawns and at many, many dusks. The pleasure of it barely diminishes, yet I recognise that it is impossible ever to maintain the temperature of any first find fever.

It was with delight, therefore, that I listened to one of my friends telling me that he hadn't been able to sleep much the night previously 'just for thinking about it'. I know exactly the feeling. I have had it at many times, in many places. Nowadays, I must confess that I tend to experience an after-glow rather than a before-blaze.

When I have been somewhere as miraculous as the Ouse Washes, I find it hard to sleep when the flight is over, no matter how physically tired I am. Packs of duck insist on inserting themselves between my retinae and my subconscious, at least until utter, contented weariness overcomes me.

At the outset of this particular expedition the weather did not look good—low mist, inclining to fog, with not a puff of wind. When one has to pick a date out of the diary to suit everyone concerned, maybe a month in advance, the weather very seldom agrees to fall in with your plans. So I warned our two newcomers that they would be lucky if they fired their guns more than twice. By way of compensation, they would see an awful lot of duck.

Our local pub is one of the most hospitable that I know. What wild-fowler deserves, or at least expects, hot water bottles in his bed?

When we arrived close on closing time, there was a local darts Derby in progress. Landlord and landlady were busy, though not too busy to serve us all a mixed grill on one of those plates that look a yard long. 'You're all in the big dorm together' our hostess said.

My partner and I had brought our dogs—more dogs than are strictly necessary can prove an embarassment on the Washes, where cover is practically non-existent. By the time we had given our hounds a goodnight stretch and bedded them down in one of the cars, the other two fowlers were already between the sheets. So we took it for granted that they had tucked themselves up in the big dorm as directed, and immediately followed them into the two vacant beds.

I had little difficulty in falling asleep. Before I did so I remember remarking that our favourite pub seemed to have gone downhill, that the beds felt damp and there were no hot water bottles. The truth of this uncomfortable situation was not to emerge until far later the next day, in fact not until long after the alarm had sounded fowlers' reveille at 5.30 am sharp.

I have màde the point previously in this column that I find no hardship in rising early and dressing fast. When flighting on my own I reckon to leave the house fully dressed and with a cup of tea inside me within five minutes of waking up. None of my three companions on this occasion has this same happy gift. Lacking it, they take refuge in vituperation and calumny of those who possess it.

We eventually got off in good order by 6 am.

The journey down the river bank can only be accomplished by Land-Rover. It is seldom less than hair-raising. To start with, there is the Slough of Despond to negotiate. Four-wheel drive is the only thing that can get a wildfowling pilgrim through that. There follows a dizzying ascent of the river bank itself. This is done in reverse while heeling over at a good twenty degrees. Once on top of the embankment, it is fairish going for two miles. The next problem is to recognise the gate that leads to our modest forty flighting acres.

Whenever one stops to make sure of one's bearings, the ear is tantalisingly haunted with a thousand quackings and whistlings. Somewhere, in the darkness, not more than a few hundred yards away, huge quantities of wigeon, teal, pintail and mallard are waiting to start their day with a rush of wings.

The gate is identified at last. Here the more panicky members disembark. I can't say I blame them. The Land-Rover must be squared off exactly at right angles to the line of the bank, and then, brakes hard on, eased down a slope that is so acute that the unfortunate driver is practically standing upright on the foot pedals. But we invariably make it and scarcely give a thought to the equally, if not more tricky, business of making the climb back when the flight is over. At least it will be daylight when that attempt is made.

Already there's a peep of false dawn. My partner and I each seize one of the newcomers and hustle them out, lumbered with guns, cartridges and camouflage nets, across the quaking marsh. There is a particularly sticky quagmire at the gate where the cattle, now mercifully off the Washes, have floundered and wallowed. My man goes down like a wounded buffalo and both flounders and wallows rather dramatically. Not even his best friends—among whom I number myself—could call him a humble man. Though dawn is coming and the duck won't wait I cannot conceal a mite of pleasure at finding him on his knees and in an attitude of supplication. 'For heaven's sake pull me out,' he says. We *afficionados* remark callously that, if he fancies that this is mud, he should try the Medway estuary sometime. A string of oaths that would delight the Middle Temple, where he normally earns an immodest living, puts up a bunch of mallard two hundred yards away.

Somehow we are in position by first light. Duck begin to take off all around with a wing noise comparable to the opening of a thousand umbrellas. Wigeon pass overhead, alas out of shot, with a growling and whistling so loud that it almost seems to press one into the soft earth of the Wash.

Then the snipe begin to scramble with a *screep* and a *scaape*. I hear geese, a rare enough sound for the Washes, and look up to see eight pinks, just in three-inch range, heading straight for me. My guest, he who wallowed in the mire, fires at a single snipe and the pinkfeet tower and disappear into the clouds. Ah well, so long as someone is enjoying himself.

This dawn the sun never makes it. Light comes as a slow thinning down of the night. It is as though someone is pouring water very slowly into a great bowl of blue ink.

Way off towards the river I can make out thirty or forty white mounds. I walk out towards them, wading through the deepening flood water. When I am only twenty yards away, I realise that my mounds are Bewick's swans. The shepherd had assured me that there had only been two Bewick's on the Washes until yesterday.

The swans must be new arrivals; perhaps they've even come in overnight. Indeed, I am pretty certain this must be the case. They only take off when I get within five yards of them and then they fly lumberingly over my head. The swans are tired after a long migration flight and give me the finest view I am ever likely to enjoy of them.

It is full light now. As I walk back, a single wigeon comes on regardless, high over my head. I fire, unbelieving that it can be so stupid and watch it parachute down on wings stopped in extended beat, stone dead.

Now the sky is full of duck. Pintail, shoveler and pack upon pack of wigeon. In few places in Britain can one hope to see so many fowl.

It does not matter to me that my total is two teal, one wigeon and a snipe and that our guests have done no better. We have seen what the Great Fens must have been like before those darned Dutchmen drained them.

The morning flight dies down by half past nine. Back in the pub for another yard long breakfast we are faced by our genial hostess. 'Whatever happened to you lot last night?' she asks. She is a lady who values her hospitality. 'Why on earth didn't you sleep in the beds I had all nice and aired for you. You went into the wrong room and now you'll all get pneumonia.'

'I doubt if many wildfowlers catch pneumonia in bed,' I tell her. Anyway, who cares? After breakfast, a whole day on the Washes stretches ahead. Even on a still day like this, there will be odd teal and snipe rocketing around until the wigeon come back again at evening flight.

In the Wash

There is a saying among the shepherds who look after the washes that if they see a Land-Rover practically on its side or bogged down to its axles, they know who has turned up.

Last time out last season I crashed through the ice and sat down on my differential in a deep rut. This time I made the mistake of trying the track at the bottom of the river bank in the belief that some kind soul had tipped some gravel into it. He had, but only for the first hundred yards. At the hundred and ten yards mark, I went off the hard stuff and almost sank from sight.

As flight time was only an hour distant, I told my companion that we would abandon ship and worry about salvage on the morrow. This left us with a good three quarter mile slog to our flighting point to that tantalising accompaniment of mallard getting up in large parties, just out of range, as we walked along.

When we reached the gate at the entrance to our drove, it was plain that things still weren't going to be easy. The flood water was knee deep for the first 150 yards. Beyond that the ground fell away quite sharply. The only cover, a couple of five bar gates, stood with their top two bars barely showing.

It was there or nothing. I told my companion that I thought his thigh waders might just keep him dry at the nearer gate, provided he didn't make too much bow wave, but I had no real hopes of things turning out that way. About the farther gate, I had no illusions. I might just as well get the water into my waders now as later. However prepared you are for the first inrush, it is invariably more unpleasant than you thought it was going to be.

Duck on these washes have a healthy distrust of anything that stands upright. Today, in the still air, patrolling parties of mallard, teal and shoveler gave us at least sixty yards of tolerance.

I have never seen so many early season shoveler. Every other party of duck was equipped with the tell-tale schnozzle. I couldn't understand why the entire population appeared to consist of hens until, at last, an over-confident singleton misjudged the range, or forgot the danger of gateposts, and fell with a splash just behind me. As I should have guessed, it was a drake not yet fully changed out of its eclipse plumage.

The flight was an infuriating illustration of why one should never go wildfowling without a dog. After we had each lost a duck in the floods, we were careful to pick only those shots which would fall in wadeable water. On the other hand, what could we have done with our dogs had we brought them with us? We could hardly ask them to tread water for several hours. The water was well over standing-room-only depth for even the rangiest labrador. In the event we were lucky to gather three shoveler and a snipe between us.

Once the flight was over, the lightheartedness with which I had abandoned the Land-Rover began to look like sheer foolhardiness. We had nearly a mile to flounder back along the bank, then a further mile and a half on the road into the village and the pub where we were staying.

We would also face problems on the following morning. My friend had left his car at the pub, so we could take that down to the river bank for the morning flight. But we would still be left with a three quarter mile walk with dawn threatening to come up all the time.

We emptied the water out of our waders, wrung out our socks, put the clammy lot back on again and began to stride out for the village lights in the far distance. We hadn't gone more than a quarter of a mile when two of those lights seemed to detach themselves in some strange fashion and veer towards us.

A few minutes later we were assaulted by a stampede of horses. We had met these earlier, grazing on the river bank. Next came a herd of heifers. It was only then that we realised the unbelievable—those two lights were actually approaching us along the top of the bank. The cattle were being driven before them. The closeness together of those headlights told me that this was a Land-Rover coming though I didn't for a moment think it would be mine.

When it approached, a well-known voice yelled out of the darkness: 'Don't tell me it is so-and-so Colin Willock here again. Every time I find a Land-Rover bogged down, I know who is responsible.'

Josh Scott, the shepherd and warden, had seen our plight and got his brother to tow the wreck out with a tractor. It had, apparently, been a near thing. Even a tractor didn't want to shift the vehicle out of the slough I had put it in. We drove home rejoicing and ordered large restoring whiskies for rescuers and rescued alike.

Next morning, at flight, I took no chances and used the track along the top of the bank. As far as the flight was concerned, the water level defeated us once more, though we shot three more duck, again all shoveler. But the morning was worth recording for an extraordinary mishap.

When we returned to the vehicle I couldn't find my gun case. Nor, it turned out when we arrived back at the pub, could my colleague find his new pair of suede shoes. There could be no question of anyone having stolen them. The vehicle stood in plain view of us throughout flight time, on top of the bank, and no one passes that way.

Then my friend recalled the horses. Both our daughters keep horses and so perhaps we have a deep, built-in distrust of the species. I have never been attacked by them when shooting though I have frequently had my vehicles savaged by cows. Cows seem to have an insane appetite for cellulose and especially for Land-Rover green. That morning the cows had been at least half a mile away down the bank. About the horses we were not so certain.

So we drove back. After a thorough search we discovered both gun-case and shoes distributed over 400 yards of river bank. All three were bitten through with those nasty nipping teeth horses keep up front. When I looked at the Land-Rover I found that they had also had a go at the canvas hood and that only the metal bar supporting the top had prevented them from gnawing their way right through.

Hiding in the Washes

On the Ouse Washes where I shoot, camouflage is the continual problem. It's even worse than on a salt marsh where there is often a creek into which you can lower yourself. Sometimes bends or angles in a salt creek can be improved or adapted to the wildfowler's needs. On our wash—nothing.

On the face of it, it should be an easy problem to solve. One keen duck shooter, who has a section of the wash not far from our piece, thought he had got the problem licked when he sunk some large metal drums into the waterlogged fields.

The washes soon taught him what was what. Halfway through the season, the drums rose out of the fields as surely as if they had taken root and were alive and growing. Then, one by one, they popped out altogether and toppled over, rejected, on their sides, in the position they had assumed when first dragged out there at such pain and cost.

Next he tried staking the newly buried tubs down with strong wire but this snapped like nylon fishing line and the barrels surfaced for the second time. An architect friend of mine is now calculating how much foundation concrete would be needed to anchor such barrels in this morass. Somehow I don't think I shall have the cash or the perseverance to build the kind of Maginot Line which I am sure his calculations will eventually demand.

The trouble on the washes is that there is no natural cover. There are drainage dykes, of course, but they have the disadvantage of being non-tidal. Consequently, they are perpetually filled with three or four feet of very cold water.

True, there are numerous gates and gateposts. On one red-letter day I stood in a gate from midday until dusk, flattening my face against the post until a duck came in range and then straightening up to shoot. That day the duck never tumbled to the fact that wildfowlers make poor gateposts.

At practically all other times I have found that duck are immensely suspicious of anything that stands more or less upright on the washes. They don't wait to see if it is going to go bang, but give it a wide berth when at least a hundred yards distant.

So I am back to the old question of portable hides. They need to be portable because the flight line here, as everywhere else, can swing about quite a bit with a change of wind. I've tried my pigeon hide, but it is not a great success. To begin with, it is too square and bulky and the metal posts stand too high. The brown and green scrim dressing is not the right colour for the washes where winter vegetation is sere and yellow.

This season I am working on a new theory. The basis of this is six yards of one-inch mesh chicken wire through which has been threaded six lengths of curtain rod. I tried using bamboo canes first of all, but these were not man enough for the job. The curtain rods need to be attached to the chicken mesh at three or four points with soft fine-gauge wire to stop them slipping out when you are carrying the whole contraption.

Last time out on the washes I took a sickle and cut armfuls of phragmites reed and sedges. These I am now in process of threading through the holes in the wire to form a light, reed-coloured, see-through screen which will stand about three feet above the level of the marsh when the posts are forced into the ground.

It is important that some of the stiffer reeds break the outline at the top so that the finished hide doesn't assume that sentry-box shape so rightly detested by duck. In theory the whole apparatus will roll up like a prayer mat and will be quite light to carry out in the pre-dawn darkness. In theory!

There remains the question of what to sit on. Both hide and shooter need to be as low as possible. There is nothing worse than kneeling for perhaps six or eight hours on end. I think I have found the answer in a certain kind of oil container about eighteen inches deep and less than a foot wide. I won't say that it makes the most comfortable of seats, but wildfowling, anywhere, is not the most comfortable of sports and anyone who values a dry backside or warm feet more than a brace of wigeon would be well advised to stay at home. Personally, all I'm interested in is being sufficiently comfortable to be able to move quickly enough when the few chances of the day come my way.

Dig Down a Build Up

Sitting the other day in our new palatial hides on the washes, I reflected on comfort, found that I was enjoying the sensation and wondered if I was getting old.

After spending a good deal of thought, and obtaining a great amount of kind and, I've no doubt, informed advice on how to build hides that would resist the worst the washes might do to them, we took the coward's way out.

Most of our advisers were concerned with digging *down*. So at first were we. The trouble when you dig down into the peaty soil of the washes is that the marsh, sooner or later, insists on pushing everything *up* again. It cannot stand foreign bodies such as metal tubes or fifty-gallon wooden barrels. The pressures of the spongey soil soon force them to the surface again.

Many kind friends suggested that we tether our hides by means of chains attached to buried railway sleepers or iron girders but, frankly, the thought of making the kind of excavation necessary to accommodate a railway sleeper, let alone a fifty-gallon barrel, utterly intimidated us.

We had a period when we were leaning towards the use of explosives, but abandoned this for fear of killing our neighbours' cows with a clod of earth straight between the horns at 200 yards' range.

In the end, we decided to build *up*. So, when we saw a dragline working nearby last summer, we persuaded the driver to dump some six foot high mounds of peat in convenient spots.

Just before the season opened, they were still in this very raw state. The earth had settled and looked as solid as the pyramids and about as useful when it came to hiding from duck. Plainly the mounds now had to be hollowed out and lined with timber to make them into spacious and lasting entrenchments.

This proved to be nearly as gruelling a task as digging down into the marsh itself. However, we did have one lucky break. One of our members had managed to obtain a pile of loading pallets, the stoutly built, slatted, two-walled wooden rafts used for lifting loads by crane and storing cargoes. These varied from about four feet square to four by six.

All that had to be done, therefore, was to dig out one side of each pile of earth. Then we burrowed away towards the middle until there was a hole big enough to swallow four of these pallets placed in a box shape.

It sounds easy enough. With two of us at work on a hide, it took all of three hours to complete each one. Once the pallets had been forced into place, all that loose earth had to be banked up again against the exposed sides.

When we had finished earth-shifting, we had four superb emplacements with sloping banks that must surely give maximum cover from duck eyesight. However, the earth still looked surprisingly bare and fresh. So the last phase of all—which also turned out to be the most exhausting—was to cover the slopes with turves.

The dragline had fortunately provided these, since its first bites at the marsh had been directed at tearing the top layer of skin off the place. This skin now lay around in large lumps, thatched with dried-out grasses. It was in fact the ripped-up topsoil complete with vegetation.

It sounds a simple task just to pick up and transport these sods and then to lay them on our earth ramparts.

Most of them had taken root again. A dragline is not a dainty eater. Many of its mouthfuls were anything up to four feet long and weighed, I would guess, around half a hundredweight.

Transporting this stuff took a further hour per hide. But the effect was well worth it. We slumped gratefully into our Maginot Line and sat in these super-hides, enjoying the cool of the evening air—for the operation had taken all day. Although it was still only July, we imagined how it would be to man these gun positions when the sky became black with duck.

The test of any construction work on the washes is time. The tranquil-looking flood meadows are possessed of extraordinary powers. The floods, when they come towards the back end of the year, can demolish most things. If the floods are followed by ice, and the ice pursued by a north wind, the ice floes can bulldoze almost anything flat.

We are pinning our faith mainly on the fact that we are above the level of the marsh. Thus, ejection of our wooden pallets does not seem likely. Floods we can do nothing about. I don't think that ice will greatly trouble our man-made banks. It will ride up or over and will have its work cut out to push all that weight of earth flat.

Several small snags have already cropped up. With the absence of rain, peat shrinks horribly. All those turves we carried have shrivelled like the flesh on a badly taxidermised mummy, revealing in places the wooden bones beneath. Lulls between flights—and so far there have been more lulls than duck—have been spent making good this damage.

What rain we have had so far is inclined to turn the bottom of the hide into a quagmire. This has been got over by building elementary duckboards. But the duckboards have in turn raised the level of the shooter so that, even when sitting on an oil drum or an Effgeeco seat, his head shows above the parapet.

The answer to this problem has been to bring in bundles of Norfolk reed—*phragmites*—and to stick clumps of it down between the two layers of the pallet, tying them in position with binder twine. The pallets are ideally constructed for garnishing.

The reed is successful if used sparsely. Pack it in too tightly and it sticks up like a sore thumb. Its colour is foreign to the surroundings.

The last problem to be solved is one of dog-sit. A straw bale might be ideal. There is certainly room enough in these palatial hides to lay one crossways for the dog to sit, or lie, on out of the wet—even the duckboards become uncomfortably muddy.

Now that we have got things right, all we need is duck in large quantities, but these must inevitably come once we have had enough rain and the washes begin to flood. It will be a real pleasure to shoot from such superb quarters when the great moment arrives.

Yes, for once, comfort is rather agreeable. A few years back I might have argued like the hairy-chested wildfowlers who say that flighting is only any good if you suffer for it. I don't feel like that any more—at least not all the time. But then I did my suffering when we had to shift all those peat mounds and heavy turves. There's no real reason why I should feel either senile or guilty.

Postscript: The hides stood up to winter floods well. After three seasons only one has collapsed.

Saga of a Hut

This is a story of superhuman endeavour, a triumph of all that is great and noble in the human spirit. It is a story of fortitude and selflessness and if you think I'm writing a blurb for an epic film, let me put your mind at rest at once. I am about to recount the saga of how a hut got built on our marshland shoot.

Some time back, someone—I forgot who, although it was possibly me—said how nice it would be if we had a hut in which we could brew up and shelter when the duck weren't flighting and the weather was unkind. I was possibly thinking of the old tarred hut on the marshes in which WAGBI began. Mind you, I had no intention of doing anything about building one myself.

But two members of our marshland group were made of sterner and more determined stuff. One of them had a great deal of spare timber which undoubtedly helped in shaping their joint resolve. He had accumulated the timber along the coast over a long period—as driftwood. This fact, therefore, dictated that the hut must be built on the coast, moreover at a point on the coast at least seventy miles by road from our wash shoot.

Without saying anything to the rest of us, these two gallant gentlemen put aside a whole week of their summer holiday towards the design and erection of our bothy. Put like that, it sounds fairly straightforward, but just wait.

They built the hut in sections, by eye—that is to say there were no plans as such. A door of known dimensions existed; a window likewise. Everything that followed had to be designed to accommodate these two fixed points. Door and window were, as you might say, the grain of sand in the oyster around which this pearl of a hut would accrete. It takes great skill and handiness to build a habitation on these lines, but then I don't suppose the builders of those magnificent Tudor mansions had much more to go on than the length of the key beams.

It took them two days to complete the roof and walls in sections. The timber being astonishingly stout, these sections were more than any two men could move more than a few inches at a time. This may seem irrelevant, since casual manpower is usually obtainable or at least bribable with a few pints. Where they had built, however, there was little manpower available. Because that's where the timber was stacked, they had had to do the hammer and nails work on an isolated sandspit on the wrong side of a harbour channel about half a mile wide.

One of this pair is a man of the sea, conversant with every mood and tide of his part of the coast. To him the problem of transport across half a mile of choppy water presented no difficulty. Cleopatra's Needle was towed all the way from Egypt and that, he argued, might have been expected to sink like a stone.

With the aid of a clapped-out Land-Rover which stands out all winter, like a moorland pony, though without growing a protective coat (unless you count a coating of salt), they towed the hut, using the roof as a sledge, along the sandy beach to a suitable creek.

At high tide, they persuaded most of the hut to enter the water, piling section on section and nailing and roping all together until they had made a sizeable raft. By now the whole caboosh was about as heavy as Cleopatra's monolith! The only difference was that the timber was required to float of its own accord. The Needle, as I recollect, was encased in a buoyant hull of steel.

The landsman stared glumly at the accumulated pile which was even then sinking into the sand as the tide fell. 'It'll never float', was his verdict, just as it would have been my verdict had I given a hand's turn to the enterprise.

'Don't you worry,' the seafaring man told him. 'Tomorrow morning at 5 am, the tide is the highest of the month. She'll float off lovely.'

Exhausted as they were by their efforts, they were down at the beach at half-past four next morning, taking no chances should the tide arrive ahead of schedule. By five, there was water under the raft, but no sign of lift-off. At the very last moment, when the tide was on the turn, the diesel engine of the towing launch just managed to pull this new Kon-Tiki free. Now all they had to do was to get the raft across to the mainland.

At once, another snag arose. At any speed over three knots, the leading edge of the raft acted exactly like a paravane and put it into a shallow dive which threatened to take the whole issue straight to the sandy bottom. This meant battling a strong headwind at around two knots which was virtually the same as standing still, if not actually going astern.

Once it turns, the tide rushes out of this particular harbour like water out of a bath. The hut still had to be tugged up a muddy creek, into the saltings, where a gravel-bottomed hard gave some chance of running a boat trailer under the timber while still afloat. The plan was that the trailer would then be towed ashore by a second Land-Rover.

Because of their slow headway, all seemed lost. There would be no water in the creek. It was then that the seaman came up with the Nelson touch, or, anyway, a touch of the Nelsons. He ordered the landlubber over the side to sit on the stern of the raft so that his weight would lift the bows clear of the waves and eliminate its suicidal urge to dive.

They made their landing while there was still just enough water in the creek. They even got the boat trailer under the contraption. But then the tide began to drop so fast that the wheels of the trailer sank through the shallow gravel crust into the primeval marine ooze beneath. Back at his house half a mile away, the seaman had some kind of vast marine jack which he now raced off to get. I suspect that at this point things had even got him rattled.

While he was away, and while the wheels were sinking deeper and deeper and the hut looked like ending up as driftwood once more, a second professional boatman arrived. This stalwart seized a long balk of timber and, by main force, levered up the tail of the trailer so that the Land-Rover could drag the whole issue on to terra firma at the last available instant.

After that, the story of how they moved the hut by road in a hired furniture van, how the driver gallantly backed this pantechnicon up a forty-five-degree river bank and drove it two miles across country which no furniture van is ever likely to be asked to face again—all this seems almost an anti-climax.

The fact that they faultlessly erected our dreamhouse in the right spot and that it all fitted together and is almost completely waterproof leaves me wordless with admiration. All I can do is to promise to drink the health of these two heroes with every cup of steaming, hot sweet tea that I brew up there.

Night in the Hut

I should be too old to want to play boy scouts. Last weekend I had a wonderful time scouting. I could have stayed in a pub to go wildfowling with two of my partners. Instead I decided to spend the night in the hut we've built on our marshland shoot.

Despite the fact that they both snored, one of them talked in his sleep about wolves coming through the walls, the rain dripped on my safari bed and the door needs a good deal of draught-proofing: despite all this, I had a perfectly wonderful time. It was a perfect antidote to meeting TV and newspaper deadlines and waiting for the telephone to ring.

Oh, one other thing. We forgot the alarm clock, so, since I am the only one of the trio who has any chance of waking up at the desired time, I was deputed to shake the entire outfit. To make sure that I didn't fail in this duty I woke up at 3, 4, 5 and 6 am and eventually called them with a cup of tea, at quarter to seven at which, naturally, they complained bitterly. But this is getting ahead of the narrative.

We decided to let the traffic chase itself out of London with all the mad fury of Friday night rush hour before we ourselves headed for the marsh. It was half past seven before we drove out on the A1 with two station-wagons loaded down with enough impedimenta to wipe out the entire wildfowl population of East Anglia. Or, as one of my companions put it: 'All this to get one duck.'

The late start, plus a hot meal under the belt, paid off. The traffic had thinned and, knowing the standard of boy scout cooking we were likely to have to endure for the next twelve hours, it seemed likely that that one square, digestible meal would prove to be a considerable asset.

On arrival there are two ways of reaching our marsh. Both have their own particularly hairy aspects. You can get there by dinghy, which necessitates a short row across a tidal river. The row itself is nothing. The floundering down, and up, a slithery, glutinous mud slope, angled at about forty-five degrees, ensures that you arrive looking and feeling like a rather badly iced chocolate cake. Naturally, if you are carrying much gear with you, such as dry clothes and sleeping bags, that arrives far from dry and chocolate-iced also.

The alternative is to drive two miles down a boggy track. A Land-Rover copes adequately. It is touch and go whether a saloon car will make it. One of the party, naturally he who had comparatively little gear, elected to go by boat.

My companion and I, laden with hides, food, bedding, guns, cartridges, changes of clothing, waders, wildfowling smocks, waterproof trousers, camouflage nets, sticks to support same, water containers and a good deal of other assorted loose packages, could not frankly face the ordeal of loading and unloading that lot, in the dark, in a downpour, into the dinghy. It seemed less than a fifty per cent chance that we would reach our destination by car, but we decided to have a go.

Had we bogged down, there was not much we could have done about it except sit there until morning flight time came around, or, walk up and get the boat, inevitably find that the tide was flowing the wrong way in the river, wait for it to turn and then ferry the gear up to the hut four hours after our colleague, the boatman, was in bed and asleep.

We had some horrible moments, including a tail slide that nearly took us into the river and a further tail slide that did take us into a gate-post. Mercifully, the boating expert had arrived before us and had got the kettle on. Furthermore, as we drove up, he came rushing out in the rain to order that we switch engine and lights off. There were, he said, thousands of duck about.

In the half moonlight we would see the encouraging gleam of water on our marsh. More encouraging, there was a great deal of splashing, quacking and *wee-ohing* going on. Plainly the place was handsomely occupied by duck drawn to our part of the country by the recent flooding. The hot, sweet tea, reinforced by a heavy slug apiece of Highland malt, made the bare board interior of our hut seem more welcoming than the Ritz.

A state of euphoria experienced only when enjoying the best

moments of outdoor recreation temporarily set in. The ride down the track was forgotten, so were the scars caused on the rear of the car by that side-swiping gate-post. We even agreed to overlook the large mouse that hopped out of the drawer where we store our modest provisions. Tomorrow promised to be a great wildfowling day.

The sheer trauma occasioned by three men and two dogs settling down for the night in a space, roughly eleven feet by nine, is perhaps best forgotten. My dog, of course, is beautifully behaved, except for a tendency to get into a sleeping bag before the owner has entered it. I don't mind this so much when he is dry, but when he has explored the chocolate-coated river bank, master is not at all pleased.

The other miscreant with whom we were condemned to spend the night is a large, young, black labrador called Tosh. Tosh is a trifle restless and since he was ordered to sleep among the pots and pans under the makeshift kitchen table, the first hour of mock sleep was spent to the accompaniment of a badly tuned and under-rehearsed steel band.

No sooner had the canine percussion section fallen silent under the oaths of the human inhabitants, than his master fell into a deep coma and immediately started this sleep-talk about not letting the wolves come through the walls. By the time we had silenced him, the wolves might not have been coming through the walls but the rain most certainly was—on to my bed.

Halfway through the night, between my third and fourth time-check, the weather changed violently. Blessing of blessings, the wind was getting up. It had also turned very cold indeed. The wind was of a keenness and force that immediately showed up the weaknesses in the lapping of our walls. One such crack was apparently next to my left ear'ole.

At half-past six I poked my nose outside the hut to feel the nip of frost. The rain had gone. The tops of the reeds were straightened out like streaming plumes of smoke in the wind.

Duck were calling everywhere. Distantly I heard the call of Bewick's swans. The horrors of the night were forgotten before the prospect of the day. Who would want to stay in a nice warm pub?

I put the kettle on and gave my companions a friendly good morning prod with a wadered foot.

'The wolves aren't yet coming though the walls,' I told them. 'But by the sound of it, the duck damn nearly are. Get up and get cracking.'

The Night I Shot Fish

I don't usually dream about shooting. I leave that to my springer spaniel who relapses into a coma at the end of shooting days and twitches and whimpers, apparently pleasurably, in his sleep, no doubt recalling a particularly clever retrieve by himself or maybe a particularly footling miss by master.

However, just before the opening day of the duck shooting season this year I had the most extraordinary shooting nightmare.

The scene was the actual one on which this event is scheduled to take place—the Ouse washes. But there verisimilitude ended. The washes had suddenly become the coast. We were on an estuary and I was waiting for Ted Eales to pick me up with the big launch at Morston Creek to take me across to Blakeney Point—which is, of course, a Nature Reserve!

When we had crossed the water, in the dark, there were, oh horror of horrors, hundreds of gunners in position before us. In fact, the scene along the bank of the New Bedford River resembled an early print from the American West with men in coonskin caps pouring lead into bullet moulds. A few hundred of them, I noticed, wore modern American duck hunters' camouflaged caps like the one I sport myself.

At last we made our way out on to our marsh only to find several total strangers crouching hopefully in the blackness.

This seemed a bit much, seeing that we actually own the damn place! However—and this doesn't ring true to character either—I recall speaking remarkably nicely to one of the intruders who, equally improbably, spoke most politely back, but made no attempt to move.

At that very moment the sky was darkened by a rush of, presumably, duck. I fired into the mass and was nearly driven into the ground by a heavy fall of, of all things, fish. By then, the pleasantly-spoken poacher was rushing around gathering up my bag. I was a bit put out about this but eventually managed to salvage two nice salmon, a couple of cod and a ling at least four feet long.

I remembered remarking at the time to the intruder, who was loping off into the gloom with the sea-trout which I had particularly wanted, that fish was a very odd thing to shoot.

'Not at all,' he said, 'they often come over at the beginning of the season when the fens are all dried up.' It seemed quite logical at the time. Later in the day. I am ashamed to say, I shot a great-crested grebe and a snow goose which I immediately and guiltily plucked.

When I recounted all this to my wife, she said: 'You know that cucumber sandwiches never agree with you,' and, put like that, I have to admit that she's right.

However dawn on September 1 turns out, it can't be as bad as all that!

In the event, I am happy to say, it didn't turn out like that at all. There were, however, other disasters, though I can see no connection between the more doleful happenings of that flight and the twisted imaginings of my dream.

The worst of these calamities—calamities are seemingly inseparable from any major fowling expedition mounted by my particular circle of friends—concerned not a fish, nor a fowl, but a fine black labrador called Tosh.

Tosh is the property of one of my fowling partners who happens to work in television like myself. Television, being the young and relaxed medium that it is, does not seem to mind dogs about the office. So, on this day, to accelerate our getaway I had brought my springer, Teal, and he, his labrador, Tosh, to share our working day.

At lunchtime we decided that Teal and Tosh needed some exercise and so took them across the road to Hyde Park. There, what more natural than that we should indulge in a little competitive 'hie-losting' in a suitable rhododendron shrubbery to see which was the more skilful at finding and retrieving a large log.

Alas, the shrubbery was cut off from the grass area of the park by one of those hideous iron fences that seem to be constructed of five foot high rusty iron spears. There was a perfectly good safe way round the end of this fence and when we put the dogs into cover this was the way we sent them. However, Tosh, having, I am bound to admit, won the first round of the contest, decided to add a bravura touch by leaping the five foot fence to return the retrieve to proud master.

Unfortunately he was not straight to the fence as we say in the show jumping business. He tried to cut a corner, put in a half pace and four-faulted in a horrifying way, impaling his flank on one of the spears.

When we got him down it was quite clear that he had a nasty wound. Richard at first thought that he had punctured a lung. Luckily there was no sign of this and the dog, although subdued, did not seem in great pain.

I don't know if you have ever tried looking for a vet in an emergency in the heart of Hyde Park in the lunch hour. Actually, it is surprising how many London dog owners there are and how helpful they can be. Within minutes we had a Sheltie and a Dane advising us. With their advice and the help of the yellow pages, Tosh was duly being wheeled into the surgery within half an hour of the accident.

The vet was, I thought, a little gloomy. He talked of exploratory operations, said the wound, though not deep, was in a very unfortunate place as far as infection went and refused to stitch it, simply pumping it full of penicillin. As to the next 24 hours, he advised making Tosh a comfortable bed in the back of the estate car and letting him rest as much as possible.

Tosh seemed quite happy with this temporary measure. The vet had assured us that all that could be done for the moment had been done. Somewhat doubtfully, we set out north. Tosh was quite relaxed in the back of the car, no doubt under the impression that master was taking him duck shooting. Since we only intended to do a morning flight, we would have him back at Richard's own vet for a fuller inspection by the following mid-day.

We were talking hard on the drive up the A1. So it wasn't until Baldock, where we suddenly had the urge for an intake of fish and chips, that we thought to look closely at the silent and uncomplaining Tosh. Then, horror of horrors, he had licked something out of the wound which a first panicky reaction said was intestines but reason immediately said was sub-cutaneous fat. Whatever it was, there was enough of it lying around to be deeply disturbing.

Now conscience hit us both hard. To hell with morning flight and opening day, Tosh was all that mattered. This time a friendly chemist came to the rescue. There was a vet five miles away. We could use the chemist's phone.

At first sight, the vet's car park did not give great grounds for optimism. In a small, rough plot of grass stood a dog-sized headstone in memory of 'Jake, always with us' and 'Joey, sadly missed'. 'By jove,' said Richard, 'what an advertisement. It's like going to your doctor's and seeing some of his not so successful cases planted out on the front lawn.'

The vet however was all that could have been desired. He confirmed the London man's opinion, chided us gently for not noticing what had happened, probed the wound and took one or two foreign bodies out, filled Tosh up with penicillin ointment for the second time and took him into casualty ward for a good night's sleep.

Chastened, late and perhaps deservedly hungry—the fish and chips had been forgotten in the panic engendered by the discovery of Tosh's condition—we drove on towards Ely, where it was too late to get a meal, and finished by putting our decoy pattern out in preparation for the morning slightly after midnight.

The other minor calamity we discovered on arrival at our hut was that the cows had eaten the roofing felt from the outside and torn off the wooden strips that help keep the draught out. Since it was a gratifyingly windy night, it was just as well that we were inside sleeping bags otherwise we might have had to weight the blankets down with bricks. To hear the wind sighing and soughing outside was, however, more than compensation for any chilliness resulting.

We were up at four-thirty and in position by a quarter to five. The first teal passed over flat-out at ten to five. They were, after the fashion of their kind, in a great hurry. They were behaving as one Norfolk member of our wildfowling group has graphically described them. 'Teal,' he once said bitterly, 'whip in, wipe your nose, take your cap off and sit down in front of you.' Nevertheless we were soon, as another great East Anglian wildfowler, 'Kenzie Thorpe, puts it, 'shooting pretty strong'.

It was about the 10th shot that I remembered that the third member of the party, who was leaving London at two in the morning to join us for flight, had *not* joined us. I had dimly registered a pair of headlights wandering about on top of the bank half a mile or so away and feared this might be he—totally lost. I was right. John only found us when half an hour and the most thrilling part of the flight was over.

In fact, it was a memorable opening day flight for teal, with a few mallard, shoveler and snipe thrown in to total over 40 head.

So, if you ever dream of shooting fish what interpretation can you reasonably put on it? Old Moore Willock says this: 1, don't take your dog anywhere near five foot high iron railings. 2, make sure you know how to find your own marsh in the dark. 3, take plenty of cartridges.

Christmas Present

The week after Christmas I took a few days off to give my younger son, Simon, home from school, some wildfowling. During that week we made two expeditions, separated by a return home to celebrate New Year's Eve. Only two days thus intervened between our two excursions but those two days made a dramatic and almost unbelievable difference, as I shall recount. Each day had its own particular highlights and fascinations. Above all, they demonstrated how undependable the sport is and how very much it depends on the weather.

The weather throughout the time was cold, often very cold. The scene of both operations was our own small piece of the Ouse Washes. The Washes are, of course, fresh water. The difference of a few degrees of frost can therefore be crucial.

We had planned to leave on the Sunday evening following

that white Christmas. In the event, the amount of snow discouraged us. We felt that the washes would be frozen stiff and that all the duck would probably have left for the coast.

There were other complications. My son chose to impale himself on a tree while tobogganing on Box Hill in Surrey, a winter sports ground that approaches the Cresta Run as a proving ground for prospective suicides. Simon limped into the sitting room well after dusk on Boxing Day, announcing rather proudly that he had just been discharged from Redhill Hospital. He seemed more disturbed by the fact that the tree had torn a large hole through his brand new waders—a Christmas present—before boring an even larger one in his leg.

Sunday was out. So was Monday. The cold persisted and the walking wounded still wasn't in any condition to walk. On Monday, I drove alone thirty-five miles to shoot some pigeon a farmer friend was troubled about, only to find that the snow had drifted and locked their larder door. The clover on which they had been feeding was now well buried. I shot one and drove sorrowfully home reflecting on the daftness of sons and the fickleness of the weather.

That evening one of the Norfolk partners in our wash shoot phoned to say that he had had an excellent daytime flight when the snow was falling the previous Saturday and that he reckoned that if there was any kind of a let-up we should drop in to a nice shoot.

By now my barrister friend and his young son had returned from a Christmas away from home and demanded to know why we were still at base. They had intended, in the original plan, to follow us up to the washes. Something in my friend's voice suggested that he was delighted to find that we hadn't already set out. Just before Christmas he had issued me with severe warnings about what would happen if we had shot the place up before he and his offspring, name of Angus, arrived.

My son was now limping around, falling down from time to

time and assuring his mother that a bit of fresh air was all that his leg needed. With the pressures building up from all directions, therefore, there seemed little alternative, whatever the weather might do in the next few days, to setting out on the Tuesday.

We left, loaded with the usual unnecessary impedimenta, including a couple of chicken wire and straw 'sandwich' hides, in time to catch the evening flight, if any.

As we drove along the river bank we found that we were in for one of those rare, pleasant surprises the weather occasionally gives a suffering wildfowler. Evidently it had not been quite so hard in these usually bleak and blistering parts. There was open water in the dykes and there were mallard flighting to and from the fen farmlands. Maybe, after all, we had dropped in to something.

When we walked down our wash we were thrilled to find that a partial thaw had set in. There was water over a film of ice on the fields and the dykes were free except for a coating of thin ice at the base of the reed stems. In these conditions duck might flight to look for food that the ice had previously hidden from them.

We humped out our sandwich hides to where we guessed the flight line might be, far over towards the Delph, the lower-lying of Vermuyden's two drainage rivers. Then we went back for Hopalong Cassidy for whom the fresh air didn't seem to have quite the quick-healing benefits he had outlined to his mother.

We told him with some acrimony marring the basic sympathy in our voices that if he couldn't hobble quicker than that we would all have to get up an hour earlier to be in position in time for morning flight next day, or leave him to make his own way.

Correctly enough, he pointed out that if we did this he would probably still be limping pathetically down the wash long after we were in our hides, daylight was up and the flight had started. So, if we didn't want morning flight spoilt by his infirmity, we had better start being a bit sympathetic and agree to help him on his way.

Bickering stopped abruptly at the appearance of a pair of teal which flew low over our heads and departed unshot. All our guns were still in their sleeves. Chastened by this experience, we took it as a warning of what to expect if we didn't (*a*) show a more charitable spirit towards the young, and (*b*) more important, keep our eyes on the ball.

There were no more duck until darkness began to fall. I have often noticed on the washes how flighting goes on until around four in the afternoon. Until then, big masses of wigeon, sometimes four or five hundred strong, pass overhead, usually at a great height; odd, low parties of duck of all kinds may be flying around to give the occasional shot. Then, suddenly, as if a switch has been thrown, the sky goes dead: not a duck moves. The Bewick's swans flight down against the sunset and then nothing, nothing until full darkness.

This is the way it went that first night. There was little moon but enough light reflected off the frost and snow. Small parties of mallard and wigeon began to move as the last daylight fell away. A teal dropped with a splash to Andrew in the Delph. Twice I was caught facing the wrong way by small groups of easy wigeon. At last I shot a high one directly overhead.

The two boys had stuck to their hides, an error of judgment. I reflected that it was our fault for not telling them to move out into the centre of the wash to stand right on the edges of the splashes for which the duck would be making. The duck wouldn't see them there in the bad light. It is when you are standing with your feet in the water that you stand the best chance at evening flight, or so I have found.

We packed up at around seven.

It was bitterly cold again, though, encouragingly, the water did not seem to be freezing round our boots. We had a handful of duck with which to start the bag and our hopes were high for next day—if only it didn't freeze in the night. None of us suspected that a red letter day lay ahead.

It was bitterly cold when we left the pub next morning around quarter past seven. There was no need to hurry. It wouldn't be light until half past eight and the duck seldom start moving until well after half-light. There was nothing in the darkness of the morning to suggest that this would be a super day.

The previous evening there had been a kinder feel about the air, but this morning again the puddles in the village street were iced over and there was little promise of wind. Overhead, the stars were brilliant. It threatened to be a bright, still, though very cold day—all the conditions that would give the worst possible flight on the freshwater of an inland marsh.

The boys were hopeful just the same. When you're their age, you can't afford to believe that it won't work. As we bounced about on the frozen ruts along the bank of the Hundred Foot River they debated seriously whether they had brought enough cartridges. One had seventy-five: the other over a hundred. It seemed a shame to tell them that five apiece might well be too many.

Simon, my own sixteen-year-old, was still partially lame, but was noticeably making better time down the marsh than at yesterday's evening flight. Now he had a crack of dawn behind to spur him along.

The straw-and-net sandwich hides were as we had left them. Often a strong wind will partially dislodge them overnight. Now they stood disconcertingly upright. My finger-tips had gone numb in the short walk down the marsh. It was certainly going to freeze. It couldn't be worse.

Crouched on my oil drum seat, kicking my toes against the frozen grasses, I felt a stirring at my back. The reed heads stuffed into the wire to break up the outline at the top of the hide were fidgeting against my hat. A breeze, if not a full-grown wind.

Suddenly, I found that I could no longer see the remaining stars. It was still very dark and some flecks of snow were drifting past. I heard the first big bunch of wigeon go over high. There still wasn't any encouraging sign to suggest that they would fly any lower than that all day long. Or so I thought. A few seconds later I was having to lean against the wire at my back to hold the hide upright. Snow almost blotted out all vision.

A storm had come from nowhere, and so had the first bunch of teal, come and gone over my head, but only just over my head. Unexpectedly and miraculously we were in business. A volley of 20-bore shots from the two boys' hides told me that they thought so, too.

While the snowstorm lasted it was a morning flight to remember. Mallard, teal, wigeon, the odd shoveler, parties of pintail. They began to move around in a way which I can only describe as snow-crazy.

Out towards the Delph, usually a regular flight line, and a good hundred yards beyond my own hide on the right flank of the two boys, the other senior partner barely got any shooting. The duck wanted the centre of the wash, though there was apparently little open water to draw them on this line.

Under such conditions it wasn't surprising that the junior members didn't score a high ratio of kills. The squall was swinging the birds all over the sky. But I believe the main reason was that they couldn't believe their eyes. They had never dreamed of, let alone seen so many duck at a morning flight.

It was well after nine before we could make out all the familiar details of the marsh. The sky had cleared again and, though there was a strong breeze blowing, the snow and the minor hurricane that had heralded it had died away. Duck still moved though not in anything like the same quantities.

When we packed up for breakfast at around half-past ten, we had over a dozen between us, mostly wigeon but with some mallard and a teal. If that was it for the day, we couldn't complain. The sky was now brilliantly blue. Such water as was still open was acquiring a skimming of crust ice. Once again conditions didn't look too favourable.

We cooked our usual three eggs, seven sausages and five

rashers each, and sat around drinking hot tea in the hut, telling each other why we'd missed, fishing for compliments about the ace shots we'd hoped the others had noticed and generally feeling pretty good about things. Of course, we kept an eye on the marsh all the time. Apart from the occasional high flock of wigeon, nothing seemed to be offering any trade.

We decided that when we returned around noon to sit out the rest of the day, we would regroup our forces. In the morning, the flight line had been so clearly defined that there was plainly little object in spreading our effort. We might as well all try to be under it. This meant pulling in Andrew who had the thin end of the flight perched out alone on the Delph, and since there were only three other hides, doubling up in one of them. Father and son may not be the ideal combination in such circumstances but at least it keeps the recriminations within the family.

Anyway, young Angus had the biggest hide—when making these 'sandwich' constructions it pays to be generous with the wire netting. They can then be expanded if necessary. The spare wire can always be used as an overlap at the entrance when shooting singly.

In fact, there was little need for recriminations. No sooner were we in position than the first snow squall hit us. You could see each one coming miles away, its arrival preceded by a howling gale. And, every time the snow came, the duck moved, though it was hard to see what made them do so. They must have been quite snug and safe where they were. The only explanation I can offer is that the storms made them restless.

The incredible thing was that, though there was barely fifty yards covering all three hides, almost every party beat a flight path to the door of the double hide. Father and son combination missed few chances. Once they had wigeon dead in the air at the same time. The rest of us got what was left, which in itself was no ground for complaint.

By four in the afternoon, the snow had gone through. The flight had stopped. We had picked thirty. It had been a day the two boys would never forget. Nor will their fathers. We didn't wait for evening flight. Enough is enough.

Wash Survey

At the end of what has been for me a fantastic, if modest, duck season—I tend to think of any bag of six duck and upwards as something exceptional—I'd like to record some impressions of the Ouse Washes.

The first is that the juxtaposition of reserves and shooting areas is working well. True, on Saturdays, when the most guns are out, the wigeon naturally tend to head for the Wildfowl Trust sanctuary as the day wears on. But, as I've remarked before, they benefit from the respite and they have to flight out sometime. There are more than enough flying around outside the reserves to satisfy the wildfowling interests.

Second, I have had a number of lessons this season on how much sport along the washes depends on the weather. Friends who have come to shoot with us on calm, foggy or otherwise useless days can be pardoned for thinking that our wash is overshot. One or two have even said so quite openly.

We shoot once a week, most weeks, and this may fairly be judged to be enough, or even too much, by most standards. But I doubt if normal standards apply to the washes. I would submit that the Ouse Washes have always been shot more than might be deemed wise. To a large extent this is due to the patchwork pattern of ownership. A single wash is a long, narrow strip, perhaps 200 or 300 yards wide by half to three quarters of a mile long.

Without owning a large block of washes—which is what the Wildfowl Trust and the RSPB have sensibly and prudently done—it is impossible to guarantee quiet between shoots: another reason for the importance of proper reserves.

Even if you rest your bit, your neighbour is quite likely to shoot his. An RSPB warden to whom I was talking the other day swore that duck shunned any wash, and even those bordering it on either side, for a fortnight after it had been shot.

If he meant a mass descent of a thousand duck, as sometimes happens on a single wash, then I would agree. But our experience is that regular shooting does not prevent frequent parties of duck from dropping in if there is something there, either food or water, that they want. Frequent parties rather than mass descents are, of course, the ideal.

So what kind of weather produces results? Wind is the key, as it is everywhere else. But wind and a clear blue sky is pretty useless. The duck then navigate at an impossible altitude—their unanswerable reply to overshooting. Wind with something nasty in it is the perfect weather. Sleet or snow is best; rain, unpleasant as it is when crouched all day in a hide, is a fair third. One definitely needs the cloud that all these conditions bring.

The first day of a freeze-up can be tolerable. The second and third days are usually profitless unless, miraculously, you have some open water. The first day of a thaw is the time to aim at but a couple of days following the retreat of the ice age can still be something to put in the book.

Over three-day periods we've had nearly conclusive evidence of the part weather plays. During a recent three-day trip with my son in his school holidays, Day One was rough and we shot a lot of duck. Day Two was a butterfly day. We fired five cartridges between us. Day Three was a really wild one, complete with snow and sleet. We had a day to remember, despite the fact that there had been a large two-gun cannonade only one day previously.

To say we only fired five cartridges on that poor day is a slight exaggeration. I daresay we could have let off one or two more if we hadn't decided to pack it in and go to see my friend, Josh Scott, warden of the new Wildfowl Trust Sanctuary. We were as much in luck as birdwatchers as we had been luckless as gunners. Upwards of 25,000 wigeon had decided to use the Sanctuary that day. It was enough to make you spit, though a gladsome sight by any standards.

The interesting thing was how restless the birds were. There was certainly no question of any disturbance, for the Sanctuary is skilfully screened from human activity by earth banks.

Every few minutes, packs of anything up to a thousand wigeon would get up and wheel round like a cloud of starlings, or maybe knot. Then, after a circuit or two, they would settle and contentedly start grazing again.

The Trust has rightly spent a good deal of time and trouble in getting their grasses just right for the wigeon—a lesson for wash shooting owners. All the same, even 500 acres of grass cannot indefinitely supply that number of birds and as the warden pointed out, 'they've got to flight out sometime'.

In fact, they moved well before evening flight time. I suspected their destination was the fen farmland. Several of the duck we shot next day were crammed full of spuds. The paddles of the wigeon were caked with mud from the fen fields. Fairly conclusive evidence.

If the wigeon were exciting, the Bewick's swans were a knockout. Over 130 of them were feeding and quarrelling in family parties in front of the observatory window. Like the Slimbridge Bewicks, they have become quite used to being floodlit at night.

It was sad to learn that a high percentage of swans examined recently were carrying lead shot. One had in it what the warden, Josh Scott called, using an old fen term, a 'whooper ball'. I gather this to be something the size of a single pellet of SSG.

It's fairly safe to suppose that English wildfowlers are now sufficiently educated not to let drive at swans of any kind. The Bewicks must get liberally peppered by several nationalities on their 2,000-odd-mile trip back to their Siberian breeding grounds.

The thing that attracts the swans in such numbers at Welney is a straightforward bribe—wheat. Apparently, whether they stay or not, depends on how easily they find the grain on their first visit. If the tradition builds up as it has done at Slimbridge, then there is no reason why Peter Scott shouldn't find himself soon playing host to two or three hundred Bewicks at Welney. After that, the only limit would seem to be the amount of shallow shoreline suitable for feeding and the quantity of grain put down there.

Key Wetland

A bulletin from the Wildfowl Trust reminds me that it is high time that I wrote about their new reserve at Welney whose opening I attended a few weeks ago. The trouble is that I have been so busy writing about the shooting on the Ouse washes that I have completely failed to cover their equally, in fact, far more important aspect: their role as a wildfowl habitat.

There are those who still deny that shooting and protection can live side by side. There are also a good many who see the arrival of the conservationists as the thin edge of the wedge which will eventually push the shooters out. I most certainly don't belong to either faction. All that I have learned in the higher echelons of the conservers persuades me that there is no such intention on their part.

One very notable aspect of Peter Scott's address at the opening was that he paid tribute to the co-operation of farmers and sportsmen on the washes—farmers and sportsmen in those parts are often one and the same thing.

Enough of politics for the moment. Let's talk about the washes themselves and why they are so vital to wildfowl over a huge area. The total winter population is around 45,000 duck, predominantly wigeon. In 1969, counts made along the twenty-one mile stretch of the washes between Denver and Earith revealed: 36,000 wigeon; 3,700 mallard; 1,725 pochard; 1,300 teal; 1,100 pintail; 938 Bewick's swans; 300 shoveler; 289 tufted; 140 whitefronts; 46 whoopers and many 'various' from coots to mute swans and even a single sheldduck!

The incredible thing is that this gathering represents an enormously high proportion of the total European population. One in eight Bewick's swan winters on the washes. One out of every fifteen wigeon can be found there. The pintail concentration is the highest in Britain, so it's not surprising to find that one out of every twenty-five of these elegant duck picks Norfolk or Cambridgeshire—the washes span the county boundary—for its winter vacation.

How much of a winter vacation is it for wildfowl? There is no doubt that the washes have always been well shot and now might be described even as heavily shot. With the growing popularity of wildfowling, coupled with the extreme mobility of most wildfowlers, there is little doubt that the shooting pressure would have increased considerably, perhaps unbearably. Reserves seemed the obvious, logical and, indeed, essential step.

There are those wildfowlers who complain bitterly that the birds simply go and sit on the reserves, as, in fact, many of them do—and who can blame them? I myself saw, one Saturday last winter, 25,000 duck resting on the 500 acres of the Trust's sanctuary. But, of course, those duck have to fly out sometime. They like to visit the fenland farms all around, and, if the weather is right, they do not always remember to make the trip out of gunshot.

I must add, moreover, that wherever I meet the Director of the Wildfowl Trust he always asks how the flighting is going and what sort of bags we've had. I am certain, knowing him, that he takes the view that both our interests are compatible.

Such liberality is not the exclusive property of the Trust. Only last weekend we entertained in our hut a young warden from the RSPB who collects wildfowl viscera for the research the Society is doing into wildfowl feeding habits and food plants along the washes. We helped him by making our modest bag available for dissection. In return he walked round our wash inspecting the vegetation, suggesting what grasses and rushes we should encourage to attract more wildfowl.

Even if I gave up shooting tomorrow, I should most certainly keep coming to this wonderful place, if only to watch. Indeed, on many fowling days, I spend most of my time watching. Welney duck are no fools and believe in performing the majority of their aerial comings and goings at a considerable height.

We have many reasons for visiting our small piece of washland in the off-season. Sometimes we turn up there to improve our modest property, but more often we come just to look and listen. The characteristic and almost overwhelming sound of spring and summer is that of snipe drumming. There can be few such prolific snipe nesting grounds.

I recently heard a recording made by the Anglia Television Natural History Unit as part of a forthcoming 'Survival' film about the washes (a short version was shown at the Trust's sanctuary opening). When I heard the soundtrack I swore that it had been dubbed on the film from a 'loop'.

A loop in the film business is exactly what it sounds—a continuous loop of magnetic tape on which the same set of sounds is repeated endlessly. I complained that the drumming of snipe on this loop was unrealistically monotonous, only to be told that this was from a continuous tape in making which the recorder had been allowed to run for an hour. The snipe had kept up their drumming at the same intensity, not only during that particular hour, but right throughout the day and even into the early hours of the night.

Garganey, gadwall, teal, shoveler, pochard, tufted and mallard: they all nest on the washes. So do black-headed gulls, little owls, skylarks, meadow pipits, wagtails, sedge and reed warblers, reed buntings and goldfinches. A couple of million sand martins roost in the osier beds. But the summer glories of the Ouse washes are the rarities, birds that have not bred in Britain for a century, until very recently.

Ruffs, black terns and black-tailed godwits have returned to breed, thanks to careful management of habitat. With the formation of reserves, there is every chance that they will do so in ever-increasing numbers.

First Goose

My younger son and I were hopeful as we stepped out of our hut on the washes after one of the wettest nights—inside the hut—of the season.

But now the troubles of the night were past. The rain had stopped. There was duck-talk in the air. It was pitch dark and 6.30 am. A sharp twenty minutes' walk would take us to our hides. With a flicker of wind, we might even enjoy a remarkable flight. We found the hides without trouble. The previous guns had left them for us 'bang on the flight line'. Privately I had doubts about this. Experience on the washes has taught us that what is bang on the flight line one day may well be bang off it the next.

Indeed, even when the duck are flighting freely, as often happens throughout the day in really rough weather, you can sit three abreast, thirty yards apart, well-concealed in hides. One hide will get two thirds of the shooting; the man next to it practically the whole of the remaining third. The third man is lucky if he fires a few shots at duck swinging away from the other two.

In other words, the flight line is often critical to within twenty or even fewer yards. Duck will follow this flight path without much deviation all day long, so long as weather and wind conditions remain constant.

No one can accurately forecast exactly what a slight difference in water levels or wind direction—and possibly twenty more imponderables which one can only guess at—will do to the flight line. The only possible course of action is to wait and see. Then, if you've guessed wrong, don't wait but move your hide right smartly, even if it means missing part of the flight.

Simon and I crouched in our hides to wait and see. It was still as black as pitch at ten to seven. Apart from the whistle and growl of a few wigeon packs passing over remarkably high, there was little sign of duck movement. The quack of mallard revving up their engines in preparation for a dawn take-off was what we had expected and hoped to hear. Instead, silence. This was very depressing. Our predecessors had reported that up to a thousand mallard had travelled this flight path three days previously and there seemed no reason for them suddenly to have departed. To my right I heard the tingling bugle call of a family party of Bewick's swans. If only they were geese. I thought.

But geese are remarkably rare visitors on these washes. Once, eight years ago, about 400 pinks appeared against the sunset and seemed about to land somewhere along the washes. My two companions swore afterwards that the skeins had started to swing in preparation for landing on *our* wash. As they turned high over me I took a deep breath and fired. After all, I had three-inch cartridges and neither of the others had anything more powerful than standard game guns. To this day I claim that those pinks were in shot and that by failing to fire I might have thrown away our solitary chance to bag a goose on the Ouse washes.

There were recriminations afterwards as you might expect. There still are—eight years afterwards. One's friends can be like that!

My thoughts were running on these reminiscent lines when I heard those Bewick's bugling in the duckless, luckless dark of the December morning I am describing. Simon must surely be in no doubt about the wild swan's identity. To be on the safe side I shouted out to him: 'They're Bewicks.' I heard his answering snarl to the effect that he knew a swan when he heard one. The wild swans passed well within shot safely above his hide. As their clamour died away, there was a different sound in the darkness. I could hardly believe my ears. Grey-lags!

Now a different fear seized me. Perhaps the same proper caution that had prevented him getting excited about the swans would now stop him getting excited about the geese. So I shouted again: 'Geese. There are geese coming.'

Almost at once I saw them, very high, surging on directly for his hide. There were four, all talking busily to each other. It was a long shot for a 20-bore loaded with sixes. I saw the outside goose drop out before I heard the shot. It was losing altitude fast in an attitude which usually says that the goose will be dead by the time it reaches the ground. I was practically certain that the goose must have fallen on our own wash, but individual washes are such narrow strips and it could easily have glided on before finally folding up. I sent the spaniel out to join the boy who was already racing through the shallow water, kicking up as much spray as a power boat, to collect his first goose.

At the moment I wanted it for him quite as much as he wanted it for himself. I could imagine how he was feeling, the sick sensation in the stomach that the goose might after all be lost.

Boy and dog were splashing about in the darkness. From the shouts, encouragements and scoldings, it was clear that the spaniel wasn't successful in his quest. A greylag goose, however, takes a lot of hiding on such a level surface as the washes, unless, of course, it has made the river. By now duck flight should have started. Not a pinion stirred the air. The sky was dead. Even if it had been alive with duck they could all have gone unshot at in return for that one first goose.

As soon as it was light enough we both searched. We set off to the farthermost corner of our wash, against the river, in case the goose had come down on the bank. Immediately Simon sighted it. It was down on the neighbouring wash in a splash of water, but too far off for the dog to see it.

This caused a slight dilemma. There was another gun out, not on the neighbouring wash where the goose had landed but on its immediate boundary, just over the dyke, on the wash beyond. He would not enjoy having his hopes of a flight jeopardised by two fowlers cavorting about on territory which was plainly not their own.

To make matters worse it looked as though I would have to fire a shot in the general direction of the goose to awaken my spaniel's mind to the possibilities. But a first goose is a first goose. One has to take a few chances in such a situation though I was well aware how things would look to the neighbouring gun.

We got Simon's goose. Afterwards I walked over, accompanied by goose-laden son, to apologise. At first our neighbour was not amused. He even suggested that we might have been poaching. I believe we persuaded him of the justice of our cause in the end. Apart from a teal and a wigeon that goose was the only success of the day but it certainly made one wildfowler's Christmas holidays.

PART VIII

The Shooter Naturalist

Doing a Selborne

I have never been much of a one for keeping personal diaries. Perhaps this is because I am lucky enough to enjoy something approaching 'total recall', at least about events that interest and intrigue me. About other boring subjects, such as overdrafts, I can invoke total switch-off which means that the receiving set is dead and nothing goes on record at all.

I do keep a shooting log, though this records the barest details. Even looking at an entry a couple of years later, I find that some such note as 'Evening flight. Gravel-pit. Three duck came in late out of windy sunset. Pulled down high drake' is enough to rekindle the whole scene. There is nothing clever about this. It is a useful trick of memory and nothing more.

However, last week while staying in a friend's lodge in Sutherland, a house that has one magnificent room looking directly out over a sea loch towards the Atlantic ocean, I found on the table in that room a large bound volume on whose cover was blocked, in gold lettering, the name of the place and the words 'Nature Log'.

The book had been presented to my friend by a very well-known naturalist who had himself stayed in the lodge for several weeks. A pencilled inscription in the front stated that its pages were open to the pen of any writer who wished to record genuine first-hand observations, no matter how apparently trivial. Later on, the donor suggested, the log might prove an invaluable record of changing species, changing habitat, even changing ecology of the area.

Since many of the people who visit this magic place are

naturalists or sportsmen, or almost invariably both, most of the observations recorded in the log are likely to be accurate and valuable. And since my friend intends by everything in his power to encourage the mammal and bird fauna of this barren and beautiful coast, the changes may indeed be quite striking.

As I read the entries for the two seasons since the log began, I gradually overcame my built-in aversion to diary-filling. This was fascinating and living stuff.

A picture of the wildlife of the area began to emerge, above all the extraordinary contrast between the obvious richness of the sea and the apparent faunal poverty of the land.

In these wild and wonderful parts of the Western Highlands, it is the sea that is the magnet, centre, provider and protector of life. Barely a mile offshore I learned, on the small rocky island that I could see through the window, greylag geese surprisingly nested. The islets beyond the sea loch were crowded in due season with razorbills, guillemots, black and white. Fulmars were almost more common than gulls. Barely a hundred yards away from the house was a tiny rock on which the not-so-common common gulls nested.

The nature log recorded that this summer Risso's dolphin had played round one of the boats in the outer sea loch while the occupants were out picking up the lobster pots which help enliven the family menu during their long summer stay in the lodge.

Compared with the abundance of the sea, the land is apparently barren. It has, after all, comparatively little to sustain life. A good deal of it is rock. The heather is not abundant or rich enough to encourage many grouse, though there are some blackcock and ptarmigan high up the mountain. In these parts, a pair of golden eagles need over 20,000 acres as their hunting territory. The visitor just passing through might be excused for imagining that nothing, save perhaps a hooded crow, lives there. And yet the diary revealed that, for the observant naturalist's eye, there was a great deal to see.

Strange droppings on a wall close to the house had puzzled

one diarist. Now the mystery had been cleared up. The perpetrator was one of the rarest mammals in Britain. This summer, a pine-marten had been seen regularly sunning himself on the wall in the early morning.

Though red deer did not come this close to sea level, roe dwelt in the little wood on the opposite shore of the sea loch. Otters commuted between the lochans, which my friend was devotedly stocking with trout, and the sea loch when the mood took them for a change of diet. Bird life, though certainly not abundant, had already produced 122 species in two seasons for the check list at the back of the book.

I looked up to see two black specks on the far side of the sea loch. Duck? Reaching for the glasses, I found a pair of black-headed divers already in winter plumage. Two mergansers flew past just then and five dots, moving in on the tide, turned out to be a party of mallard.

I reached for the diary to make my first entry. The inscription in the front of the log invited any observation 'no matter how apparently trivial'. With time on my hand and nothing to do except to fish occasionally and watch this beautiful scene, I found that I was dying to burst into diarist's print.

Perhaps in future years it might be of interest to know that black-throated divers called in, wearing winter dress in late September. On such small items was parson Gilbert White's Selborne epic founded. Even though we diarists might not match his illumination of thought or clarity of style, we should do our modest best for the natural history of this part of Sutherland.

As the days passed, I did manage to pick up some interesting trivia. Apparently, at this time of the year, Highland bats hunt in the broad blaze of noon. Against a bright blue sky, I found pipistrelles hawking insects at mid-day all around the house. Not only that but one or two landed on the slates of an outbuilding roof and lay there sunning themselves.

One even permitted me to get a ladder and climb up to photograph him from a foot range. After he had posed, I somewhat fearfully stroked the fur along the little fellow's back. By then he appeared, luckily, to be fast asleep or, anyway, didn't have the willpower to nip my finger, for which I was grateful.

What was the reason for this divergence from customary bat behaviour? Is it perhaps that winter comes quickly and insects disappear faster than down south and consequently northern bats have to work a day shift as well?

Another 'first' for the diary concerned the fishing. My host had asked me to sample a small burn into which he hopes to introduce sea-trout after blasting some waterfalls to assist their passage to a mountain loch. He wanted to know whether any sea-trout tried to run the burn as far as the falls.

I waited for a spate and then collected some humble worms, not an easy thing to do in rocky Sutherland. There were no sea-trout at home, not on that day, but there were some extraordinarily large salmon parr. We had established one thing—that salmon ran the stream without need of aid by dynamite. Another one for the book.

Just before I left, the first songbird migrants were coming through. Parties of mistle thrushes, great tits, wrens and whitethroats would suddenly arrive in front of the window, indulge in wild chases, settle and then abruptly take off to cross the sea loch on their way south. But now my pencil was getting quite blunt.

London Kestrels

Every now and again I take a holiday from shooting in this column and make a few natural history notes instead. The editor, bless him, thinks this is entirely consistent and even makes a nice change. Shooting men and naturalists are often one and the same thing, though only shooting men and naturalists understand how this can happen. The ordinary member of the public simply just doesn't believe it possible.

This time I have even more excuse than usual for wearing my other hat, albeit a city one, for the events I have to report took place slap in the middle of the biggest town on earth.

It happened like this. The very first 'Survival' wildlife documentary Anglia Television transmitted was in 1961. The setting was London. The principal characters were the birds and beasts who make their home there.

The film was a considerable success yet it had its disadvantages. For one thing it was in old-fashioned black and white. Frankly, we cheated a good deal. We used film of, say, a peregrine, a falcon that periodically visits London, but which obviously wasn't shot among the chimney stacks. So we were determined that the modern version should be 100 per cent authentic.

A good deal of field work in early spring, ably helped by members of the London Natural History Society, had us poised to pounce on almost any interesting location or creature that turned up. We not only knew where the nearest toads to Piccadilly Circus spawned (Chelsea), but we discovered a rare middle eastern spider that had colonised the roof of the Natural History Museum.

High on the list of filming priorities was a genuine London kestrel. Kestrels nest regularly in such places as St Paul's Cathedral, the Victoria Tower of the Houses of Parliament and a church spire in Hampstead. But none of these eyries is particularly handy for a film camera or cameraman, no matter how intrepid the latter may be.

We were getting a little desperate about the kestrel when we got the tip-off. If we would contact a young lady who lived on the sixteenth floor of a block of flats off the Old Kent Road, we might hear something to our advantage.

We phoned and were invited round. The view was magnificent anyway, but it was made spectacularly splendid by virtue of the fact that you could actually look down on the soaring kestrels and face them eye-to-eye as they stood up against the wind to make a touch-down on the lady's window-sill.

Only one other place do I know where you can thus enjoy an overhead view of soaring birds of prey. This is the cliff above Jerez de la Frontera in southern Spain. From that eminence you look down on griffon vultures and lesser kestrels galore.

There were no vultures along the Old Kent Road—at least not at sixteenth floor level—though I read lately that as recently as a hundred years ago marsh harriers soared over the unreclaimed reed beds there. These sixteenth floor kestrels must certainly have provided the finest wildlife sight since the harriers vanished.

The young lady, a West End secretary without special wildlife knowledge, pointed to a window-box, barely four feet away from her own main window. There, at the far corner, in a shallow scrape, lay four beautifully marked falcon's eggs.

The big question was: would the birds sit or would they desert? On the plus side, they had chosen their unusual eyrie well. The window box was uncultivated and dotted with small pebbles. It closely resembled the sort of nesting ledge they would have looked for in the wild.

As to an unscalable cliff-face, they had a beauty. They'd nested in a corner that gave morning sun, protection from prevailing wind as well as shade in the heat of mid-day and early afternoon.

Against their successful rearing was the fact that they were only divided by a pane of glass and several feet of air from the nearest humans. Humans, what was more, who had a TV set winking away in the not-to-distant background. Supposing the kestrels did not care for westerns, or, worse still, for wildlife programmes!

The actual owners of the flat on whose ledge the birds had settled down were unknown to our kind secretary friend, who gladly handed over the key to her own flat for filming purposes. The next door people were, she said, in the manner of London flat dwellers, just 'neighbours'. Supposing the neighbours did not realise the rarity value of the guests who sat on their window-box?

But as time went by it became only too clear that these good people did. They kept their telly turned down and their window shut, even though heat waves came and went several times during the incubation period.

On the twenty-eighth day, the first egg chipped and soon there were four perfectly healthy young falcons yelling for grub which the parents unfailingly caught for them in the squares and parks below. Both birds hunted and both parents shared the chores throughout the whole rearing process. The little tiercel was a model father and took over from his larger wife without even a single squeak of protest.

We never actually found out where the adults did their hunting. But it was a fine sight to see them high-dive off that window-sill and peel off in the wind, slanting away like fighter bombers going into the attack. Wherever they actually went,

they were seldom away long. As might be expected, their main quarry in London was sparrows, which they presumably caught on the ground, with an occasional sprinkling of house mice.

At the outset, we had hardly dared hope our kestrels would stay to incubate, and, if they did, that the eggs would hatch. Beyond that we never really believed that all four chicks would reach the flying and self-supporting stage.

They have all left the window-box now and have become fully fledged London kestrels. The day they left, the unknown neighbours raised their window and turned the telly up loud again.

Thumping and Booming

In our business of making the 'Survival' natural history series for television, we have recently been set a fascinating bird problem. On the East African grasslands—in this case the Serengeti—lives a spectacular bird called the Kori bustard. He's a relative of those which once inhabited Salisbury Plain and now, once again, hope to do so, except that the Kori bustard is far more impressive.

He comes into the category known as 'huge'. He looks even more immense when he indulges in his mating display, for he puffs up his neck feathers like bittern, only more so, until they resemble something between a football and a powder puff. He also goes down on his 'knees', or rather 'ankle' joints, when wooing the female who squats unimpressed on the ground.

But the most fascinating thing is the noise he makes. This, too, is not unbitternlike. It is more of a muffled thump on a bass drum than an outright boom and it is very loud indeed. In attempts to get sound recordings of this thump, I have contacted three first-class naturalist recorders of great experience, all armed with the most sophisticated equipment.

Though each one has heard the thump at an almost deafening level, the recorder has almost totally failed to pick anything up.

This is rather disturbing. It is exactly like taking a picture of a friend and finding when you develop it that there is nothing on the negative except the place at which he posed. Supernatural to say the least, or maybe just supersonic, or do I mean ultra? Whatever the explanation, it poses a pretty problem both from the ornithological and acoustical points of view. Theoretically, what the human ear can hear, the microphone can also hear and the tape recorder, too.

Perhaps few of my readers are actually likely to hear a Kori bustard in mid-thump or non-thump as the case may be. Many may already have heard, or will hear, one of the most exciting sounds of the British outdoors, the boom of the aforementioned bittern. Now here is another acoustic mystery. Fortunately this one has recently been solved by that well-known naturalist and conservationist Aubrey Buxton.

Aubrey Buxton is a Norfolk man who spent much of his boyhood mucking about on salt marshes and bird-watching in reed beds. Besides being one of the best wildfowl shots it has been my privilege to see in action, he is also a great authority on water birds in particular and waders perhaps most of all. Since boyhood, one of the ornithological questions that has intrigued him most is: how does a bittern make its boom and what does it do to produce it?

Until a couple of years ago, quite frankly, no one really knew, although not a few, including some most distinguished bird artists, were willing to hazard a guess and pass it off as gospel. These experts depicted the bittern standing bolt upright, much as it does when pretending to be a bed of reeds, in order to utter its shattering sound.

The boom *is* quite a shattering sound. It carries across the flat surface of the great reed beds of the Broads for at least a mile. The trouble about the bird's natural reed bed habitat, and indeed the bird's natural habits, is that the former are dense, and the latter extremely furtive. The chances of seeing a boomer at close quarters are, therefore, slim.

At his home at Stansted in Essex, Aubrey Buxton has built up the most beautiful and remarkable bird collection. The collection, as you would expect, is largely a waterfowl one which must come fairly close to Slimbridge in extent and variety. The reserve also has its exotic highlights—rheas, those strange South American 'ostriches'; Sarus cranes, which fly honking about the grounds and actually rear young from time to time in unlikely Essex. Ne-nes, Hawaiian geese, breed, so do red-breasted geese. African fish eagles call with that spine-tingling half-whistle, half-shriek that is pure nostalgia to anyone who has travelled in the wilder parts of Africa.

Eight winters ago, in that minor ice-age we endured in 1963, some kind soul brought in a bittern that had had a road accident. The main injury seemed to be that the lower mandible had been displaced to give the bird a cross-billed appearance. Aubrey was thrilled and immediately built the injured bittern its own private marsh and instructed Jack Bunting, his brilliantly adaptable bird-keeper, to try it on live eels and then, later, to wean it on to fishmonger's sprats.

Not long after this, a second starving bittern was brought in for succour. Aubrey now realised he had the ideal situation for a boom of bitterns. But would the blighters do it, even in this ideal state of captivity? Were they even a booming pair, for, presumably, to boom there had to be a he and a she present, and it takes a bittern to tell.

The bitterns settled down. Nothing happened the first spring. Then, suddenly, a couple of years later, the reserve shook to a boom. It was broken-beak that was booming, but, alas, as if he had guessed the world was waiting to know, he remained remarkably modest about it, preferring always to boom in a thick clump of grass.

But, at last, one spring morning, he slipped up and there he was booming in full view. The performance was a revelation. Far from standing upright, Broken-Beak held his body parallel to the ground. He began to nod his head and fluff out his neck feathers. Then—and this is the only phrase that aptly describes the operation—he appeared to pump himself up, drawing in great gulps of air in order to release it in what should have been an ear-splitting detonation.

When he finally boomed, the whole body shook as if in recoil. But here was the next surprising thing. Though the boom can, as I have said, be heard in the wild for every bit of a mile, close up, within a matter of feet of the bird, the sound was almost non-existent.

So, I am forced to wonder: do booming birds have something acoustically in common that enables the sound they make to be heard at a distance while being practically inaudible at close range?

Of course, there are still mysteries to be cleared up about booming bitterns without even starting on bustards. For example, *why* does a bittern boom? The obvious guess is that it is either a territorial warning or a come-on to a female.

The late James Fisher thought that bitterns probably boomed whenever another bittern, of either sex, passed close by. Finally, there remains the explanation of the vocal mechanics that can produce such a sound. Is there, for instance, some kind of resonance chamber?

I have a sad and rather touching footnote to my story. Last winter, Broken-Beak died, apparently of a stroke. He had been at Stansted for eight years and, of course, no one knew his age on arrival. Aubrey Buxton realised he had a marvellous chance to get the bittern sexed and even to have his vocal 'chords' examined at a post-mortem. But by then Broken Beak had become part of the family and he simply hadn't the heart.

Eating Habits

Are there colours in nature which tell predators to keep off? Take the yellow and black of the wasp or cinnabar caterpillar. I have always understood this colour code meant: 'Don't touch me, I'm either dangerous or taste nasty.' Some African butterflies which birds definitely find unpalatable are faithfully imitated in colouring and wing pattern by others that are said to be delicious. Nature is endlessly ingenious in the devices it thinks up for keeping its citizens alive.

I wrote recently that no less an authority than Peter Scott had suggested to me that black and white, and even black on its own, was intended by the wearer as a gentle hint to predators that he might not eat very well. Peter made this suggestion with particular reference to the oyster-catcher.

If there is one thing that rivals the endless variety to be found in the natural world, it is the diversity of opinion to be encountered in the naturalists who study it. Indeed, wouldn't a lot of fun go out of natural history if all, or even part, of the answers were definitely known?

In the matter of sea pies, or if you prefer it oyster-catchers, Sir John Craster, that well-known shooting man naturalist from Northumberland, takes issue on the inedibility of the species. He tells me:

'In my young wildfowling days (when oyster-catchers were not protected) I ate scores of these birds, some on Fenham and Waren Slakes, and others coming—with curlews—to roost on two small rocky islands called the Emblestones, a few miles north of Craster. In my view, the flavour of oyster-catchers is rather like that of mallard and young curlew mixed and the birds are usually very plump.

'I think that in those far-off days I shot just about every wader that flew and they were all good, although of the smaller species one certainly required a large number to make a good "sea-pie". I defy anybody but a real expert gourmet to tell a redshank from a snipe.'

Sir John is one up on me in that I have never eaten oystercatcher. I would take issue with him slightly on the redshank-snipe score. I don't shoot 'shank any more, though I hasten to add that I have no prejudice against anyone who does so. In the past, I have eaten a good many of them but I would never rank them with snipe. Snipe have that gloriously juicy, sweet flavour, whereas I have always thought of redshank as highly edible but made of rather darker and stronger meat.

I've eaten my share of curlew and found them very good indeed, especially in the early part of the season. I once knew an ancient wildfowler on the north Norfolk coast who specialised in curlew stew made in an iron pot. Guests who were invited to share his speciality usually noted with alarm that the top layer of this savoury mixture was coated with something that looked remarkably like feathers. This, indeed, turned out to be the truth.

The ancient man invariably cooked his curlew without plucking them. One visiting wildfowler of rather refined tastes was visibly set back by this feather sauce. It was, he saw, rather like being invited to dinner by a sheik and being offered a partly cooked sheep's eyeball as the principal delicacy.

The visitor would like to have declined, but his host was more terrible to offend than any sheik. 'Don't you worry about that,' said the old man, 'before we start on it, I always skim that lot off with a stick of firewood' and proceeded to do so.

Shortly after dawn one Sunday I was sitting with Land-Rover and horse-trailer, horse and jockey, waiting to rendezvous with friends *en route* to yet another of these jumping tourneys I keep complaining about. We were parked in the yard of a country pub in Surrey.

The Saturday night visitors had left the usual courtesy card of litter which the British drinking public—or any other part of our public—seems to find indispensable to its enjoyment of the countryside. The litter consisted mainly of potato crisp bags.

I was woken out of my early morning trance by the sound of a crisp bag being heartily shaken. Normally I should associate this sound with my daughter, but even she doesn't eat potato crisps shortly after daylight on a summer's morning.

I looked around to see what was causing the noise and discovered a cock blackbird. He'd picked up a bag in his beak and was giving it a thorough shaking. He seemed dissatisfied with the results and quickly moved on to the next bag, about a yard away.

This one evidently produced something. After a couple of violent shakes he nipped around picking up invisible scraps of, presumably, crisps from the car park tarmac.

He then made a complete circuit of the area, shaking in the process up to twenty different bags. He bothered with no other item of litter and, believe me, there was a fair amount to choose from. Once he found it necessary to have a few sharp chirps with a couple of sparrows who were hanging around one bag but despite their reputation for smartness, were not bright enough or big enough to give the bags a shake.

That bird had learned the trick for himself. No doubt he lived locally and gave the pub yard a good going-over most mornings. One tends to think that it takes birds a very long time to learn these strange feeding habits. But then tits learned to open milk bottle tops in a few short years. By the same token Egyptian vultures may only just have discovered that it is profitable to throw stones at ostrich eggs. One thing is perfectly certain, here was one early bird who was getting more than the worm. He'd got his chips.

One-upmanship

Loch Tay was, to me, a revelation. One expects all of the Highlands to be lovely but Lochtayside seems to have a particularly happy blend of softness and severity. I'd never been there before my trip of a week or two ago though I know the Highlands farther north as well as only a man who has been made to walk through two of the finest passes in the Cairngorms can do.

Remind me to tell you some time how the editor of *Shooting Times & Country Magazine* once conned me into walking through the Larig Grhu and Glen Tilt (forty-four miles) in one solid stint, starting at night and walking most of the way on what he promised would be 'a midsummer's night as light as day'. In fact, it was as black as the Devil's Point, an appropriately named mountain round which to blunder in Stygian darkness. (See Introduction to this book by Philip Brown.)

Tay is a steepsided loch, sixteen miles long with a mountain, Ben Lawers, which just fails to make the 4,000 foot mark, overlooking it. Tay is friendly, though not to sailing men which is perhaps a blessing since it never gets the brunt of the holiday traffic and probably never will do. There are few places at which to approach the water's edge except at Killin at the head and Kenmore, where the Tay itself begins, at the opposite or eastern end.

My friend had done that rare and difficult thing in Scotland, bought the freehold on a solid stone, two-up, two-down farmhouse. He'd taken four years, using largely family labour, to tidy up and convert, burn the rubble of centuries, plant trees and shrubs as a wind break and to encourage birds, and now he was ready to sit back and enjoy the view. And I was only too ready to help him.

He'd begun a check-list of birds and already had thirty-nine species on it from the previous summer. We set the target for twelve new ones during my week's stay.

The house is the sort of place in which one is quite content to sit behind two huge picture windows with a pair of binoculars within easy reach. It is a rather boring *cliché* to say that you need never be bored with such a view constantly available. In a place like this it happens to be true. There is perpetually some movement on the far hill, some bird that might be a buzzard swinging over a crest far down the loch, some glint on the water far out that suggests wildfowl are resting there.

In the event, we got our twelve new species. Some were simply confirmations of the obvious. There had been thousands of geese around the Loch all winter but to my friend they were simply 'grey geese'. The betting was that they were greylags but now it was April and it seemed likely that the evidence would long ago have flown north.

On the second morning, however, we spotted twenty birds wavering along high over the mountain. After a while they began to whiffle down. A breathless car chase over five miles of twisting roads brought us to the approximate spot at which they must have pitched. Close to a stone wall, five hundred yards from the road, 200 geese were feeding in a field of spring wheat. Greylags without a doubt. But why so late in flying to Russia? My betting is that these were not mere laggards, but birds who hadn't yet reached breeding pitch and hadn't felt the imperative urge to pair up and depart.

So one more for the list. Others were easily got without moving out of the house. A pair of yellowhammers and a cock reed bunting that came to feed with about 200 chaffinches—mostly males—on a field of newly drilled oats at the end of the garden. A coal tit made the score four and a common sandpiper tittuping for insects on the stony edge of the loch, 200 feet below, became the fifth.

Seven to go. The loch itself does not seem much more friendly to waterfowl than it is to dinghy sailors. There is little sheltered shoreline and few weed beds or reeds. However, there is a good deal of limestone around and this usually favours the production of molluscs, crustacea and other water life which keeps both fish and water birds happy.

We took the dinghy out ostensibly to fly-fish for trout, though we knew it was far too early in the season and the water too cold. Birdwise it was rewarding. Four goosanders got on the wing as we drifted along under the trees, followed by a female merganser. Nine.

Plenty of mallard, already clocked in, but not much else, then suddenly a flash of four pale underwings and a spring of teal twisting out against the mountains. Only two more needed to reach the target.

We got one on Ben Lawers in textbook fashion. My friend, whose bird knowledge is sharpening daily, had just said as we passed a small rocky burn at around the two thousand foot level: 'Just the place for a ring ouzel.' I think he said it to impress his wife who is still at the small-brown-bird stage. Anyway, there it was standing on a rock, a mountain blackbird and a very worthy number eleven.

Farther along the lochside towards Kenmore is a fine mountain called Drummond Hill. It is heavily forested and it has a special place in Scottish ornithology, a place that is commemorated by a splendid effigy that stands atop the schoolhouse in Kenmore itself.

A bronze caper, better than life-size, throws back his head at the mountains in defiant and raucous display. As well he might, for it was here, on Drummond Hill, that Lord Breadalbane's keepers turned down the colonists from Sweden who were to repopulate the Highlands with turpentine-tasting grouse as big as turkeys. From Drummond Hill, the caper spread out to make its famous Scottish come-back.

We climbed among the conifers hoping to see the genuine article posed in a pine-top, telling the brazen image in Kenmore that, as far as capercallie's went, it was a hollow mockery.

We failed to find our caper. Probably we weren't up and about on the hill early enough, but we did get our twelfth new species for the list up there. With a whirr, a fine blackcock went soaring down the treeline, lyre tail set and red topnotch glowing.

My friend's list is now over the fifty mark. No doubt it will climb much higher yet, especially when summer gets into its stride. Species-spotting around one's home is relaxing entertainment. It introduces just that touch of competitiveness and one-upmanship so essential to some temperaments, including my own.

It is also a very easy way to get the uninitiated interested in birds, an interest which often extends to mammals and the natural history of the region in general. I am always amazed how quickly the new recruits catch on. My own wife, who can hardly be called a new recruit, is a case in point. At home I doubt whether she would notice if a Uganda crowned crane flew through the garden. On safari she is often the first to spot what we are looking for.

Footnote for my wife's benefit. Not long ago she said to me: 'You will never guess what I saw flying over the garden today—a Uganda crowned crane.' I won't even hint at my reply. Pay-off line. Three days later, the local paper headlined: 'Crested Crane Escapes. Seen at large in Surrey.' That's all and thank you.

PART IX

Various

Hitting Things

This question of how you hit things with a shotgun has always greatly intrigued me. I suppose that it's only right that it should, since it is pretty basic to the whole business. So, when Town Gun went for a refresher lesson at the West London Shooting Ground recently, he was greatly relieved to hear no less a deity than that remarkable teacher Percy Stanbury advising him to 'give it a bit more lead'.

Now I have always supposed that the really superb performers were not aware of such vulgar ideas as 'lead'. That the fine shot simply hit the bird out of the sky as if taking a half-volley, or maybe an overhead smash, at tennis.

You, no doubt, have had the experience of asking some god-like game-shot how much ahead he was of the almost stratospheric pheasant he has just brought down like a spent rocket stick. What's more, he killed it with what seemed not much more than a casual flick of the gun.

If you've asked this question, you have probably got the same sort of reply that I have. This is either a polite but blank stare. Or, if the great man speaks at all, he says with a puzzled frown: '*Lead?* What do you mean, lead? I just pulled when the gun passed his beak' or, more puzzling still; 'I just shot straight at it.'

The trouble is that he probably did, or, rather, thinks that he did. If so, he is in that rare class of shot which I privately call a 'swinger'. A swinger is doing something pretty close to playing a ball game. His timing is not dissimilar to that of a superb tennis player volleying.

What this character does is to pick up the line of flight of the bird, just like any normal mortal must do, then he swings his gun along it at an instinctive speed, probably accelerating as he reaches the tail and sweeps out towards the beak. The moment of impact for him is when the gun (which he probably isn't aware of holding, anyway) clears the beak. This, if you like, is the tennis racket hitting a smash volley.

He pulls the trigger and thus retains the impression that he has shot *at* the bird. So in a sense he has, but even performers of this calibre have a certain amount of built-in timelag in the brain. So, by the time the brain has said 'pull the trigger' and the messages have flown down the various cables that convey such impulses, quite a lot has happened.

In particular, the swing has taken the gun well ahead of the bird. Thus by the time the cartridge has actually gone off, the gun has moved through an angle that will put the shot where it is most needed.

One other refinement: the best of such paragons actually fire (or so the books tell us) at the precise moment at which the butt beds into the shoulder. None of this mount-the-gun-and-then-have-a-crack-at-the-bird kind of nonsense. The whole process is nearly as fluent as a cat reaching out to catch a mouse.

On my very good days, this is occasionally me—or so I like to imagine. It's especially me, and, I suspect *you*, when we don't have time to think. It's us when the snipe gets up and zig-zags away or the mallard flicks out of the night sky and is seen just for an eye-blink. Then, we average shooters simply fire and down it comes to our utter amazement. For a brief, triumphant moment we're really swinging.

However, having said that, I have to admit that, most of the time, this *isn't* me. Maybe it isn't you, either. If I hit that very high pheasant, I am definitely aware that my gun, or at least my 'pointing sense', was ahead of it. I'm achieving the same result as the crack shot, maybe, but by a very different and much less instinctive and more laborious process. The Americans have a good term for it: they call it 'pointing out'. We call it simply 'giving it some lead'.

It goes without saying that certain of the requirements of both the swingers and the pointers-out are the same. We must both estimate the line of flight correctly and sweep the gun through it. We must both keep swinging the gun until well after the moment of firing. The difference is that those who 'see a length of daylight' between gun and bird have to achieve this situation with a bit of a muscular and optical struggle, whereas the First Eleven Man doesn't have to think about it at all.

Those who give lead have somehow got their gun ahead of the bird by an estimated amount, dependent on its flight speed and angle of approach, or departure. Then they've kept it there, and still moving, while they pull the trigger.

When I am conscious of doing this, which is at least seventy per cent of the time, I am also conscious of a sense of inadequacy. I feel that I have not done things as the real top-notchers do it. It was therefore a great relief to hear such an expert as Percy Stanbury admit, without the least sense of shame, that he was aware of giving lead. I shall never mind confessing in future that I was about a field-and-a-half ahead of that very high, gliding, downwind cock which I killed in such a grand-standing manner on the bottom ride of our shoot.

But this question of a field-and-half, or five-foot-six, or 'about two birds' length', or whatever is the fancied length of sky we measure off for any given shot, brings us right back to square one.

As everyone who uses a shotgun knows, what one man sees as about the length of a five-barred gate another gun declares to be about 'six inches from his beak'. In other words, the whole question of lead is highly subjective and may even vary with an individual shooter according to the state of his eyesight and reflexes on any day you care to name.

Speed of swing for the swinger, amount of lead for the pointer-out, they both add up to the same thing. The question

is, and everyone has been arguing this from Charles Lancaster onwards, how do you gauge and apply lead or speed?

What is a certainty is that you cannot apply them on any mathematical basis. Poor old Lancaster's theories of forward allowance have long since been tipped on to the empty cartridge heap. What does as a substitute for calculation then?

The only possible answer is experience. For any shot that you may find yourself called upon to take, your gun is guided by a kind of computer. Maybe the human brain is a poor sort of computer, but then it's the only one you've got.

Your eyes feed it information. If you like, they programme it. They give it angle of approach, approximate speed, not, surely, in miles per hour, but merely as a slow bird, medium bird, or sizzler. They also convey, as late as possible, any last minute characteristics of the target's flight; jinking left; tail coverts slewed over for right-hand turn. All this can only be based on observation of a thousand other targets, on other days, at other times.

This is the stuff from which the human computer has to produce speed of swing or amount of 'lead'.

Then what's the snag? If you can knock 'em down one day, surely, with your kind of experience, you should be able to do it the next? Unfortunately, programming the human computer doesn't end there. There's a lot of other data that gets fed in as well.

Did your wife speak crossly to you before leaving home this morning? Did your accountant mean it when he said that you really must settle with the Inland Revenue by the end of the month? Your host is at the next stand. He's put you in a hot spot. If you miss them, will you ever be asked again? If only we could programme that sort of data *out*.

A Matter of Footwork

In a London evening paper the other day I saw a picture of champion golfer Tony Jacklin holding a shotgun in what seemed a distinctly businesslike fashion. He was, the caption said, enjoying a couple of days' grouse shooting as a relief from golfing stresses.

The picture set me thinking about what has always been a pet theory of mine, namely that shooting with a shotgun has a good deal in common with most ball games.

In ball games, the placing of the feet is all-essential. The same goes for shooting, although I know that wildfowlers will quite justifiably tell me that there isn't much chance to place your 'plates' correctly when stuck in the bottom of an oozy gutter. Pigeon shooters will no doubt point out that, when in a hide, they shoot most of their birds sitting—I mean that *they* are sitting, not the birds, though some of us shoot them sitting as well.

Nevertheless, the fact remains that circumstances in each of these cases, in other words the paramount need to remain hidden, deny the use of the feet. But I'm sure that all classes of shooter would much rather stand up to fire—and what's more stand up with their feet planted comfortably, which means in the position most likely to produce accuracy.

If you don't believe the importance of the feet, then, tell me, have you never sorted out a comfortable standpoint when waiting for pheasants? When passing those anxious last few moments at your peg out on the plough, the moments when you hear the first sounds of the approaching beaters in the covert ahead of you, surely you've found yourself stamping down a nice level gun platform from which to be able to swing at your most free and easy.

If you have, then you may even agree that the action is rather like that of a batsman taking his stance at the crease or a golfer addressing the ball on the fairway. The answer in all cases is that what happens to the top half of your body when that split-second comes to swing at ball or bird depends on how well and truly planted are your pedal extremities.

I shall always remember having a lesson on walked-up birds. The coach made me put out my left leg in the direction of the rising clay as I mounted my gun, exactly as a batsman would do when putting his weight into a drive. That leg movement gives you a wonderful feeling of reaching out to hit the thing for six which is, after all, the object of both exercises.

The ball game comparison became firmly established in my mind when, some years ago, I worked with Jack Hargreaves, and I cooked up the idea of taking a skilled games player, who had never fired a shotgun in his life, to the West London Shooting Grounds to see how he made out.

The games player was Patrick Campbell, the distinguished Irish humorous writer and, more recently, TV personality. Paddy also happened to be a scratch golfer. To tell the truth, he had always made rather light of our outdoor activities. Jack Hargreaves, of course, is an excellent shot and a first-class fisherman.

So we handed him over to Percy Stanbury, more or less as an act of revenge, but also because we wanted to get a magazine picture feature out of the result.

There was little doubt whose faces were red at the end of the lesson. Paddy powdered clays as if he was smacking tee-shots two-fifty yards down the centre of the first fairway at St Andrew's. It was a performance, which even allowing for the miraculously soothing effect of Percy Stanbury's coaching, would have been a credit to a veteran.

When we asked Paddy Campbell how he had managed to hit so many, he said: 'Once I got the feel of the "club" in my hands and *found out where to put my feet*, it was easier than hitting a good crisp No 3 iron.'

I wonder what Tony Jacklin would say to that? I imagine he would agree. And since his gun in the picture I referred to was an over-and-under with a raised rib, I wonder whether the champion golfer isn't a clay bird shot into the bargain.

I only hope no stuffy traditionalist turned up his nose at Mr Jacklin's workmanlike weapon when it appeared in a grouse butt. You never know these days when everyone seems ready to tell everyone else what weapons they should be using for what occasion.

A Deadly Disease

Every now and again I suffer from attacks of gun-itis. The symptoms are a tendency to reach for the cheque book whenever a tempting fowling piece is offered at what seems to be a knock-down price. I have had to speak very sternly to myself twice recently, telling myself that I really can't afford any more guns, but knowing full well that guns are probably as good an investment as you can make—provided you can force yourself to sell them again at the right moment.

I watch with envy friends who are still suffering from the complaint at its most virulent stage. One such, a sportsman whom I helped introduce to shooting some twelve years ago, is in the throes at this moment. In the past few months I have watched him buy: two monster muzzle-loading punt-guns which he hangs on the wall, though the way things are going he will almost certainly buy a punt to go with them; a single-barrelled muzzle-loader and a very nice double 10-bore with a cracked stock.

He got the latter for £12 and was quite prepared to have a patching job done on the stock—he even spoke of copper wire. However, when he showed it to his gunsmith, the latter said that it was such a lovely weapon that it would be a shame not to restock it. The result is that he is now finding another £40 to make his purchase even lovelier.

With all this I have the deepest sympathy. The truth is that I have begun to feel the itch again myself. What has exposed me to gun-itis once more is the fact that I have rediscovered a use for my magnum. I bought this gun—a Greener—more years ago than I care to think. I bought it in the belief that it would pull down impossibly high duck for me and that I was fit enough and quick enough not to feel handicapped by its seven pounds of metal and wood when shooting pheasants. It never quite pulled off those miraculous wildfowl shots that I dreamed of. On the other hand I grew used to its unnecessary avoirdupois and found that I could hold my own with it on game.

Then we got a very hilly forestry shoot. I had inevitably acquired a bit more avoirdupois myself while, no doubt, slowing up fractionally in the process. So I decided that I would retain my splendid magnum but buy myself a double 20-bore, a gun I had always secretly coveted, for game shooting.

It was a splendid theory and it worked very well in practice. The 20-bore weighed just over five pounds and was a dream to shoot with. It killed, as far as I was able to tell, as well as a bigger gun: the only disadvantages I found was on pigeon-decoying days when my eye was not quite in. Then I discovered that I was apt to send away rather more than usual of those feather-streaming, edge-of-pattern birds which you pick later, round the outskirts of the field, if you are very lucky.

So all was balanced and cosy in my armoury until my younger son came to shooting and, indeed, began to shoot very well indeed. Naturally he started on my 20-bore. From that moment on, it and I, were as good as lost. So, in his second season, I gave it to him as a Christmas present, having first had a chunk carved off the butt so that it would fit him.

However, I had an additional chunk made which, when attached by two screws, still made the gun the right length for me. As you may have guessed, that extension has seldom had a chance to be fitted, though he has once or twice lent me the little gun when my magnum has been in for repair.

Lately, I had all but convinced myself that it was high time that I got rid of the magnum and bought myself a sensible game-gun. Then, this season, I discovered that the big gun really did have its uses and that occasionally it was worthwhile investing in the high-powered and high-priced ammunition to fit it.

The duck on the Ouse washes are often very high. This winter I have proved to my own satisfaction, anyway, that the three-inch Greener, suitably primed with Magnum 4's, brings them down when the normal game gun should not even open fire. So, of course, I have to keep the Greener now for its proper purpose. I am once again faced with the necessity for providing myself with light armament.

Who knows? If I *do* buy myself a lovely 12-bore sidelock ejector with standard game boring, I may even get my 20-bore back. Shooting sons, like woodpigeon, have a nose and eye for what is sweetest and best. This time, however, I shall try to be firm.

I may manage to resist the urge to buy myself that sweet sidelock. Temptation came my way only last week when someone totally unknown to me phoned and asked whether the Charles Lancaster was still for sale. Unfortunately, I don't own one, so I was understandably speechless. I was even more so when it turned out someone had advertised this weapon in the local paper, giving my phone number. I have yet to discover who the advertiser was.

I might have been tempted to go and look at the Lancaster but for the fact I realised that I wasn't going to get much further with the transaction if I simply phoned myself. Perhaps it was a warning from the gods to keep my money in my pocket.

I *may* resist the purchase of a new game gun for a while but I know that I could never refuse a first-class muzzle-loader if it came my way at a suitable price. The best of them really are such beautiful things.

I have made some of my craziest as well as most rewarding purchases in this field. Time was, when the muzzle-loading craze had hardly got under way, when you could stroll into Bapty's, the theatrical costumiers in Whitcombe Street just off Trafalgar Square, and look through their stock of property firearms. The manager was always prepared to tell you if he had any shootable muzzle-loading shotguns and, if the luck was with you, you could pick up a gem at the standard price of a fiver. I doubt whether any such blissful state exists now.

The nicest muzzle-loading buy I ever made came from a well-known antique shop in, of all places, the Edgware Road. This was a Joe Manton 14-bore in its original case, complete with all fittings, powder and shot flasks, nipple wrenches, spiral worms for removing charges, cap boxes—the lot. It cost fifteen guineas. This was barely as many years ago. I doubt whether you could get it for five times that price today.

I gave it away to a young man for his twenty-first birthday present. I am sure that he has had much joy with it, but I have regretted my generosity ever since, which, perhaps throws a poor light on human nature and my nature in particular. But it *was* so beautiful. It had a walnut stock that glowed like a newly-hatched horse chestnut.

Every word I write is increasing the risk of my suffering a severe weakness in the bank balance, the inevitable symptom and after-effect of gun-itis. Perhaps if I tell my wife that I am sickening again she will say a few magic words that will hold the malady at bay.

Keep Your Powder Dry

There is something about shooting in thick woodland that makes muzzle-loading especially attractive. I think it is the way the smoke hangs around between the trees.

I once remember roost-shooting pigeon near Wokingham with Dick Arnold when we were both using what Americans graphically call 'smoke-poles'. It was a still, cold day with a powdering of snow on the pine-needles. The pigeon had been tucking into green stuff and came back early and kept coming, presumably to make sure of a nice, warm berth for the night.

They had stuffed themselves with kale and you could see the bulge of their distended crops even when they were high above the trees. I remember thinking that it looked as though they had stuck a pillow underneath their pink jerseys. There wasn't time, however, for much metaphorical observation of that sort. We were too busy ramming it down and pumping it up: black powder and shot that is.

The flight proceeded and the pile of slain gratifyingly grew, for a muzzle-loader, held straight, shoots as sweetly as any gun though, being innocent of choke, not so closely: but as the afternoon shortened, the light seemed to be fading unnaturally fast.

The reason was not far to seek. It was all around us. We were shooting in a dense fog of our own making. The white smoke made by the black powder remained wedged between the pine trunks until the whole scene resembled an engraving of an ancient battle. I seem to recall that from time to time one had to fan the stuff to observe the fall of shot. I definitely remember being forced to take one pace to the right to see round my own muzzle cloud . . .

Recently, our local roosting flight, which was pretty brisk a few weeks ago, has begun to taper off. So I thought once again of my muzzle-loader and what fun it would be to take it out in the woods for the comparatively few shots each evening provided.

The Chief Constable of Surrey kindly renews my powder licence each year and this entitles me to buy eight pounds of black. I found that my powder flasks were empty and so went to my favourite gunsmiths to buy a couple of pounds of Curtis and Harvey's No 6, now made by IMI Ltd.

I have owned a good few muzzle-loaders in my day. They have included: a double 6-bore, a double 8-bore, a lovely little Joe Manton 14-bore and my present single-barrelled smoke-pole made by a gunsmith called Hammond of Winchester. I wish that I had them all now but, alas, one cannot go on accumulating weapons unless one is either very rich or has a lot of wall to hang them on—or both. I got rid of them one at a time for purely mercenary reasons, namely that someone offered me a good price for them. Except the Hammond.

It has a 32-inch barrel with a beautiful twist pattern, mellowed and brown like the bowl of a well-smoked Meerschaum pipe. The stock is what they used to call 'roach-bellied'. The lock 'talks'—*chock-chock*—when you ease the hammer back. The trigger pull is sweeter than most nuts. There is only one snag to the weapon.

My 10-bore is a pigeon gun. Not the sort of pigeon I now shoot with it, but the kind that used to be released alive at Ranelagh and elsewhere, before the sport was banned for humanitarian reasons. They were then shot dead for large sums of money.

Since the Hammond was never intended for field use, it doesn't boast a ramrod housing. The live pigeon shooter had a small table before him on which he laid out his powder, shot, wads and caps. His ramrod he stuck in the ground beside him. I didn't realise this fact when I first bought the gun.

The first time I came to use it on the marsh I discovered myself at a distinct disadvantage. I had to devise some method of carrying a ramrod, loose. When roost flighting in a pigeon wood, however, you are in very much the same situation as the Ranelagh shooter of the mid-1800's. I stick my ramrod, point first, into the ground.

My friends scorn—a little jealously I suspect—the whole proceedings. 'Loading must take you an impossibly long time,' they say, deprecatingly. I hotly deny this, swearing that I can be fully charged and ready for re-engagement in half a minute.

Needless to say I have never checked my facts, but for the purpose of this article I now intend to do so.

The test I have just now conducted tells me that, simulating actual field conditions, with flasks, wads, caps and so on disposed about my shooting jacket in their proper places I take twenty-two seconds to load my single barrel. The time is split up as follows. To pour powder—five seconds; to ram felt over-powder wad—five seconds; to pour shot—three seconds; to ram card overshot wad—five seconds; to recap—four seconds.

When roost shooting, this is generally fast enough, since the first discharge usually puts the pigeon out of shot for about half a minute. I'll agree that in a really 'hot' roosting flight, when the birds are just pouring in, I may sometimes be caught unarmed. However, in the days when I owned double-barrelled muzzle-loaders I found I could usually deal with most situations. You can certainly reload both barrels of an empty gun in well under forty-five seconds, possibly faster since you already have powder and shot flask in the hand and can pour for both while you're about it.

Soon after the war, when I was exceptionally broke, I used to shoot with muzzle-loaders for economy reasons, mainly because I could not afford to go out and buy a good modern double and there were then no good cheap foreign guns available. When wildfowling we used to have considerable trouble in keeping our powder dry, not, of course, in the flasks, where it was quite weatherproof, but when actually loaded into the gun. The rain would invariably find its way down the nipple. Even with a copper cap in position, it still crept down that pinprick of a hole.

I do not know how Colonel Hawker coped with this. The nearest thing to an answer we discovered was to buy those valve rubbers which start off wide and become narrower ending in a sealed tip. The wide part, when cut off, enclosed the cap and sat as a kind of skirt over the nipple. Caps had to be prepared before one set out and it was fiddling work, but it did save many a misfire.

Out on the marsh, we smoke-polers really knew the meaning of Oliver Cromwell's famous order of the day: 'Trust in God and keep your powder dry.' But for the short duration of a roosting flight, all you have to do when it rains is to keep your lock well tucked under your arm during lulls in the action.

Gun and Punt

The way of it was this. In about 1955, Jack Hargreaves, now of Southern Television, and self, now of Anglia Television, worked together on a magazine called *Lilliput*. Jack had shot all his life but had never been on a saltings. I accordingly introduced him to Stoke Ooze in the Medway estuary where, at three o'clock one bitter December morning, he stepped off firm ground into the aforesaid ooze and instantly lost both waders.

Despite this initial wetting, and despite the fact that we were cut off on an island for nearly twelve hours thanks to the highest North Sea surge since the 1953 floods, Jack Hargreaves had, as they say, a ball.

Thereafter nothing would do but that we design a sneak boat that would enable us to maintain mobility on the flooded saltings, carry two with safety to a suitable position, leaving one gun ashore and one free to go sneaking where he wished.

For anyone who wishes to follow a similar watery course, I can only retrace the steps we took in the depths of our supreme innocence. The fact that we are still undrowned is testimony to the fact that I can fairly confidently pass our meagre information on to others.

We found, as all who try will find for themselves, that there aren't really any plans extant for such a boat. The classic old-timers such as Sir Ralph Payne-Gallwey dealt mainly in battle wagons when it came to punts, huge double efforts with fifteen-inch armament.

We started by consulting these old masters. Hawker was definite and disconcerting. 'There is not a boat-builder in a thousand,' he roared as loudly as his own big gun, 'who knows anything about punts.'

However, the Colonel did come up with a recipe for a 'light boat', fourteen feet long, three feet eight wide at the gunn'ls amidships and eight inches less across the keel at the same point. However, Hawker's light boat was meant for shoulder gunning which might account for its generous width amidships. The Colonel, fully accoutred for winter fowling, was a formidable and bulky figure, moreover his duck shoulder gun, which I have seen, had barrels over four feet long. Try swinging that at a bunch of wigeon in a toothpick sculler!

We searched the basements of second-hand bookshops in Charing Cross Road and came up with a costly load of gems. These included the well-known and the mildly rare. They included: Payne-Gallwey's *Fowler in Ireland*; *Shooting: Moor and Marsh* (Badminton Library); *Wildfowl* by de Visme Shaw; *Practical Wildfowling* (1895) by Henry Sharp; *Modern Wildfowling* (1880) by *Wildfowler* (Lewis Clements, first editor of *Shooting Times*) and *Wildfowler in Scotland* by John Millais, the latter for the pure joy of ownership.

If nothing else came out of the exercise, we had acquired a wonderful library of wildfowling books, from most of which we got invaluable hints how to do the job. Payne-Gallwey laid down: 'All fowling punts should be built with a swell aft of midship section. That is to say, the beam half way between midship section and stern should be from three to five inches wider than that halfway between midship section and bows.'

Here are some of the other gleanings from the classics.

On seaworthiness: 'The difference in length between the measurement overall and on the floor gives the rake of stem and stern; the former always to be given an inch more rake than the latter.'

On avoiding sticking to the mud: 'The spring of a punt's floor should run from the stern to one foot aft of her midship section, with a drop of not more than one inch and then gradually increased out to the stem.'

On safety: 'The life and buoyancy of a duck-punt depends greatly upon the flare of the sides—a punt with well-slanted out (flared) sides, though they do sometimes cast a dark shadow, especially when viewed sideways, will meet a wave far lighter.'

On camouflage: 'As to colour, a dull unreflecting white or very light slate is best. Not green to imitate the sea, as I saw not long ago on a fowler's punt and was informed by its owner (a novice) imitation of the water was the reason for its peculiar hue.'

And finally, Payne-Gallwey on strength: 'Punts are nearly always built far stronger than they need be.'

In the end we stole a little from each of the old masters. Sharp had adapted Hawker's light boat. We adapted his adaptation by adding a pointed stern, and cut down Hawker's width to a maximum beam of three foot four at the gunnels. On the subjects of rake and spring, we followed the old-timers religiously. As to the lightness, which they had all so rightly stressed, we had modern technology on our side. Hawker and Sharp had never heard of marine-bonded plywood and the new glues like Aerolite. For colour we plumped for what one of *Wildfowler*'s correspondents had poetically described as 'the colour of a kittiwake's back', in other words matt, light grey.

For those who may be interested in doing it themselves, I have, since starting this article, just come across our actual dimensions. They are: length, stem to stern, fourteen feet; length at bottom, thirteen feet three inches; width at bottom midships, three feet; spring fore and aft, one and a half inches; depth at bow, five inches and at stern seven inches.

When we had worked all this out, we made a model of our craft and tested her with proportionate weights. If our calculations were right she promised to carry 700 lb while drawing one and a half inches of water.

I have to add that if we were building her again we'd cut down on beam and get rid of the knees on the coamings. They throw a shadow. But we didn't stop at a punt. We were also determined to build, or rather convert, a gun.

A good friend, called Mark Dinely, well known as a firearms expert and collector as well as an adviser to various government departments on lethal weapons, knew of our enterprise. One day he walked into our magazine office with one of the heaviest brown-paper parcels I have ever encountered. When unwrapped, this turned out to contain a beautifully made breech block.

Mr Dinely explained his breech thus: 'At one moment during the war I thought I was a rather clever boy and would develop a smooth-bore mortar capable of giving not only perpendicular but horizontal fire against armoured vehicles, using hollow charge projectiles. It was perfectly effective but rather heavy and not much better than lots of other things: it was used only once when with dummy charges it drove some rather frightened Home Guards out of a strongpoint. I shudder to think what it would have cost to make today. All the engineers in England would want a fifteen per cent raise on the spot. I can only hope it gives you lots of fun and saves some expense.'

The breech looked solid enough for a four-inch naval gun. It had a vertically closing door that locked by rotating lugs operated by a breech lever. The internal diameter of the breech was 37 mm, which seemed just right to fit into into the barrel of a half-pound punt gun. All we had to do was to find a barrel.

We consulted that redoubtable and kindly expert Dick Casely of Bland's. He opined that if we intended to turn a barrel ourselves we needed a threequarter-inch thick steel tube about seven feet long.

A well-known firm of tube makers in Wolverhampton confirmed that they could produce such a thing. This chunk of metal would cost £17·50, not an outrageous price when you come to think of it. I went to examine the barrel 'in the white' or rather 'in the rust'. It is one thing to think of a beautifully tapered seven-foot gun barrel, another to confront the raw material for same. The weight of this object was appalling. The thickness of its metal daunting. I judged, rightly I think, that it would have taken the resources of Woolwich Arsenal to whittle it down to size.

There seemed only one other course open: to find a suitable muzzle-loading punt gun, take out the breech plug, clean up the interior and somehow attach Mark Dinely's breech to it.

We advertised in the *Shooting Times* and received a reply from a Mr Shearer in Spalding—a likely area from which to acquire such a piece of ordnance. Mr Shearer described his weapon, ominously, with that magic phrase 'a lovely, hard-hitting gun', opining that he had never heard of a gun from his parts that needed to be proved (few of them probably ever *were* proved) and asked a modest £10 for what came to be known as the Wash Cannon.

The gun, he thought, was about fifty years old, had been used before him by a Mr Robinson (now dead) on Cowbit Wash. He himself used an eight ounce measure for both powder and shot.

He had once killed twenty-seven wigeon and on another occasion, when the gun was 'pegged' on the bank, twenty-nine pigeon.

The next step was to find a willing substitute for the Woolwich Arsenal. Again we were in luck. We managed to interest a skilful young craftsman called Bill Roper of Charles Hellis, gunmakers, late of the Edgware Road. Bill agreed to work on the cannon for fun and for such publicity as might accrue from his efforts. He, and we, got plenty of fun, but I fear that Bill did not get much other reward.

To begin with, the interior of the Wash Cannon's barrel looked like a very old factory chimney with a lot of bricks missing. Proof Masters are more lenient about the internal condition of punt guns than they are when it comes to shoulder weapons, but the London Proofmaster would plainly not pass this gun.

So a great deal of boring and skimming and lapping was necessary before the inside began to look anything like a tube required for the accurate presentation of shot.

Before we spent any more money on the project we decided to ask the London Proofmaster to 'view' and give us a provisional proof just to make sure that Mr Shearer's gun was worth proceeding with. The Wash Cannon passed this test with distinction, though the Proof House suggested that when we did get the breech on and send it for definitive proof, they would like to see the bore a little less pitted.

Meantime, Bill Roper was having trouble with Mark Dinely's breech. He had evidently fashioned it of metal so hard that the usual tools of the trade would not even scratch it. It blunted everything he had in the workshop. At last, however, he managed to find something strong enough to come to terms with Dinely's cast steel.

Bill Roper's method of attaching breech to barrel struck me as slightly terrifying. He proposed simply to soft-solder them together with the breech slipped over the end of the barrel while very hot on a reverse taper. Solder, he assured me, would make the strongest possible joint. The reverse taper would do the rest.

Finished breech and gun looked magnificent. There was only one snag. When the finished piece went to definitive proof, firing a charge not much larger than at its provisional testing, it blew itself up. The barrel split along about a foot of its length, revealing a flaw that had probably been there for the past fifty years, all the time Mr Shearer and his friends were whanging away on Cowbit Wash. But then they would never have risked their gun at the Proof House.

The Proofmaster's definitive charge had brutally murdered our lovely creation at a point about half-way along its barrel. The resulting wound was eight inches long. Revealed in it was a long dark stain, obviously the cause of the disaster.

The old muzzle-loader which had done such sterling service on Cowbit Wash had at some time long past developed a crack. Possibly, even, it had been made with a flaw in its barrel, but it had taken the Proofmaster's charge to find this out.

That dark stain showed where rust had begun to eat in below the surface of the metal. I wonder how many of the oldtime professionals' muzzle-loaders operated with similar potentially fatal blemishes hidden beneath their patina of grey paint and rust.

Even while we surveyed the wreckage, a comforting thought came to both Jack Hargreaves and myself. This must be the sole consolation for anyone who puts a beloved weapon to the test and finds it wanting. The thought is this: 'Thank heavens I wasn't behind that lot when it happened.'

The barrel was beyond redemption. The explosion had hurled it against the roof of the proof chamber and bent it like a boomerang. The foresight had nearly sheared off. Only Mark Dinely's indestructible breech remained unaffected.

Neither of us had the heart to start building another gun. We bore the corpse back to the workshop of Bill Roper, the faithful and skilful young craftsman who had spent so many hours attaching breech to gun for us. We left the breech with him as a souvenir. If he still has it he has the consolation of knowing that he possesses a fine bit of wartime workmanship that must have cost the British taxpayer a bomb.

So now we had a beautiful new boat but nothing to fire from it. The search started all over again. Both Jack Hargreaves and I had our hearts set on a genuine half-pounder, preferably one of Bland's double-fours with five foot barrels and stubby stock adapted for punting use.

Alas, they were no longer manufactured. Dick Caseley of Bland's explained that it was not possible to get the tubes in sufficient quantity to make manufacture an economic proposition.

Then we had a much-needed stroke of luck. On a business trip to Cambridge, Jack got talking to a man in a pub who happened to be a wildfowler. This character knew where there was a beautiful double-four going begging. Such tip-offs should usually be regarded in the conviviality of the moment.

This one, however, could be taken at face value. The gun turned out to be a double-four Reilly with conventional butt, forty-four inch barrels and only very slight pitting. It weighed 25 lb and, what was most important, had been proved for nitro within the last year. The owner wanted only £20. He had a sale.

We took our purchase to Dick Caseley. He pronounced it 'lovely' and only very slightly inferior to Bland's own out-of-production double. The difference in barrel length, he said, was due to the fact that the Bland fifty-inch gun was designed for black powder.

Our gun already had a hole through the butt to take a small breeching rope. There were metal loops at the tips of each trigger for attachment of a firing lanyard. Dick Caseley suggested one modification: that we bore a hole in the rear of the trigger-guard so that the lanyard could be given a direct pull when firing both barrels.

Would the gun stand up to such treatment? Caseley's answer held echoes of Colonel Hawker. 'You realise,' he said, 'that it's virtually impossible to fire both barrels simultaneously, even if you wanted to. One always goes slightly before the other. Anyhow, even if you got them off at the identical split-second, it wouldn't trouble this gun in the slightest. You've got a bargain.'

A combined discharge of both barrels would give us the load we had originally intended for our Wash Cannon—six ounces. All that remained to find out was how well those six ounces of shot would be distributed about a target.

We persuaded Percy Stanbury of the West London Shooting Grounds to let us test against the school's plates. Percy Stanbury was once a keen punter so we didn't have to twist his arm too hard. When we turned up he already had a large plate and buckets of whitewash laid on.

The whole experiment of building punt and gun had followed closely in the steps of the great turn-of-the-century masters. So it was natural that we looked to Sir Ralph Payne-Galwey for plating instructions.

Sir Ralph, always one for a mechanical or ballistical lark, had most elaborately plated his own famous double twenty-ounce gun. He had used a plate eighteen feet long and six feet high, in the centre of which was a twenty-inch aiming circle. Distributed around this in two lines were eighteen cut-out wigeon.

Sir Ralph's score was impressive. Out of the 3,280 pellets in his total charge fired at seventy yards, 1,353 struck the six foot square plate in the centre. The centre six wigeon were hit by between eight and nineteen BB's apiece.

Our own line-up was slightly more modest. We used a group of seven cutout duck, stuck on to a six-foot plate with rubber solution.

I remember that we were a bit chicken about pulling both triggers at once, or as close to 'at-once' as we could get it. I don't think that either of us believed the gun would succumb to the strain—for hadn't Dick Caseley reassured us on this point? The recoil might be something quite impressive, however.

Eventually we drove two iron pickets into the ground and

ran a breeching rope from these through the hole in the butt, propping the muzzles on one of the shooting school's gun rests.

The gun jumped about six inches when both barrels went but that was all. A count showed 332 pellets out of 347 on the six-foot plate: all the duck had been hit with between one and four pellets. The range was seventy yards. At last, we were in the sneak-boat business.

A Nasty Hiss

Since the days when I used to assist in the letting off of large calibre weapons, more or less in anger, I have always had a healthy mistrust of misfires. I remember numerous IGs (the dread figure of the Instructor Gunnery in his red hatband still haunts me: I was much more frightened of him than the distant enemy). . . . Anyway, I remember these august figures dinning it into us that should the weapon misfire, the gun number operating the breech would instantly report 'misfire' and on no account open the breech.

Number One in charge of the gun then waited half a minute while the round in the chamber made up its mind. If it didn't go off, he then ordered the breech to be opened. To him fell the doubtful distinction of examining the primer to see that it had been struck. If it had, he ordered 'unload', making sure that the ammo number caught the damn thing before it hit the deck, and instructing him to take it 'twenty five yards clear'. The ammo number ran trembling with his touchy burden and laid it down where, it was hoped, it would be far enough away to do little damage should it belatedly decide to explode.

All very nice and according to the drill book. Service regulations cover most situations and emergencies. But what is the drill for a misfire when the weapon is reduced in size to a 12-bore and the gun crew to a lone pigeon shooter sitting in his own kind of emplacement, a hide?

By now you will have guessed that a misfire recently happened to the writer in the circumstances outlined in the previous paragraph. It did and the writer behaved in a slightly ludicrous fashion. The story is certainly not to my advantage but since it has serious aspects I will tell it.

I can remember only three misfires in my shooting life. One was with a British cartridge of considerable antiquity, bought in a job lot, so I really can't hold the makers to blame for that. The other two were both with foreign ammunition. One, several years back, was when using a transparent, plastic cartridge from Belgium. (I never really felt the cartridges you could see through were *meant* to go off, so perhaps this doesn't count.)

My misfire last week came with a cardboard-cased Czech cartridge of which I have grown rather fond. It is loaded with seven eighths of an ounce, is mild on the shoulder, head and eardrums over a long day's pigeon bashing and seems to kill, for me, at least as well as anything I have ever used. Despite the makers' single lapse I shall certainly continue to shoot pigeon and possibly game with its plastic-cased successor.

The pigeon concerned had a lucky let off. He was coming in to decoys nice and steadily and I had him cold. I pulled and was aware of a soggy kind of plop. This noise was so off-putting that I forgot, or perhaps did not feel inclined, to pull the other trigger. I realised at once that I had had a misfire.

It was at this point that the spirits of a hundred IGs rose up and waved their batons at me. 'On no account open the breech,' I heard their ghostly voices intone. I sat there feeling a bit of a Charlie with the gun on my lap while another pair of pigeon invited me to clobber them. If one gave a four-point-seven half a minute, how long did one allow a possibly sizzling 12-bore charge?

Being impatient to get back into action I waited, I'm sure quite unnecessarily, twenty seconds and then opened the gun. Remembering the drill book, I inspected the primer. Most certainly it was squarely struck. Still following the procedure laid down, I removed the shell-case. It was empty, though looking suspiciously black inside. It smelt rather awful, too, like an old firework.

Next for a bit of drill of my own. 'Whenever in doubt, look up the spout . . .' I tilted the barrels down so that I could apply my eye to the breech end and was horrified to hear a nasty sort of hissing noise from inside. The charge *was* smouldering. Any second a great gout of orange flame would roar backwards from the open chamber and do me a horrible injury. I snapped the gun shut again and sat there holding it in a safe direction.

All sorts of crazy notions went through my head. The main one was that opening the gun had allowed air to get to the slow-burning charge and had started the processes of ignition again. Commonsense should have told me that nothing much could have come of any explosion so caused because any gases generated were hardly likely to be in a state of compression. I wasn't taking any chances, though.

The pigeon were now showing a suicidal tendency that hadn't overtaken them all day until this, my most helpless of moments. I opened the gun once again, taking care that the breech was well away from my person. This time I lifted the muzzles skyward to take a cautious look up the bore. I hadn't elevated them through more than ten degrees before the snake in the barrel hissed again. If anything, the sound this time was even more aggressive.

So I closed the piece for the second time and sat down to think things out. I devoutly wished that I had Gough Thomas with me in the hide at that moment. He would know straight away what the trouble was.

At last, feeling a complete chump, not to say coward, I crept out of the hide and laid the gun down, breech open, in the grass. Watching it as though it was a black mamba, I went back and poured myself a glass of brain-cooling beer.

Five minutes, and about thirty potential pigeon later, I decided that this nonsense had got to stop. I advanced on the gun, seized it firmly, held the muzzles skywards, bravely ignored the savage hiss it emitted as I did so and peered into the right chamber. My eye met total blackness. The barrel was most effectively blocked.

In the days of the muzzle-loader, the remedy would have been simple. But one does not commonly carry a ramrod around these days. Luckily, I had brought some thin bamboo canes for jacking up decoys above the height of the pea crop I was defending.

The bamboo met the first obstruction halfway up the bore—the overpowder wad. This yielded to a good prod and the prod instantly produced that intimidating hiss. At last I realised what had been causing this sound. The sussuration was the noise of the shot charge running loose in the barrel between the two wads which had apparently separated by several inches. Every time I had tipped the gun, the shot had trickled up and down the barrel.

I felt, I confess, a BF for being so pussyfooted. If my knowledge of ammunition and ballistics had been stronger, I might have had another ten pigeon in the bag. But in one thing, my personal gun drill had been fully correct. 'When in doubt, look up the spout.'

I do not like to picture the consequences of firing another cartridge behind those two separated wads and that wandering shot charge. I would hazard that the misfire had created the optimum conditions for blowing at least one's hand, if not one's head, off. So, after all, maybe I owe something to all those Gunnery Instructors who threw a healthy scare into me all those years ago.

On the Hill

I am constantly aware that there are degrees and differences of taste and inclination in one's own attitude towards different field sports. For some reason that I cannot analyse accurately I have never been attracted to the hunting with the gun of mammals, except possibly rabbits, even though I am addicted to what the Americans call bird-hunting.

Certainly, I had never shot, nor felt the need to go and prove that I could shoot, a stag. This was not from any sense of squeamishness or disapproval as I shall quickly make clear. This month I was invited to try my hand on a famous Perthshire deer forest. I went. I shot. I killed. And these are my purely personal reactions to, for me, a new exercise.

As with all expeditions that I seem to make, my stalking had to be sandwiched in between a lot of other things. This meant catching the night sleeper up to Rannoch, taking my chance on getting my stag in a single outing on the hill and returning by night sleeper the next day.

My host met me at the tiny Highland station, took me to the local and very hospitable inn, bade me change with the injunction that the train had been half an hour late and that he could allow me about five minutes to get myself ready.

We then roared off up the valley alongside a once-beautiful river that had been stripped of its muscles (and its salmon) by one of the Highlands many hydro-electric schemes.

Dick Sutherland, my host's stalker, was waiting and ready. I thought that I had better start by confessing my utter greenness not so much as to the habits of deer, of which I know a fair amount, but of the business of stalking. He accepted this with the grave courtesy of his kind and said that we would zero the rifle on the way up the hill.

By one of the hydro-electric dams, in the middle of a heathery nowhere, he stopped the Land-Rover, produced a two foot square sheet of white card with a black four inch bull in the centre of it and retired about one hundred and twenty yards into the heather. Then he retreated to a cautious distance himself.

I have not shot with a rifle for some time, though I used to be a moderately good hand at it. However, it is many years since the last conflict and an even longer time since my days with a .22 match rifle and before that to the school shooting eight, the

SMLE and the Ashburton at Bisley. One has grown older, the breath shorter, the eyesight, if still as keen, then at least different.

I took the .275 Rigby and lay down in the heather with a good deal of trepidation. I confess that I had hoped for telescopic sights: these were open. The first shot was just outside the bull at two o'clock. I was told that I would have killed with it. The second shot nearly key-holed the first. At least this was consistent, though one could not discount that it was more likely to be a fluke.

I remembered what various people, including Royal Marine small arms instructors, had told me and made what seemed to be an appropriate allowance for how the rifle, or, much more likely, I, appeared to be shooting. The third shot was slap through the centre of the bull. If this was a fluke, then I wasn't going to admit as much. 'That,' I said rather grandly, 'will do.'

Accompanied by two companions, whose day on the hill I had probably usurped by my very presence (they were guests of my host), we now set out in pursuit of my stag. I was prepared to make a fool of myself in front of the stalker whose natural good manners and sympathy for the tyro would, I felt sure, have let me down lightly. To have an audience of two experienced stalkers into the bargain was, I thought, just a trifle too much.

Expert stalkers will have to forgive me if I record the obvious, but everything, you must understand, was new to me. We began our approach march up a long, gentle, boggy mountain. I began to feel a little short of breath and thought with apprehension what might happen if I was forced to take a shot before I got my second wind. I need not have worried. The shot was yet a long way off.

I am used to looking for animals that insist on blending into the surroundings, so I found little trouble in spotting deer with the naked eye. If you can see a bunch of teal at a mile, said I to myself, then you ought to be able to spot a stag on the sky-line at the same range. However, I found that I was no match for my companions. Their trained eyes spotted deer in places which I had passed by. To identify these we repeatedly squatted, steadied our glasses against our sticks and spied.

The hills seemed exclusively peopled by hinds: hinds in family parties, hinds with calves at heel; hinds always willing to bark and give the alarm or run across our front with their youngsters trailing behind them. There were hinds posted on every skyline like Red Indian sentinels.

During the first two hours' walk we found few stags. Those that we did see were noble beasts with good heads that any proper management plan—and this deer forest was beautifully managed—would leave severely alone as breeding stock.

What we were looking for, Dick Sutherland explained, was a beast that the forest could well afford to get rid of. Again this will be obvious to experts, but Sutherland's definition of 'rubbish' included: stags that were 'going back', that is to say past their best with antlers deteriorating with each passing season; 'switches', stags with straight-up points above the brow tines, antlers that become lethal in rutting fights; stags with poor heads that were never likely to improve; and, of course, a hummel, that mighty muscled creature who never grows an antler but puts it all into bone and sinew with which he lords it over a large harem of females to the exclusion of more worthy contenders.

No such creatures appeared in our glasses. Indeed, it was a credit to the way this forest was managed that 'rubbish' was notably absent. The recommendation of the Scottish Red Deer Commission was that my host culled forty stags and seventy hinds each season. Careful and selective shooting over the past five years had produced the fine-looking animals that now confronted us.

During the first two hours, the Rigby was never once in danger of coming out of its case. The beauty of the day itself more than compensated. It was sunny and warm and, for stalking, diabolically still. Every sound could be heard by the deer at a far from comfortable range. If there was no wind to carry our scent, then there was blinding sunlight that cut down our chances of concealment.

At lunchtime, the stalker, myself and the two guests who had insisted on accompanying us, sat down on a rocky outcrop above Loch Ericht and ate our sandwiches, washed down with a delicious face-down drink of burn water. One of the pure pleasures of being in such lovely, untouched places is to be able to drink the water just as nature delivered it.

Below us, hidden by an escarpment, were two stags that would 'do', that is to say they had poor enough heads to qualify as part of the forty stag cull recommended for the forest by the Red Deer Commission. The chances of getting close enough for a shot, said Dick Sutherland, were very small indeed.

Our approach would have to be made by crawling down a corrie beneath us. We would be hidden from the stags all right, but in full view of about fifty hinds grazing the slope beyond. Though they were feeding into the wind, that is to say, away from us, one of the wary old ladies was bound to look round and spot us before we had gone far. The way things were, it was worth a try.

The young man who had come with us asked me: 'Isn't your heart knocking?'

As a matter of fact, it wasn't. I wasn't particularly excited by the whole performance. My pulses race uncomfortably when the teal start coming at evening flight. I have been known to feel a distinct kick in the stomach when a cock pheasant erupts out of the reeds at my feet. I've also been known to miss same, no doubt due to an overflow of adrenalin pumped into the bloodstream.

My pulse rate at the moment, was, however, truthfully normal, even below normal. The explanation was that I was contributing very little to the stalk myself. I realise, of course, that I knew so little about the finer points of the game that I should not have succeeded in stalking on my own. Nevertheless, this was what all my instincts and tastes cried out that I should be doing. So I told the young man that I felt no quickening of the pulse. 'You *will*,' he assured me, 'when Sutherland says "tak' him noo".' I decided I would wait until the moment came before I passed judgment on that.

We crawled down the corrie and through the edge of a black peat hag. All I saw was Sutherland's boots just in front of my nose. The rifle was still in its leather case so there was plainly going to be no summons to crawl up alongside him for the shot. I judged that at this rate of crawl we must be within one hundred and fifty yards of our two stags.

If it came to it, could I score at that range? Despite the fact that I had covered myself with glory when sighting the rifle before we started, I wasn't too confident about the real thing. The audience left high above us, and no doubt watching every movement through their glasses, didn't make me feel any better.

The matter was never put to the test. Three mountain blackfaces came thundering past. I saw, even with Sutherland's boots blocking my vision, some of the hinds on the far hill look up. That was it. They moved away, taking our two stags with them.

The rest of the afternoon passed in a fairly wearisome to-ing and fro-ing over the same mile of hill tops. We had one more attempt to get close to a poor six-pointer with stick-like antlers, but this time a covey of grouse rose and gave the game away. It had been an improvement. The Rigby had actually been handed to me.

Around five in the afternoon it looked like a blank day. There had been many compensations. We'd seen two parties of ptarmigan, four in one and five in the other, at a range of about twenty yards. Then a peregrine came prospecting along a ridge where we sat spying out the land below. She was doing the same.

The view was magnificent. Cloud shadows raced across the valleys far below and a chain of lochs led the way to where the dark hills marked the even darker Pass of Glencoe. I thought again that if I had been up here doing this on my own, pitting my own skills, then I might have been caught with the fascination of the sport. As it was, I felt like a spectator.

Dick Sutherland now decided that we ought to make our last throw on some new, lower ground. We set off in Indian file to descend a steep slope above Loch Ericht and then to worm our way round a nasty face of scree. There were some tufts of grass to cling on to. It was a fairly hairy place, all the same.

More ptarmigan. They weren't particularly troubled by us. They flew above thirty yards and sat on an outcrop, watching. We emerged into a country of rock and corries. Plenty of stags here, some far too good to cull, but several that would have been better out of the way.

The hind situation was quite as desperate as before. Hinds that barked the alarm. Hinds that ran across our front with calves obediently at heel. No matter how cautiously we crawled, they seemed to have us pinned down.

Our audience had once again been left at base. Sutherland and myself were now horizontal for every yard of the way. Crawling up to crests, crawling back again, then down again to a lower, rocky ledge.

After an hour and a half of this, the rifle was out and in my hand. There were two shootable stags just over the next ridge. I would have to be quick. They were already uneasy.

We poked our heads above the last line of rocks. There they were about a hundred yards away, both poorish heads that were probably going back. 'The right hand one. Tak' him *noo*!'

He wasn't to be taken the noo. He slid quickly into dead ground. 'The left hand one.' I won't say my heart was thumping but I obviously wasn't as calm as I thought I'd be. The rocks made poor elbow holds. I was afraid to get into a decent upright firing position for fear of spooking the remaining beast. I should have taken a second longer but I was afraid this stag would disappear, too. Excuses, excuses! In the event I failed to make the three inch allowance my sighters had told me I needed to score dead centre. All the same the stag went down as if hit by a train. 'Well done, sir,' said Sutherland.

But it wasn't well done, really. I'd hit him him too high. A second shot was needed to finish him.

'Well done,' said the audience when it climbed down from its

vantage point to join us. Everyone seemed pleased except me. I felt that I'd made a bit of a mess of things. The stag was certainly one to be rid of. He had one fewer points than last year and was starting to go back. Perhaps I was, too!

Two Lakes Teasers

It is always a pleasure to fish or shoot with a master craftsman, even if the occasion shows you up for what you are, by comparison. In my case the discovery almost invariably reveals that I am only a fair to average hand, though, I hasten to add,

I'm quite happy to be one. I imagine that when Arthur Oglesby fishes with Barrie Welham the odds are fairly evenly matched. When I fished with Barrie there was no doubt who was the long-odds outsider.

The scene was Two Lakes, which is now much more like five lakes, just outside Romsey. Barrie has been kind enough to ask me to share a day with him there for several seasons. This was the first time I had been able to take advantage of what promised to be an angling experience.

The day did not look like one in which the trout would give themselves up. The sun turned on its full power at about ten in the morning and stayed that way until well into what should have been the evening rise.

The traffic on the abominable A31 made me half an hour late. I found that Barrie, quite rightly, had taken off for one of the upper lakes to make the most of the comparative cool before the giant rainbows wound down their periscopes and scuttled themselves.

I didn't get to the water for a further half hour because I fell into conversation with a tall gentleman who came out of the lakeside house to make himself known. This was Alex Behrendts, the founder and designer of Two Lakes. Normally, I would have developed stomach ulcers just having to stand talking while fish rose steadily on the nearest lake as an angler in a white shirt cast unavailingly to them.

Could it be that the white shirt was making them shy? Might not I, if I could only get at them, and being more suitably camouflaged, be in there with a chance of landing a 4 lb rainbow before Barrie had caught his first fish of the day. If so, what a triumph, for Barrie Welham is not only a tournament casting champion but practically the uncrowned king of Two Lakes.

I forgot my impatience, and to tell the truth was quite happy to do so. With many apologies for keeping me from the water, and while urging me to go at once if I wished, Alex Behrendts told me something of how he had built this outstanding fishery.

Two Lakes is rather like Jeffery Harrison's WAGBI-Wildfowl Trust reserve at Sevenoaks. Both have been turned into watery paradises from the most unlikely looking basic material. In the case of the WAGBI reserve, the setting is a working gravel-pit. Two Lakes was more or less a derelict property when Behrendts bought it. With the aid of bulldozers, he has dug out a complete minor lake district, the lakes interconnecting and allowing for a continuous flow of water.

He has catered for the giant fish they support with every piscatorial convenience. To protect his trout in all extremes of the English climate he has given them fourteen-foot deeps and sunny, food-rich shallows.

For his stew ponds he is not content with just any old water. In freezing winter conditions, the warmest water is to be found in a layer close to the bottom. In summer the opposite is true. Rainbows need cool water in the summer heat and, though they thrive in cold, appreciate something well above freezing point. So he runs concrete pipes from his rearing ponds out into the centre of one of the lakes to draw off the most congenial water in all seasons from the depths there.

Recently he has had a serious problem with over-fertilisation of one lake due to washings from a nearby chicken farm seeping into it. The result was that the lake became far too rich in algae and was soon covered with weed that made it impossible for the fly fisherman.

Alex Behrendts' answer to this was an unusual one. He covered the bottom of the lake, a vast area, with pegged down black polythene sheeting, the kind farmers use for protecting haystacks. No weed, of course, could force its way up through this and the sheeting seemed to make no difference to trout, while it was invisible to the anglers.

But the most impressive thing about this fishery is its mature beauty. I agree that the set-up does sound comparatively tame, especially to fishermen used to the wilder rivers. It even *looks* tame when you get out of your car by the neat house and see the well-kept banks and the positions cleared for casting in most, but no means all, of the best spots. When you first view Two Lakes you began to feel that spending your day with eight or nine other rods in this well-ordered paradise will be a slightly claustrophobic experience.

For some reason that I can't fully explain the feeling soon passes. Perhaps it is because the different lakes present different problems. Perhaps because it is easy to lose yourself, especially on the lakes away from the house. But even right beside the house, you are soon involved in the kind of fishing problems that put all thoughts of tameness or stock fish out of your mind. These Two Lakes trout are not only of legendary size, they can be of almost legendary perverseness, at least when you first start to fish for them.

I won't disguise that I did not have a successful day. I would like to pretend that the glaring sunshine was to blame. I would like to, but then most of the other rods caught their limit of five fish and most of those fish were between 2 and 3 lb.

I fished like a maniac all day. I chucked floating and sunken flies, nymphs, well-weighted nymphs, dragging flies, dry flies that merely sat there waiting to be snapped up. With me attached to the other end of the line, I believe they'd be waiting yet.

Meantime, all around me, the other rods of the day caught their share, fighting titanic battles with what should be fish-of-a-lifetime but which here are scarcely worthy of more than an appreciative 'nice fish'. The rainbows were downright scornful of my efforts, doing what I have never seen fish do before and for which I can find no explanation. At intervals throughout the day, 3 and 4 lb fish 'bombed' across the surface, back and dorsal fins out of the water, bow waves shooting up ahead of their snouts.

I watched Barrie Welham take two rainbows close on the 3 lb mark in the space of a quarter of an hour, fishing what he called a 'well-sucked' Grey Wulff in the surface film. No matter how well I sucked a similar fly, I got no offers and certainly no takers. He insisted that Two Lakes had beaten many real experts at their first encounter and that he himself had nearly given up out of frustration after his first season. I suspect he was just being nice.

Town Dog

In the experience of this Town Gun, one of the hardest jobs such a shooter can take on is the training of a Town Dog. I do not, of course, mean a town dog in the poodle-boxer sense of the word. I mean a dog who, like me, has to spend five days of the week, dreaming about what he's going to do on the sixth day—that is, go shooting.

Now I am sure that Peter Moxon, Jack Chudley and all the crack men in the gundog business have the answers to this situation. But I hope they'll forgive me for even suggesting that they may not have the forces to deal with what oppose us city slickers. I'm still waiting for the masterwork that tells the pavement-bound shooter how he makes the best of a bad job. Maybe what we are attempting is very nearly impossible.

Some of my shooting friends take the easy, and expensive, way out. They send their labradors and spaniels away to doggy finishing, or even beginning, schools. There, some kind and masterful keeper or trainer teaches the dog to be a little gentleman as well as an industrious—if you will pardon the phrase—son of a bitch when he reaches the shooting field.

Apart from the fact that it costs a lot of money, sending your pup away to boarding-school does, to my mind, remove some of the pleasure from the subsequent relationship.

Now the books will tell you—and up to a point they're right—that miracles can be achieved by a few minutes' morning and evening training in a garden or even indoors. Basic obedience, elementary retrieving, answering to whistle and so on. But the books also say that gundog puppies, like children, quickly get bored. They're right there, too. However, what the experts are talking about is boredom in terms of *time*. They never seem to take into consideration boredom in terms of *space*, which is quite as strong an anti-training force, I assure you.

My own garden is, by outer London standards, quite a large one. I suppose it's about three-quarters of an acre. Half of it is a nice wild place with rhododendrons and azaleas, holly bushes, laurels and all kinds of attractively snuffly hide-aways. At any time of the day or night it must prove quite an exciting hunting ground for any dog equipped with an enquiring nose.

Nevertheless, a good gundog puppy soon gets moderately blasé about the current smell menu, especially since it's not likely to vary a great deal. Worse still, from a teaching point of view, is the fact that there are comparatively few training situations that one can devise and the pup quickly becomes blasé about these, too.

The hiding places for retrieves, the ground over which the pup can be sent to hunt, even the finding and fetching of a selection of dummies become routine and too well known. The permutations and combinations of problems that can be set are not limitless. After some time you can begin to see the dog 'think': 'Ah, yes—Exercise 3b. Find old sock under fourth rhododendron bush to the right of the compost heap. No need to hurry over that one.'

Later on, he may even vary his reaction with: 'Oh, heavens, not 3b again. This time when I bring it back, I'll jazz it up a bit by taking a couple of turns round the rose bed before I give it to him. That'll teach him.'

This, as the books say, is the moment to discontinue that particular lesson.

I did recently try to put some variation into the curriculum by introducing a little water training. A dummy thrown into the middle of the goldfish pond is just out of range of spaniel-reach from the shore. Up to a point, this was a great success. My puppy was not water-shy and just took one flying leap. He came out with the retrieve *and* a rather expensive new water lily plant my wife had just anchored. This earned us bad marks, as did his subsequent arrival in the kitchen, after his work-out, dripping wet and plastered with dead leaves from the pond bottom.

I haven't even mentioned the hazard of children who insist on treating your darling as a pet. Up to a point this is fine. As Jack Chudley says of gundog puppies: 'Children humanise them.' So they do, if children can ever be said to be fully human themselves. In fact, I believe a bit rubs off in both directions. If it humanises the dog, it also 'dogmatises' the kids. With past dogs, when the kids were much smaller, I have found them not only sleeping in the same basket as the dog but also eating off the same plate.

The experts who read this will rightly say that I should build an outside kennel and treat my dogs like any sensible countryman would. Leave 'em outside the house and thus make them view any training period as a welcome release from close confinement.

For a Town Gun, even this raises its own problems. Is there room to build such a structure in the first place? Dogs left outside have been known to bark. This is all very well if your nearest neighbour is quarter-of-a-mile away but not so good if he's just over the fence. Then Town Gun's kids are awfully prone to come home from school and just go in to see how the dogs are. I know they shouldn't, but the disciplines of the town are not those of the country. I'm making excuses? Maybe, but I'm not the only one to have struck these difficulties.

Despite all these handicaps, most of us manage to reach a fair level of basic training and text-book efficiency. We achieve this against great odds and often through great ingenuity. I have Town Gun friends who even go as far as co-opting their children's pet rabbits and guinea pigs in backgarden steadiness-to-fur sessions. What our young dogs lack is the actual experience which only the field can bring. So, when that first season at last begins and we have our year-old paragons trained to a hair among the flowerbeds, we are, alas, dying to show what they can do with the real thing.

This, of course, is where we far too often fall flat on our faces. No matter how good they are on pet bunnies and old socks, the first sniff of a running cock pheasant is like sticking a double brandy inside a baby. Town Gun, naturally, wants to see his Teal, Trigger, Bruno or whatever the thing's called, put the bird up and retrieve it just like he did to that blank cartridge pistol by the compost pile.

Town Gun, I submit, shouldn't be doing anything of the sort. If he has to train his dogs in the conditions I have described, then for a good while at the start of his dog's first season he should be willing to leave his gun at home and concentrate completely on his pupil. Keep that up for a month or two and he's got a fair chance. And that's the hardest lesson of all.

Who Trains Who?

Last week I was finally brought face to face with the facts of life about my dog. He is *not* steady. In fact, this particular day he would have done very well at a greyhound track.

I will make such excuses as are possible in the circumstances and then say no more on his, or my, behalf. We were shooting in Norfolk on a farm shoot very generously supplied with pheasants. In fact, there were pheasants beyond his, or my, normal expectations.

Birds clattered out from behind every clump of sugar-beet, every turnip, every twist and turn of every hedge. The day was wild and windy—and I do not think this helps—and the country was open with none of the thick cover that is generally present on my springer's home territory to help slow up his enthusiasm.

So we had a few wild courses, especially after hares. My hosts were very nice about it. I wasn't—not to the wretched dog at least. We had some cross words then and are still not on very good terms, even though the next day, in a howling rainstorm, he did a miraculous retrieve of a mallard from mud that threatened to come up over his ears.

I suppose all that this goes to prove is that you can't have everything. I certainly can't in my circumstances and I wonder, if they were being totally honest, just how many average gun-dog owners would admit the same.

Peter Moxon will quite properly read my confession with the scorn it deserves. Just the same, if it prompts him to give we owners of all-purpose inconsistent dogs a ray of hope and advice, my confession will not have been made in vain.

To begin with I trained (?) him myself. I achieved a fair degree of obedience and manage to impose this on his undoubted inherited talents. I wanted him primarily to hunt—for our country is bramble country—to be reasonably steady, to come to the whistle, to take hand signals, to be able to find runners, and, above all, to be first-class in the water.

I achieved all this with the dog's help, except perhaps for the steadiness bit, though 'reasonably' is an elastic word.

In the sort of shooting I usually do, Teal is an excellent dog. But then we have few hares and even fewer rabbits. When he was young I did not possess, or have access to, a rabbit-pen and my children were unwilling to lend their tame rabbits for dog training. Therefore, I never achieved steadiness on fur. I didn't really have a hope. Now, if I shout gruffly enough when a hare starts, I have a good chance of anchoring him to the ground. I did not have much chance in all the excitements of that Norfolk shoot.

In close, thick country, such as we shoot in Surrey and Sussex, he is apparently a paragon of a dog, with very few lapses. He sometimes gets a whiff of a cock running fast ahead of him up a hedge and this produces the occasional lapse quicker than anything else. But then what can I expect? I spend most of my time encouraging him to find scent and to hunt the most hideous places for me when he does so. I suspect that, in similar circumstances, other dog owners—and spaniel owners expecially—find themselves, to say the least, sometimes out of touch with their dog. If we want them to hunt for us, usually—and I'm sure the dogs see it this way—*in competition* with one or two other keen spaniels, then how the heck do we discourage them when they get on a hot one right under their noses?

Pace, Mr Moxon, I know what you're going to say and you're absolutely right. We should train them to be obedient in the first place and then they would be proof against temptation. All I can say is that I wish that I could do it.

I use my springer a great deal for wildfowling, where he is at his best. Though springers are reputedly not as hardy as labradors, he will sit for a long time with the tide rising slowly around him. When it gets too deep for comfort he simply stands and wags his tail. This is keenness of a high order, especially as his teeth frequently chatter so loudly I can't hear the duck. It may be unkind to let them do this, but it would be far less kind to leave him in the warm and dry at home.

I have seen him retrieve all day in conditions that were so cold that his coat froze into sharp spikes of ice almost as soon

as he hit dry land. One day on the Medway he retrieved twenty-seven duck for a friend and myself in a fast running tide.

I mention all this simply to offset the fact that he frequently runs in to retrieve a duck while it is on its way down from the sky. I know that this is reprehensible and not to be allowed at any price. Nevertheless, he does it unless I keep a very firm eye on him, which I frequently forget to do in the excitement of a flight.

There are undoubted disadvantages to a wildfowling dog that is so quick off the mark. The most obvious is that a dog moving about in the open is liable to put off any duck that may be coming in behind the one just shot.

There is also the very real danger that one day he will outsmart himself and move across the line of fire of a second barrel fired quickly at a bird coming in low. This happened to a friend of mine and neither he nor I ever wish to see it happen again.

Despite the heinous nature of the offence, I calculate that my springer's quickness to retrieve in water has so far this season got me at least twelve duck that would otherwise have been swept away by the current or, being runners, have dived, never to be seen again.

So, at the end of it all, when the accounts have been totted up, what sort of a dog do I have? I may be flattering myself, but I rather suspect that I have the kind of dog possessed by most shooting men of the same persuasions as myself. I certainly don't have a well-trained dog. I wish that I had, but perhaps I should train myself better first. I shall try harder next time.

Already I have started to think ahead to that next time. Bitches are more tractable. Why should I handicap myself with headstrong males all the time? Can I find a really calm strain of spaniel whose natural docility will make up for my own faults as a teacher?

Several of my shooting friends have had such dogs in the past. Indeed, I remember two such cases, one a labrador, the other a springer. In both instances, my friends gained the reputation for being advanced dog trainers. Their animals were obedient to, or rather without, a fault. We wondered with envy what was their handlers' secret. They didn't seem to possess any qualities that the rest of us lacked, nor did they have special training procedures that we hadn't read about in Moxon.

The truth only came out when these super dogs passed on. Their successors were exactly like the dogs owned by the rest of us—good all-rounders who not infrequently forgot their shooting manners. The fact was that it had been the previous dogs who were born excellent, not the men who had made them so. The trouble is that no one can guarantee that you're going to get one like that next time round.

Dog and Duck

If I have ever doubted that a dog is essential for wildfowling, perhaps beyond the need of any other kind of shooting, I had ample demonstration of the fact recently.

I had been working in the Anglia Television studios in Norwich. The director of the programme concerned is a very good friend of mine who has comparatively recently taken up wildfowling and, because of domestic complications, has not yet got a dog. I had not taken my own spaniel because I did not relish the idea of keeping him shut up in my Land-Rover for two days while we got on with the real business of the day.

I have always been a firm believer that business should be leavened with pleasure. My friend has this season taken on a very nice little duck marsh alongside the River Bure where he had been feeding flooded areas. These, he had generously suggested, we sample for the first time.

When we had finished our first day's work in the studios, we tore off to be at the marsh at dusk. It had all the promise he claimed for it. It was no more than forty acres in extent. But it was bordered down one side by the Bure and criss-crossed with drains as well as dotted with delectably plashy places in which duck could obviously be encouraged to feed.

The marsh was a natural breeding and jugging place for pheasants also. Though we were dogless, birds rose every ten yards. Most we saw were youngsters and so we kept to the business of the evening, which was flighting.

The first bird that came my way, once I was emplaced in the chest-high nettles that acted as a hide, was a pigeon. I downed it. At the shot, a mallard rose from the river and came past high over the tree-tops. I saw him before he saw me so that was one for the bag. Or was it?

The duck had fallen on dry land but it had dropped into the dense nettle cover that covered almost every square yard of the ground. I blundered away after it, fell in a dyke up to my waist—this, too, was concealed by the nettlebeds—and arrived sweating and wet at where I thought the bird had fallen.

I searched for ten valuable minutes while several duck passed within range of my hide. I did not think that there was any chance that the bird was still alive for it had fallen in a way which unmistakeably said 'stone bonkers'. It is a great temptation in these circumstances to abandon the search and get on with the shooting. With a dog I might have done so, being content to let him find it after the flight. But when evening flighting, a bird in the hand is worth several far off in the sky. I found the duck at last by the simple expedient of putting my thumping great foot on it.

By now my companion was getting a few shots and I saw a very high mallard drake plane down into the far corner of the marsh in a state that plainly said it would run out of fuel before it could make a forced landing. It did so, collapsing some fifteen feet above the ground and a good 400 yards from where I stood. That one we would have to find after the flight. As the light finally went I got another mallard that crashed on the far side of the Bure.

We marked this bird for a morning pick-up for there was no

way of crossing the river other than swimming it. The drake which had crashed far off was in the tall nettle country once again. After half a blistering hour in which we had both received enough nettle stings to give an elephant the itch, we sadly gave up and went home to dinner.

My director friend is a man who deplores as much as I do the shooting of a bird for no purpose other than to see it come down. We were both due at the studios again by nine next morning so we set our alarms early to drive down to the marsh before breakfast to pick those two missing duck.

Myself, I had the severest misgivings about finding the birds, but I held my tongue for once since my friend's intentions were so proper that it seemed most improper to discourage him.

Our first move was to call in at the farm to borrow such dogs as they had. Jack Russell's are fine at killing rats and digging out foxes and sheepdogs have their merits also, and, though this mixed pack was quite pleased to come with us, once on the marsh they obviously did not share our fixity of purpose.

After a long search we found the drake, or rather what was left of it. A fox had found it first.

We then advanced to the river bank to see what could be done about crossing to retrieve my bird. Perhaps there was a footbridge that we had missed in the evening light. As we inched our way through the reed beds, four mallard got up from the river and swung away towards the far bank.

My friend confessed afterwards that he had hesitated just that fatal split-second when instinct tells one that there is some reason why fire should be withheld. Often it is a question of safety that makes one hesitate, and rightly so. In this case it was a mental check which said to my friend: 'If you shoot at those duck they will inevitably fall on the far bank and then you will have an even worse problem on your hands.'

But keenness overcame caution. He fired half-heartedly. His swing was checked by indecision, and though he hit his bird he did not kill it. It came down, an obvious runner.

My friend had brought his twelve-year-old son with him so he now said to this youth: 'Off you go, then, take your clothes off and nip across.' The boy is a strong swimmer but he quite rightly in my view—and later events were to prove him right—looked at his father with an expression that said 'do you mind!' Father and son set off up the bank in a further futile attempt to find a crossing.

I stood there for a few minutes alone, looked at the mud, the reeds, the current, the width of the stream. Then I put my hand in it. It was quite warm. Sadly I began to strip off my clothes. I left my socks on as I did not fancy the idea of walking barefoot through the nettles on the far side.

When the others returned they were greeted by the vision of a naked, wet, rather angry man fiercely attacking a huge nettle-bed on the opposite shore with a large branch broken from an alder. I fancy that for one moment my colleague must have suspected that Neanderthal man had returned to darkest Norfolk.

The saddest part of this story is its end. I did not find either of those duck. Any sensible dog would have gathered the lot quicker that it takes a middle-aged wildfowler to strip down to his striped underpants on an early October morning.

Toto and Harry

In the ten years that I have been owned by a Jack Russell I have become convinced that no matter what happens, I can never again exist without a terrier in the household. In view of what my JR has done to me, and to others, this is no inconsiderable tribute to their charm and appeal.

Like several of the mistakes I have made in life, our terrier was due to the euphoria produced by alcohol. My wife and I went to a Christmas cocktail party, blundered into an upstairs room where the hostess's Jack Russell bitch was nursing a litter of puppies and immediately fell. The result of this fatal moment should perhaps have been christened 'Gin and Tonic'. This potion undoubtedly had some bearing on his purchase. In fact, he was subsequently launched on an unsuspecting neighbourhood as Toto, Toto, or rather *M'Toto*, being Swahili for any young animal, even a human one.

Toto quickly made his mark ... on slippers, rats, a three-quarter grown fox cub, which he killed and my springer spaniel admiringly brought home for him. He also made a dent or two on the Kleeneezee man, a nice post lady and a neighbour's *au*

pair girl who inadvisedly struck him with her handbag. He gave the handbag a passing shake as well. All in all he has a fairly criminal record, not, I believe out of malice because he has the nicest disposition when in the home. He simply cannot resist a moving target if it appears on what he considers to be the boundaries of his, or our, territory.

I took Toto shooting from an early age and he acquitted himself reasonably well. He would keep going all day and gave the impression of being willing to face any cover, whereas, in fact, what actually happened was that he is so small that he can pass under any obstacle that leaves a three-inch clearance between itself and the ground. In this way he got quite a reputation for being intrepid.

He also, from time to time, put up a pheasant or two for which he received quite undeserved good marks. I always got the impression that he was entirely about his own business which consisted of: field mice, voles, rats and, of course, rabbits. A pheasant was simply a bonus over which his nose, while otherwise occupied, happened to take him.

I once saw him retrieve a pigeon, though he never repeated the performance. There are a heck of a lot of feathers in a well-shaken pigeon. One had to be very quick to beat him to any pheasant that fell in his vicinity. If he wasn't all that interested in the live article, he saw the dead one in much the same light as he saw post ladies and *au pair* girls: something to be seized and shaken. Toto still comes out occasionally, though his feet are playing him up a bit now and he is apt to go on three legs after an hour or two in the thick stuff.

Because of the besotted attitude I have developed towards small terriers. I was rash enough recently to offer to take some friends' Jack Russell with me to Selsey for a day's rough shooting. Harry—his full name is Harold Wilson—is as smooth as Toto is rough (I believe correct Jack Russell parlance for his special shagginess is 'broken-coated'). Harry is a charming little dog with whom I have enjoyed a close two-year friendship. But I have to admit that a day together at Selsey came close to straining it.

There are those who say that terriers are closer to the wolf clan than to the jackal branch of the dog family and, as is well known, wolf dogs walk alone. Harold not only walks alone, he runs alone, digs alone, disappears alone and suffers from the over-confident belief that those to whom he is loosely attached will be waiting for him with welcoming arms two hours later when he decides to reappear above ground, or from the next county, or wheresoever his mysterious business has taken him.

I lost him at the first drive. He hit a line of his own and

disappeared like a remote-controlled torpedo that has lost contact with its control and is now only intent on becoming infinitely remote. Toto, who had been brought to keep Harold company, took his own independent line, as usual, but at least remained within swearing distance.

From the outset I was filled with dread that such pheasants as we might see that day would appear, rocketting out of the ground, at distances of up to one mile from the guns. From time to time I caught sight of Harold's backside, working a hedge here, inspecting a ditch there, as the mood took him, and always at a considerable range. Once I came upon him purely by accident, shaking what remained of a large rat. Another time I glimpsed him in pursuit of a rabbit.

As the morning wore on I began to realise, thankfully, that he had even less idea than Toto what pheasant scent was and couldn't care less. He may have put up a bird or two by accident but if so I saw no evidence of it.

By some strange coincidence, Harold and I met walking a large ditch from opposite directions just before the final drive before lunch. By a miracle I was able to slip a piece of binder twine round his neck and hold him until the drive began.

We were to walk a very nice small plot of artichokes, bordered by two hawthorn hedges, one of which contains a large rabbit warren. I was detailed as one of the walking guns. Provided I could keep Harold with me until the 'off', I didn't see that he could do anything but good. If he put up a bird or two it would simply go forward over the standing guns.

Harold and I set off together. That was about all. The moment I slipped the binder twine, Harold took off at right angles to the line of the beat in the direction of the rabbit bury. This didn't perturb me. It would keep the little fellow out of trouble.

We finished the beat, collected up the slain and prepared to head back for lunch in the barn. Or rather, the other guns did.

Harold was nowhere to be seen. I recalled the words of his owners: 'You never have to worry about Harry. He *always* comes back.' Yes, but back to where? He'd never seen the shoot before and he had no idea where the barn was.

So I walked round the artichokes, whistling, calling, knowing that it would all be in vain and remembering that I'd once waited forty-five minutes in the dark for Harry to decide to extricate himself from a large Forestry Commission block, which, likewise, he had never seen before.

He wasn't my dog. I couldn't return without him. I had little doubt that he was digging himself through a large section of subterranean Sussex, perhaps beneath my very feet. For fear of losing the little brute, I ate my lunch in the artichoke patch. By then it was raining hard. I thought of the others sipping sloe gin in the warmth of the barn.

At last, as the first beat of the afternoon was about to start, Harry surfaced as if nothing had happened. He was yellow with clay and had blood on his muzzle. I didn't ask him whose though I hoped it was his.

Harry spent the afternoon in the car. When I got him home, his owners asked if we'd enjoyed the day. '*He* did,' I said. Before anyone writes to me to complain that I have maligned the 'breed', it is only fair to say that I *have* known Jack Russells who were an asset to shooting. I just happen never to have been the owner of one, even for a day.

There is a sad sequel to this account of Harry's underground activities. Even as I was correcting the proofs of this book, Harry took off on one of his normal highly individual forays. He is assumed to have gone to ground and, like many lion-hearted terriers before him, become trapped in a fox earth or rabbit warren. This time, alas, he did not return to base.